INDIAN POSSE

A John Treehorn Mystery

Dinah Miller

ISBN: 978-0-9979826-7-1

INDIAN POSSE A John Treehorn Mystery is a work of fiction. Names, characters, places, and incidents are either the product of the author's vivid imagination or are used fictitiously. Any resemblance to actual persons, living or dead, events, or locales is entirely coincidental.

Published by New York Productions, LLC
P. O. Box 175
Churubusco, NY 12923

Cover Artwork by Leonie Cheetham
www.facebook.com/leoniecheethamart/

www.dinahmiller.com - Books and merchandise.

www.facebook.com/SpecialAgentJohnTreehorn/
Please join my fan page for John Treehorn publishing news and updates.

Line Editor: Jessica Keet
www.proofreadersproofreader.com/author/jessica/

Line Editor: Annie Darek Morgan

To Bart

Peace, love, and blessings.

Justice, she'll never be denied.

—FBI Special Agent John Treehorn

Chapter One:

A Murder

Navajo Indian Reservation

They emerged from the darkness as one collective soul. Their hooves pounded the ground as if crushing an evil that lived on this land. Black, gray, and red, the mustangs galloped wildly across the Rez, untamed, untouched, forbidden for on their hindquarters, they carried a brand, Property of Indian Posse. As they passed back into the shadows of the night, the mark and what it stood for were remembered by all—including those who carried the same.

Four Corners Monument

The mustangs awoke the spirits as they passed a hundred feet from the fire, a stone's throw from the Four Corners Monument. Meanwhile, the two men drank, embraced, and danced around the campfire. They continued their celebration until the bullets struck their bodies.

1

As a wolf howled in the distance, John Treehorn's eyes snapped open, searching into the darkness beyond the campfire. The man in him saw nothing, yet the Navajo in him sensed something, something moving. His hand shook slightly as he reached for the old, broken branding iron left there not so long ago. As the metal stoked the fire, the sparks flew high into the night.

The first bullet that struck each man wasn't life-threatening. It simply carried out its intended purpose, the prevention of the targets from escaping.

As Treehorn leaned back from the campfire, a paper in his pocket crinkled, reminding him it was there—and it wasn't going away. He removed the wrinkled envelope, addressed in care of his mother, Anna Treehorn. Mailed to her address on the Navajo Indian Reservation, Land of her People, from the post office in Gallup, New Mexico. Usually, he received them at his FBI office in Washington DC, the land of his father. Eight years of envelopes and he kept each and every one of them because one day, he knew the question inside would be answered.

The Indian, Paul Greyhorse, leaned against the boulder and slid to the ground. The bullet had shattered his femur. He knew his fate had finally arrived. The Texan, Bart J. Baker, clawed the ground in a panic to reach his SUV where he had stowed his gun. His leg wound created a trail of blood emanating from the campfire by which a boy scout, if required, could track him.

The rear tire of the SUV exploded as the sniper's bullet struck it. The force knocked Bart back as he struggled to open the back door to his weapon cache.

The tethered horse, attached to the front of the vehicle, broke its leather lead as it reared back from the noise of the blast. He galloped away as if his life depended on it—which it probably had.

No one gets out of here alive.

Several logs fell deeper into the campfire's coals and sparks flew upwards. The Navajo watched, wondering whether it signified an omen.

Treehorn stared at the envelope he held. It contained one name in the return address, *Nettie Tsosie*. Nothing was written beneath her name after all this time. The agent removed the note inside. A faint smell of sage wafted from it as he unfolded the slip of paper. He knew the words by

3

heart. The same question he'd been asked weekly, for eight years. *"Did you find Daniel's killer?"*

Treehorn reinserted the paper into the envelope and returned it to his shirt pocket for safekeeping. He stared out at the darkness, then into the fire for answers, but he knew he wouldn't find any tonight. Then, he added several logs to the pit and poked it with the iron until hundreds of sparks flew high into the air, hoping one of the spirits would hear his call for help.

Back at the Four Corners Monument, the night-vision scope from the sniper's rifle surveyed the two men's faces. Paul, the Indian, his lean, muscular body remained at the boulder staring into the fire. Bart, the white man, neither lean nor muscular, resumed his panicked, earth-clutching attempt at escape. His frightened eyes sought the shelter of the white SUV as his injury slowed his progress into his vehicle.

High on the ridge, the light from the campfire interfered with the sniper's scope, but he decided to keep it on. His night-vision device checked the perimeter and its surrounding area for intruders, but there were no witnesses to be found. As his focus returned to the two wounded men and the vehicle, he silently reminded himself to add two

4

more to his growing tally of death by bullets—if he could claim these two within the next fifteen minutes. The odds were 50/50 on that goal.

The older man held a night-vision recorder with audio. "Great shots!"

"I struck the Indian first, then your little thief second, as you ordered."

"You've always followed orders well, Ronan."

"Stay behind me as we get close until I give the all-clear."

"Good idea," the older Texan agreed.

Bart yelled at Paul, "Why are you just sitting there? Get up and fight!"

The Indian refused to move. "I am not fighting inevitability."

"I have guns and ammo in the trunk."

"I have something I need to do."

"What's more important than saving your own, red ass?"

"Telling Indian Posse to find your killer."

The shooter and his partner watched their targets through their devices.

"Your sticky-finger boy made it to his vehicle. He may have a weapon inside."

The rifle scope located its target.

"Slow him down," the Texan drawled, "but don't kill him."

The shooter took careful aim, squeezed the trigger, and the bullet struck its mark.

"I call that a hip replacement."

"Let's go." The older man set a brisk pace as he added, "I want to hear the last words they speak."

The two men could hear Bart's screams from the time they descended the hillside vantage point, louder as they crossed the mustang's markings stamped in the red clay, and pathetically annoying as they neared the crackling campfire.

Paul Greyhorse watched as both men approached and he chose silence in his contemplation.

The older man filmed the Indian in his sitting position as the stone and fire provided the backdrop for his video. The camera focused for a few seconds on the flow of blood as it oozed out from the leg wound at his shattered femur. Neither man commented as they walked away from him.

The older man then moved the camera to Bart as he screamed in pain from the bullet's impact in his hip. The Texan's nose twitched from the smell of his fellow statesman who lost his bowels. Such an undignified way to die. The man's life expectancy decreased with every second as the ground became saturated with his blood, urine, and feces. Neither of the standing men seemed perturbed by having their actions caught on their video recorder.

"Ronan, do you remember my Polaroid camera?" the older man recollected.

"You bring it up at the most unusual time. Yes, it's in storage and all of its photos have been carefully preserved."

Ronan watched his target as he answered.

The older man grinned salaciously at that news. Then his smile turned to anger and annoyance as he listened to the man sniveling in agony next to the SUV.

Bart pleaded to them, "There are money and weapons inside the truck. Take them all. Just let me live."

Both men stared silently at the bleeding, whining man.

"Why are you doing this?" Bart demanded.

Ronan slowly withdrew from his shoulder holster a six-shooter revolver with the letters "DWJ", in mother-of-pearl inlaid on the grip. Handing it to the older man he said, "I cleaned and loaded it for you."

"Thank you."

The older man swapped the camera with Ronan.

"Would you do the honors? Step back to make sure I'm in the shot."

"No problem."

The sniper checked to make sure the red-light recording button remained active.

The older man raised the revolver and shot Bart in his healthy thigh.

"I'll predict that stealing someone's gun, again, isn't a crime in your future."

"I don't remember stealing anything from you," he shouted as tears streamed down his lying, filthy face.

The older man angled the revolver so the fire's glow highlighted the profile of the gun to the bleeding man.

"Does this look familiar?"

Bart's eyes grew wide with recognition as he realized his judgment-karma had arrived.

"This is what we do to thieves."

The shooter raised the revolver, aimed, and shot Bart's left hand, his right hand, and paused to enjoy the agony of the screams. Then, he carefully took aim and fired a final cartridge between his eyes.

The man's spirit quickly departed to locate a better host.

Paul sat and waited for the certainty of his pending bullet. He couldn't help but overhear the conversation of the men before the final blast had ended his friend's life. The boulder suddenly felt cold beneath his back—or maybe it was the spirit's way of saying goodbye as it departed, leaving his body a cold, empty shell. He pressed his right palm into his left thigh where blood flowed from the bullet hole. Then he pressed his blood-covered palm and fingers into his right thigh. It left a perfect handprint like the ones found on painted ponies going into battle.

The two men ambled from the lifeless body of Bart Baker to the feet of Paul Greyhorse.

The Navajo knew he and Bart had lived their lives by their own rules instead of conforming to those of society. The irony of their deaths wouldn't be lost on their friends and family. He looked up at the two men. One held a rifle, the other a handgun.

The revolver's barrel slowly raised and aimed at Paul, brother of Parker and Peter.

"No one is going to remember a dead Indian."

"There's one that will," he waited for death's resolution.

Paul uttered those last words as the first bullet struck his heart, after passing through his Indian Posse tattoo. The second bullet entered his skull as his lifeless eyes stared at the dying campfire's embers.

The vulture knew no boundaries as he circled over Arizona, New Mexico, Colorado, and Utah at the Four Corners. The smoke from the morning campfire rose gently with the morning breeze. FBI Special Agent John Treehorn leaned against the door frame of his grandfather's hundred-year-old hogan. Built on the red soil of the Navajo Indian Reservation, it had stood the test of time. The sunrise warmed his soul as he held coffee in one hand and binoculars in the other.

Treehorn watched as a vulture with its five-feet wingspan flew over. Its screech broke the silence. A bird's gotta eat. He watched as more gathered for the feast at hand. Round and round they circled their prey near the Four Corners.

A pale hand appeared around his ribs and caressed his abdomen, then inched its way to his coffee. He gladly surrendered it.

"Good morning." Treehorn raised his arm and kissed her forehead.

Dr. Samantha Reynolds smiled.

"Good morning. I love the coziness of this one-room hogan."

"I do, too."

"See anything interesting?"

"You," he whispered before his eyes caught a movement on the horizon.

A herd of wild mustangs galloped along the desert mesa. Their dusty haze at first obscured, then showed, the Navajo Nation Police vehicle as it appeared on the horizon. The SUV's flashing lights were a testament that something bad had happened and help was on the way.

Treehorn looked through the binoculars and recognized Police Chief Samuel Bear as he drove intentionally near their location to catch the Fed's attention.

"Anyone you know?" Samantha smiled as she guessed.

Treehorn thought, *Good one, my friend.* Smiling he said, "Samuel. Let's take the horses for one last ride."

11

"Since it's our final day here, I was thinking of a different ride there, Chief..."

"I was thinking of a different ride there, Mr. Special Agent Man." Treehorn teased.

Samantha laughed as she finished the coffee and walked toward the campfire.

Treehorn spun her around, picked her up, and placed her over his shoulder. But instead of heading inside, he aimed for the horses.

"Treehorn, you're going the wrong way!"

"I'm going right where we need to go."

The horses whinnied in the corral.

"It could be a dead body," he said, trying to pique the medical examiner's curiosity.

"Today's our last day," Samantha mused, eyeing the beauty of the land. The red soil laid the foundation for the sandstone outcroppings and sage brush.

"It could be *two* dead bodies," Treehorn coaxed.

"We could ride in that direction," she proposed as he lowered her feet to the ground.

Treehorn chuckled. "I'll get my weapon."

He hurried into the structure and emerged a minute later with his gun, badge, and handcuffs secured to his belt. A lightweight shirt covered his t-shirt and gear.

Samantha grabbed her fanny pack from its hook and checked it for her own ID, camera, and other essentials.

Treehorn quickly saddled the horses while Samantha covered the campfire with dirt.

"I can take your picture at the Four Corners Monument," he offered.

"Isn't that federal bribery across state lines?" she teased.

"You stand in two states and I'll stand in the other two."

"Let's enjoy the ride. We don't know if there's been a crime."

Treehorn knew Samuel wanted his attention. He wouldn't have driven out of his way otherwise.

Four Corners Monument

NNP Chief Samuel Bear watched as the two Feds arrived on horseback and thought, *Some people can't stay away from a crime scene.* He also knew his friend would satisfy his curiosity after he intentionally detoured near their location.

Treehorn and Samantha tethered their horses to

Samuel's vehicle. A young Navajo boy approached and asked, "Would you like me to water your horses?"

Treehorn opened his wallet and the boy saw the Federal identification. The agent handed the boy a tip.

"The horses and I would appreciate that."

The boy whispered to the Navajo, "Two dead."

"What's your name?"

"They call me Lenny, but it's Leonard. I'm named for my grandfather."

Treehorn nodded. "Thanks. I have a bad guy to catch."

"Do you want me to watch the lady while you work?"

Samantha winked at Treehorn.

"I got this."

She knelt at the boy's feet.

"Thank you for the offer but I have work to do here, too. I'm a doctor and medical examiner. I figure out how they died, then I help solve the crime."

The young boy's eyes rounded.

"I'll help you. Both guys were shot."

Samantha smiled.

"Thank you. You just made my job easier."

"I'll be here if you need more help."

Low elevation hills and sandy gravel surrounded the Four Corners Monument that led to a gravel parking lot.

Treehorn observed the NNP deputies cordoning off the visitor attraction from its Indian staff and the early-morning tourists.

He and Samantha approached the perimeter yellow police ribbon. Treehorn lifted it for her to walk beneath.

She presented her identification to one Deputy Torrez.

"Dr. Samantha Reynolds, Medical Examiner. He's with me."

The deputy pushed the ribbon down after the doctor passed and ordered Treehorn, "Stay behind the yellow tape."

Samantha chuckled and walked toward the monument.

Treehorn lifted his t-shirt and showed his FBI badge to the officer, "FBI Special…"

The deputy placed his hand on Treehorn's chest and shoved. "It's not your case."

"Torrez!" a man shouted, "Let the federal agent in."

Torrez lifted the ribbon, "Boss says it's okay, then it's okay."

Treehorn opened his identification and presented it to the officer for documentation, "FBI Special Agent John

Treehorn."

The deputy's eyes enlarged with recognition. He opened his mouth to say something then thought otherwise when he saw the annoyance on the Fed's face.

Treehorn ducked beneath the ribbon without commenting and entered the crime scene.

NNP Chief Samuel Bear watched the two Feds approach while he waited next to the white-sheet covered body.

Samantha greeted Samuel, "Did you *have to* drive by the hogan?"

The older Navajo smiled and said sheepishly, "Guilty."

Treehorn frowned as he eyed the taped-off area. The campfire, the sheet-covered body next to the vehicle, and the second body in the distance.

"Good morning, Samuel."

"Good morning," the lifelong friend greeted the younger man.

"Jurisdiction?" Treehorn asked.

"I gave you five extra minutes to arrive before I would have called the FBI Criminal Investigative Division.

It's definitely Feds, but more precisely, you'll want this case. Two dead males, one Indian and one not so much."

Samantha made an offer: "I can do the preliminary in Farmington and Dr. Gallagher can have his Sunday."

Treehorn nodded.

"Call it in, have Farmington send the Crime Scent Unit and the wagon."

Samuel handed Samantha his investigative kit containing gloves, plastic evidence bags, and needed supplies.

"Help yourself to anything else you need from my vehicle."

"Thanks, Samuel."

The police chief lifted the corner of the sheet that covered the first dead male.

"This one is Bart J. Baker, half-Indian, half-brother to Theo Nez."

"I haven't heard that name in years," Treehorn stated. Then, added for Samantha's benefit, "An old murder case."

"Mr. Baker took a rifle shot to the leg and hip. Revolver to the leg, both hands, and one in the skull. A little overkill if you ask me."

Treehorn countered, "Farmington could have handled this. Why do you think I need this case?"

17

The two Feds followed Samuel along a taped perimeter.

"The Indian was killed here," Samuel said, pointing to the stone, "Then someone dragged him from here to the Four Corners Monument."

The chief's hand showed the direction to the stone historical site.

Treehorn examined the large blood pool next to the boulder where the Indian sat as he bled out. Then he looked at the grooves in the dirt where the man's body dug into the soil as he was dragged the distance.

They walked toward the second sheet-covered body. It covered the man's face but not his arms and legs. They poked out from beneath it. One arm positioned in New Mexico, the other in Arizona. Someone had placed large stones on each hand, so they wouldn't move from their state's location. One leg stretched into Utah while the other lay in Colorado."

"The killer definitely wanted this case to be federal."

"Who is he?" Treehorn asked, lifting the sheet.

"Indian Posse."

No name, just a title is how Samuel answered. No name needed.

Treehorn uncovered the face of Paul Greyhorse, brother to Parker Greyhorse, leader of Indian Posse, the ruthless, vicious gang that operated throughout the Navajo Indian Reservation. They ran their criminal operation from a clubhouse west of Gallup, doling out justice against the white man when it suited their purpose, one case at a time. Their fingers were in multiple criminal pies, but they stood by one rule: no narcotics.

Law enforcement and residents questioned why, but only two men knew the answer and one of them was the Navajo agent who held the corner of the white sheet in his hand. The agent's clenched jaw highlighted what would be appearing on the horizon: *Trouble.*

Samuel said what Treehorn thought, "Everyone's loyalty will be tested on this case."

"Who's Indian Posse?" Samantha asked, eyeing the corpse.

"A Navajo gang," Treehorn answered succinctly.

Samuel remained silent.

"Could you elaborate a little bit?" she asked.

"When you examine both bodies, you'll find they carry an iron-branded 'IP' tattoo; it's the mark of their gang. Usually found on the right top wrist, some cover it with a leather wristband, watch, or jewelry."

Treehorn released the edge of the sheet.

"What kind of gang?"

"They're a vengeance-seeking posse who target white men who've evaded justice in the courts for crimes committed against Indians. They fund their operation by dealing in weapons and marijuana, no hard drugs."

Samuel added, "Once in a great while, they'll target one of their own if they're a traitor."

"Why haven't the Feds shut them down?"

"They've served another purpose for law enforcement."

"They provide information on crimes the Feds couldn't obtain within the boundaries of the law?" Samantha guessed.

Treehorn nodded.

"It doesn't make it right," Samantha stated.

"Tell the staff to take infectious-disease protocols with these bodies."

Samantha looked at the Fed, "We're trained, *Agent Treehorn.*"

The agent didn't smile.

"We have two murders to solve," Treehorn said, eyeing Samantha and Samuel, "That's our focus. Let's not forget it."

Chapter Two:

Brothers

The noise from the tourists watching the police caught Treehorn's attention.

"Samuel, how many men can you order here ASAP?"

"Eight are on the way," Samuel replied, looking at the parking lot to see if any had arrived.

"Get these people back now." Treehorn barked.

Samuel shouted to his standing deputies, "Torrez, Ramirez, you heard Agent Treehorn. Get those people back. Close the monument entrance until further notice."

"Samuel, we need to set up a perimeter."

Hearing the urgency in Treehorn's voice, the police chief asked, "How far?"

"The distance of a rifle shot."

Treehorn and Samuel scanned the area as the sun evaporated the morning dew and the wind stirred the ashes in the campfire.

"Order your vehicles to line the perimeter and that single ridge."

Treehorn pointed to the only higher elevation vantage spot where a rifle shot must have been taken toward the boulder and SUV.

"Three hundred feet?"

"Go five hundred to be safe and three hundred feet wide. Whoever did this was methodical. He knew where to position a rifle shot with night vision."

Samuel picked up his radio and began issuing orders to his deputies and the ones in their vehicles as they arrived at the area.

Special Agent Treehorn found a quiet, private location to call his supervisor on his direct home line in Washington DC.

Assistant FBI Director Leo Mancuso answered on the second ring, "Mancuso."

"Treehorn here."

"This had better be tragic for you to call me on a weekend."

"Two male gunshot victims, one on the Rez in Arizona, the other spread out in all four states on the Four Corners Monument."

"What's the point of calling me at home?"

"Paul Greyhorse."

"Shit," uttered Mancuso.

"Preliminary evaluation appears they were shot with a

rifle and a revolver."

Mancuso didn't readily respond as he processed the information.

"What's the status?"

"NNP Chief Samuel Bear arrived first. Dr. Reynolds is processing the bodies. We're waiting for CSU. Reynolds and I were scheduled to return to Washington tomorrow."

"Stay there. You want Agent Shelly?"

"Yes."

"You got him. Dr. Reynolds can assist Gallagher. I'll notify Quantico."

"I'm sure Gallagher will appreciate that."

The local, thorough medical examiner had worked on previous cases with Treehorn. He appreciated any help and never turned it away.

"Who's the second body?"

"Theo Nez's half-brother, Bart Baker."

"You take anyone you need to get ahead of this. If anyone has a problem they can call me or the director. I'll notify Eli Henderson. Do you understand?"

"Yes. I need one more person."

"Who?"

"Peter Greyhorse."

"Impossible," Mancuso stated.

"You know he'll come when he finds out his brother's been murdered."

"I'll look into it, but I won't make any promises. I'll send a couple roving agents to your area tomorrow to assist you."

"If possible, send rovers with ATF or DEA connections."

"Why?"

"Indian Posse deals in weapons and marijuana. I'll lay money one of those contributed to this case."

"Keep me posted and send updates daily," Mancuso reiterated, "Get ahead of this."

He terminated the call.

Treehorn watched Samuel assemble his deputies. They were loyal and efficient when the boss was on point. As other officers arrived, the NNP vehicles formed a secured perimeter with the yellow police ribbon tied to each SUV.

Samantha handed out plastic evidence bags, plastic numbered markers, pens, and disposable cameras.

Samuel ordered his men, "Look for shell casings, footprints, disturbed soil, anything out of the ordinary. Bag it and tag it. Get to work."

24

Using Samuel's binoculars, Treehorn stood on the hill and watched the NNP deputies work the area. Upon his arrival atop the rise, he recovered three rifle shell casings from where the shooter had knelt down and positioned his gun for the shot. Two sets of footprints still remained in the dirt. The agent took detailed images of both.

Samuel crested the hill and asked, "Find anything?"

"Three rifle shell casings and footprints."

"So, they didn't care if they left evidence?"

Handing two plastic evidence bags to Samuel, Treehorn requested, "I need you to look for something."

The agent provided a detailed plan to the police chief to follow. He knew his friend was the best Indian for the job because he excelled at one job in particular: tracking.

Samuel looked around, saw no one could overhear their conversation, then uttered a spirit's name, "Daniel Tsosie."

Daniel Tsosie, an NNP deputy, found gunned down over eight years ago. Agent Treehorn knew the case because it was his case, unsolved. An officer was murdered while changing a flat tire on his patrol car. Not a single witness and the only evidence on his body were two gunshots that entered the man's skull and ended his life that fateful night. The only evidence recovered at the scene were two bullets and two casings shot from the same revolver.

Treehorn had one bullet and casing locked in his safe at his Gallup office. Samuel kept the other secured with him. ATF wanted both bullets with its casings. Treehorn refused to turn them over. A pissing contest ensued, Treehorn won, ATF Assistant Director Colin Finch lost, and the two had butted heads ever since.

Treehorn suspected information on the case remained intentionally concealed, but Finch never once provided any clue that could have solved the homicide. The only thing the Fed and the Navajo Nation Police force knew was that Officer Tsosie had dedicated his life to working the Indian Posse crimes. Treehorn and Samuel both suspected this contributed to his death. Someone had moved his body, so it wouldn't be found the night he died. For eight years, Treehorn's investigative mind had wondered: *why move a body when no one witnessed the crime?*

Samuel grabbed Treehorn's arm to refocus his attention.

"We *both* want to know who murdered Tsosie."

Treehorn didn't deny that fact.

"You and I both know that Indian Posse knows what happened. Nothing occurs inside the gang without Parker

Greyhorse's knowledge."

Treehorn didn't deny that fact either.

Tightening his grip on Treehorn's arm the police chief added, "I want Daniel Tsosie's killer. We both know Parker knows who committed the crime. He'll give him up to you if you identify Paul's shooter. Promise me you'll do whatever it takes."

Samuel saw the indecision on his friend's face.

Treehorn hesitated and offered no response because he knew Parker Greyhorse.

Samuel uttered words to his lifelong friend he never expected to say: "Swear to me you will…" he whispered, "…on Skyler's grave."

Anger flashed across Treehorn's face as he heard his dead wife's name spoken. He grabbed Samuel's wrist and removed the grip from his arm. He considered his loyalty and met Samuel's eyes.

"I promise."

At that moment, he had a premonition that the price he'd pay would come at an exceedingly high cost to him, personally. Parker Greyhorse never surrendered information that wasn't beneficial to his own ruthless agenda.

Samuel nodded once and walked away to perform his job.

27

Treehorn stayed on the hill and watched the men carry out their evidence-collection search until he felt calm enough to resume his duties. The CSU and Coroner's marked wagons arrived from Farmington, as the agent found Samantha working on Paul's body.

Examining the bloody thermometer, she clarified, "He died around 10pm last night based on liver temp and his rigid state."

Treehorn remained deep in thought about his promise to Samuel.

"Tell me about Indian Posse," Samantha coaxed.

"The tale of three brothers, Porter, Preston, and Peyton Greyhorse. The story repeated for over twenty-five years tells the tale of a drunk driver—a white man named Johnny Dupree—who killed Paul's uncle, Porter Greyhorse, as he drove home from work one night. Dupree received a short and pathetic sentence in the local jail for killing the Indian. Many felt he didn't pay his debt to society." Treehorn had read the file years ago.

"What happened?"

"Two weeks after the white man's release from lock-up, he was found dead of alcohol poisoning. Someone literally ran a tube down his throat and filled him up with high-proof hooch. We're not talking a legal variety. When

28

law enforcement located his corpse, an "IP" brand mark was seared into the man's forehead—and thus Indian Posse was founded. Since then, a lot of criminals who receive lenient sentencing for their crimes have been targeted."

"A vigilante gang?" Samantha surmised.

Treehorn didn't deny it.

"Indian Posse grew. They mainly targeted rapists, child molesters, and domestic abusers, and the perpetrators usually had connections to Indian Posse members. They fund their organization primarily with marijuana dealing and distribution. They have just two rules: loyalty connects them and narcotic-dealing is prohibited. If you're caught possessing hard drugs or trafficking them, you're immediately kicked out of the group and your tattoo is covered permanently."

"Why are we hearing about Indian Posse now?"

"Social media and Daniel Tsosie's death. He was an NNP deputy who worked Indian Posse crimes exclusively. He was gunned down at the time of Theo Nez's death. Bart was Theo's half-brother."

"Are these criminals who've been deemed as not having paid their debt to society killed?"

"A few over the years have turned up dead, but none have been proven murdered by Indian Posse. Some are branded, while some are tattooed. Rapists get an 'R', repeat offenders get castrated, child molesters received a 'CM' brand, repeaters get their fingers cut off or they disappear, and domestic violence offenders get thoroughly beaten up from head to toe, and—usually with the instrument they used against the woman—they receive the brand 'DV'. All of the burn marks are flipped so when the perpetrator looks into the mirror they can see their mark."

"What's the latest estimate?"

"I believe the count is at one hundred fifty-one reported cases documented with the NNP and FBI. The hospital reported those cases by their legal guidelines."

"And have any of those cases been solved?"

"No."

"Why not?"

"Because not a single one of the victims filed a criminal complaint against their attackers."

"You're joking, right?"

"The victims would be signing their death certificate if law enforcement conducted a follow-up investigation. Everyone knows the unwritten rules. Treat people with respect and dignity."

"This wouldn't happen outside of the reservation." Samantha judged.

"We're not outside the Rez," Treehorn said, walking away.

The CSU Team, led by Irene Logan, immediately began their work measuring the area and collecting evidence from the NNP deputies. The boxes soon filled with bags of disposable cameras the deputies took of images of interest, their documentation, soil samples, pieces of trash, and papers from every deputy signed and cataloged. No stone was left unturned or taken for granted.

Su Hawkins, a ballistic technician, supervised her team on their measurements, the collection, and documentation of the rifle and revolver casings.

"Su, how did you get the Farmington detail?"

Treehorn had worked with the extremely competent, dedicated employee on many cases over the years, including Theo Nez's murder investigation.

"Covering a co-worker's vacation, but I'll be in Gallup tomorrow."

Treehorn transferred the three rifle shell casings he had collected in evidence bags to Su who accepted them with her signature.

Her staff also handed her the two casings recovered from the Paul Greyhorse campfire location. She examined the revolver brass, then studied it more closely where the firing pin struck the casing. It appeared as if the imprint held a familiarity from either a previous case or just a professional interest in her job.

The medical examiner's staff delivered a black body bag to Samantha for Greyhorse's corpse.

As Samantha removed Paul's wallet from his back pocket, a couple of tiny pebbles fell out from the front.

"Why would he have stones in his pocket?" she asked with surprise.

"Stop!" Treehorn ordered, observing the dried bloody handprint left on the man's trousers.

"What is it?"

"Empty his pocket," Treehorn requested, "Count the stones."

Samantha took an evidence bag and removed several tiny pebbles, half an inch in diameter and two large ones over an inch in diameter.

"Two large, several tiny."

"Tag and bag them."

Deep in thought, Treehorn walked away from Paul's body to his kill location.

Hurriedly, Samantha placed the stones in an evidence bag and followed the agent back to the blood pool. Her curiosity about crime mythology spiked her interest.

Samuel and Samantha watched as Treehorn searched the stones near the boulder and where Paul sat on the ground. A few stones appeared displaced, but one appeared strategically placed next to where the victim would have sat.

Treehorn lifted the stone. Beneath it, two letters were spelled out in tiny pebbles: TP.

Samantha wondered, "What does it mean?"

Treehorn answered, "Paul wants Indian Posse to find his killer."

"Then why not write 'IP'?" Samantha pointed out.

Treehorn met Samuel's eyes as he replied, "I'll ask Parker Greyhorse today when I see him."

Samuel knew Treehorn recognized the personal message of 'TP' that Greyhorse left for him. The Police Chief knew his friend didn't need Parker's help finding out what it meant. It was *Treehorn's Mark*—but he had concealed the truth from Samantha.

The medical examiner removed and bagged Greyhorse's right leather wristband. Beneath it, the 'IP' branding scar stood dark in the paler skin area. Her team loaded the body into its designated and tagged, black body bag, and wheeled it to the coroner's air-conditioned wagon.

Treehorn, Samuel, and Samantha now turned their attention to the body of Baker.

Samuel scanned the victim's fingerprint while the agent opened an evidence bag that contained his wallet. Several hundred dollars in cash remained untouched, a Texas driver's license, a couple telephone numbers, and a Texas parole officer's contact information with a release date and prior 'check-in' dates.

Treehorn snapped pictures on his cellphone of all the information.

"His release from prison occurred a week ago. Also, he reported to the prison near the dates of Theo Nez's and Daniel Tsosie's murders."

"Coincidence?"

"Don't believe in them," Treehorn said, returning everything to the labeled, plastic bag.

Samuel read his device, "7 to 10 for assault and drugs. He injured an ATF agent during a drug deal gone bad. Hey, since when do ATF agents conduct drug deals?"

"Joint operation or wrong place at the wrong time?" Treehorn questioned.

Samantha examined Bart's 'IP' brand and found a solid circle blackened tattoo.

"This victim's Indian Posse mark has been covered with ink."

Samuel answered, "Indian Posse kicked him to the dirt."

"What would a criminal have to do to get kicked out of a criminal gang?"

The ink application appeared to be a few years old.

"He dealt drugs."

"Isn't that their business?"

Treehorn clarified, "Indian Posse doesn't deal in narcotics, only marijuana. Any member found doing so is disavowed, their mark permanently covered by ink or burn marks."

"Even some criminals have standards," Samuel replied drily.

"Has anyone searched the SUV?" Treehorn asked, eyeing the brand-new vehicle.

"Torrez checked it for a body but found it empty."

Treehorn opened the rear, tinted-window doors. Two red duffle bags sat atop a black carpet liner. Inside one bag sat clean laundry, a 9mm gun, and a box of shells. He removed the clip and checked the chamber. The other bag appeared to be toiletries and dirty laundry. The agent motioned for Su.

"Another gun?"

The ballistic tech opened a gun box and Treehorn sat it inside. Su closed it and slid it into a slot in a larger box with its barrel facing the ground. She placed the bullets in a designated box. All safety precautions taken.

"Tag it and bag it. Have Irene check the items in the bag and collect anything of interest."

Examining the back of the SUV, Treehorn found a hidden latch that activated a concealed, removable compartment. When he opened it, he found that it contained at least one hundred pistols, revolvers, and ammunition.

"Su, get back here."

The ballistic tech walked back, took a look at the stash, and whistled.

"Wow!"

Samuel and Samantha looked over to see what had warranted Su's reaction.

"You don't see that every day," Samuel exclaimed.

The sound of a siren separating the crowd caught everyone's attention.

Treehorn and Samuel looked at each other, uttering the initials simultaneously.

"ATF."

The agent immediately snapped several pictures of the guns and container with his cellphone, then turned to face the new arrivals.

Looking through the windshield, Su identified the lead agent and whispered to Samantha, "This is going to be good."

Samantha asked, "Why?"

Su quickly answered, "No time."

Samantha's eyes darted from Su activating her cellphone camera to the approaching ATF-vested agents.

"Get away from the weapons!" yelled one of the agents.

Treehorn and Samuel blocked the man.

Su didn't budge.

"Hey, Fink." Treehorn mocked.

"It's Assistant Director Finch, you half-breed prick."

Samuel tag-teamed, "You sure spend a lot of time out in the field. Staff in the office hate your guts?"

Finch pushed against Treehorn's chest and the agent returned an even stronger push.

Samuel shook his head toward the three ATF agents who stopped in their tracks. He already knew his NNP deputies stood behind him.

Samantha moved to protect her corpse.

"We're taking the guns," Finch issued the order.

"They're in *my* possession." Treehorn sneered.

Ignoring the Fed, Finch instructed his agents, "Load them into our vehicle. Any Indian stands in your way, shoot him."

The ATF agent then promptly stepped in a pile of horse shit.

"Fitting…" Treehorn said, raising the corners of his mouth.

"Where's the money?" Finch demanded, scraping his shoe.

"What money?" Treehorn and Samuel asked simultaneously.

Finch angrily faced Samuel and accused, "Your deputies steal it?"

Samuel pulled out his revolver and aimed it at Finch's face.

"Say that again?"

As Finch dodged him, he stepped into the manure again.

"You wear it well," Treehorn said with a smirk, which infuriated the ATF agent.

Samantha moved the sheet so Bart's bloody wounds were visible to the ATF agents.

"Do you want to search the body for the money?"

She watched as two of the seasoned officers grimaced at the corpse. She then billowed the sheet, so Bart's body odor whiffed in the men's direction.

"Have you touched the weapons?" Finch asked, looking toward the vehicle.

"I just started counting them," Su replied, peeking out from behind the SUV.

Her blue FBI CSU overalls identified her to the ATF.

This time it was Treehorn who pulled out his pistol and aimed it at Finch's face.

"How many guns? How much money? Who were the players? Answer the questions and I'll allow you to remove the cache."

Finch didn't take kindly to staring into the barrels of two handguns. Even worse, he knew neither of them would think twice about shooting him.

"Paul Greyhorse brokered a deal. One hundred handguns, two grand each. There was a gun dealer we were after in Texas. He decided he could make more money selling weapons illegally than legitimately."

"What's his name, for the record?" Treehorn asked succinctly.

"Right now, you're on a need-to-know basis—and you don't need to know." Finch snapped.

Treehorn squinted at Finch's arrogance. He had contacts who could obtain the information, and the ATF agent knew this.

"Where in Texas?"

"Brownsville."

Treehorn holstered his pistol and motioned for Su to step away from the SUV.

Samuel holstered his revolver and motioned for his deputies to back away.

Samantha covered Bart's body and stepped back from the vehicle. No one ventured near the smelly corpse, and she kept her bloody gloves in plain sight for all of the agents to see.

An ATF agent quickly counted the weapons.

"We have ninety-eight, two's missing."

Finch looked at the two lawmen.

"Where's the other two?" he asked accusingly.

"No idea," the Fed answered truthfully.

Samuel added in seriousness, "There were two killers here last night and the vehicle wasn't locked when my deputies and I arrived first."

Finch believed that both men were telling the truth because neither had a reason to lie.

Treehorn added on a more professional note, "If you provide the serial numbers we'll keep an eye out for the two weapons."

"We'll find them ourselves."

The ungrateful agent turned around and stepped in the manure once again.

"Load them and let's get out of here." he barked at his agents.

Treehorn's and Samuel's amused faces angered Finch more as he stomped away trying to dislodge the shit.

Samuel wanted the last word, "You really should get out of the office more."

Finch gave both men the finger.

It didn't take long for the ATF men to transfer the weapons and speed out of the parking lot.

Finch whispered to his subordinate, "Send an immediate message out to every ATF agent. I want those two guns found, understood? It'll be a never-ending nightmare if those weapons fall into the hands of those assholes."

Walking around the horse excrement, Treehorn touched a broken tether where a section of the leather remained attached to Bart's bumper. Paul Greyhorse owned a painted pony. Seemed the horse may have escaped last night's shootout.

Treehorn turned to Samuel and clarified, "We know there were *two* killers. The two large stones in Paul's pocket told us that."

Samuel continued, "We know the killers were white. Indians don't touch dead bodies."

Treehorn countered, "True, but did one of the killers move the body or someone else?"

Neither man mentioned Greyhorse's final message written in stones.

The agent stated matter-of-factly, "Funny how Finch appears every time Theo Nez's name is mentioned."

Samuel drily added, "Now, he's attached to your investigation."

Su Hawkins, ballistic technician extraordinaire, asked the lawmen, "What do you want us to do with these two pistols?"

Treehorn and Samuel turned. Bewilderment changed to realization on their faces.

Holding up a .38 in a bloody plastic bag, Samantha teased, "You don't mind that I hid one in Bart?"

The ME winked at her co-conspirator.

Su removed a .357 revolver from a hidden pocket beneath her FBI insignia.

"Fink owed me a gun. I haven't forgotten."

Treehorn remembered the incident. Finch took possession of Nez's murder weapon years ago. The agent remembered the revolver, a six-shooter with initials created by inlaid mother-of-pearl that spelled 'DWJ.'

"You women amaze me," Samuel commented.

"We know," Su said with a giggle, removing a plastic bag and a small box from her ballistic toolbox.

Samantha removed the gun from its bloody bag and handed it to Su.

The ballistic tech placed both pistols inside the box and handed it to Treehorn.

"They both have their serial numbers intact. That should give you some answers as to what Finch is up to because I don't believe his story."

Treehorn agreed but he didn't repeat it out loud.

The medical examiner's staff made quick time of loading Bart's body into the black bag and wheeled him toward their wagon.

Treehorn somehow believed this wasn't the end of the line that Bart envisioned when he signed up for a weapons deal from Brownsville to Arizona.

Removing her gloves and touching Treehorn's arm Samantha said wistfully, "I'm sorry we didn't get that ride in this morning..."

"Me too."

"I'll see you in Washington."

"Have a safe trip."

He shielded her with the door of the SUV. The kiss and hug were quick but meaningful.

"I miss you already."

Samantha smiled as she walked away.

Treehorn watched her while Samuel stayed silent.

"My mother likes her."

"Anna has good taste."

Samuel smiled, glad that his friend had finally found some happiness after being widowed for so many years.

"Is she seeing grand-babies?"

"Probably," Treehorn responded, "She's the first woman I've brought home since Skyler."

"She would have expected you to find happiness."

"I know."

"What now?" Samuel changed the subject. He didn't want to think about his murdered niece, the same time Treehorn became a widower. That sadness never goes away.

The agent looked over the crime scene one last time.

"I'm going to Cibola."

"Parker Greyhorse's home and prison. I don't think your horse will get you there today." Samuel quipped.

"Can I borrow a vehicle?"

"Sure." Samuel shouted out to his deputy, "Torrez!"

The deputy hurried to his boss, "What do you need, Chief?"

"Clean out your vehicle and give the keys to Treehorn."

The agent nodded, "Thanks, Samuel."

"I'll pick it up in Gallup tomorrow. Let's get the horses on their way."

Treehorn and Samuel removed the saddles and bridles from the two horses and slapped them on their rears.

"Over 27,000 acres and those two horses will find their way home."

The men took the time to watch and listen as the two horses galloped away. Their hooves pounded the red earth where thousands of horses had traveled before them for generations.

Samuel and Treehorn loaded the saddles into the rear of the SUV, as Torrez took a spare gasoline can that was attached to all of the NNP vehicles and filled the tank for the drive.

"Thanks," Treehorn offered in gratitude.

"No problem. Can't have you running on empty while chasing a bad guy."

Samuel waited until his deputy walked out of earshot. "Parker Greyhorse."

"Indian Posse," Treehorn countered.

"Are you ever going to tell me what happened

between you and Parker?" Samuel asked, looking his friend in the eye.

"No," came the short-clipped response from the Navajo agent.

Samuel knew whatever knowledge Treehorn possessed regarding the ruthless gang's leader, it had nothing to do with the law. It was personal because the anger on the man's face reinforced that.

"We've always suspected Parker knew who killed Daniel Tsosie," Treehorn said, stating the one investigative fact from the dead deputy's investigation.

No one from the renegade group would break their code of loyalty and speak to any law enforcement officer. Unity was their strength.

"Daniel's caseload was 100% Indian Posse criminal investigations. We knew that alone could get him killed."

"We examined his caseload at the time of his death. We could have Raven run the cases again."

Samuel felt the weight of his dead deputy on his heart.

"You and I both know these two murders are the key that will solve my deputy's death. If Parker has any information, he'll surrender it to you."

"Yes, Samuel, but at what price?"

Treehorn had been hearing everyone's misbeliefs about Parker Greyhorse for years. The difference between them and him was that he knew from personal experience what capabilities the Indian Posse leader possessed because he had witnessed it firsthand.

"Whatever it takes this time. Fate has presented an opportunity for you to get answers. We owe a fallen officer that. We're the ones still walking on the red dirt."

Chapter Three:

Cibola

Treehorn drove the one hundred-eighty miles to Cibola County Correctional Center with only the police radio dispatcher's voice intermittently interrupting his thoughts.

On the first section of the drive, he thought about how Paul Greyhorse's and Bart Baker's deaths came before their time. The crime scene, the bodies, and the obvious target that the two men had become for someone who had planned the killings. The skilled marksman's rifle shot became the profile of one of the assailants. He wasn't the killer. His job was to disable the men. If the gunman wanted them dead, the rifle would have accomplished that. The two sets of footprints from the hillside to the campfire proved a pair of men walked the area. The man who shot the revolver had become the true killer.

Why drag Greyhorse to the Four Corners Monument? A non-Indian moved the body. Was it a sick individual who thought it was cool to place the deceased on the tourist attraction or to make it a given that the Feds would take a case when the body was placed intentionally in four states?

49

Treehorn came to a different conclusion. Someone knew he would be at his grandparents' hogan and the first federal agent to arrive on the scene, thus taking the lead on the case. Someone knew that he knew the victims. The agent deducted someone had planned the scenario to ensure his involvement.

Treehorn headed south on Route 491 toward Shiprock and its 27-million-year-old monadnock that was created from volcanic rock. It towered over the landscape in this corner of New Mexico. The elders told the story that once upon a time the Navajos lived on the rock and would come down to tend to their crops. One day, lightning struck it and trapped the people on it with no way to be rescued. His people refused to allow anyone to climb it, so the ghosts of the deceased wouldn't be disturbed. The NNP arrested numerous trespassers over the years who had violated the will of his People.

He had another ghost's home to visit before his arrival at Cibola. He pulled up to the isolated hogan of Paul Greyhorse. The agent wondered why the victim didn't arrange to meet Bart here. It was private and secluded.

Paul's late-model truck sat alone next to the small barn. No other occupants greeted him upon his arrival.

Treehorn telephoned in his location to dispatch before exiting the NNP vehicle. He removed his gun from its holster as a precaution. The agent approached the home, knocked, but received no response. Opening the unlocked door, he found it neat and uncluttered.

The Indian approached the barn and found its sole occupant, Paul's painted pony, wearing a horse blanket and a set of saddlebags. His broken harness dragged on the ground. The horse reared back as Treehorn approached, a testament to the scare he had received. A scoop of oats and a few calming words and the horse allowed Treehorn to remove his blanket and bags. The animal received a quick combing, examination, water, and a bale of hay before the man secured him inside the barn.

Donning a pair of latex gloves, he opened the saddle bags and found what he expected to find: cash and a .45 revolver, serial number intact. He returned to the hogan, made a quick cursory search, and documented a few items. His CSU department would arrive tomorrow to conduct a more thorough search and inventory. Two white envelopes sat atop a Navajo spiritual book, one addressed to Peter, the other to Parker. Both covered in a years' worth of dust.

Treehorn placed both inside an evidence bag for safekeeping.

Treehorn updated his location with his dispatcher as he departed Paul's home—once again with more questions than answers.

As Treehorn drove past Shiprock he knew any trespassers there had nothing on Indian Posse. The ruthless gang was run by a tribal police officer and Preston Greyhorse after Porter's premature death. The story, repeated over the years, was that Preston was arrested and convicted of aggravated assault of his neighbor, a white civil servant employed by the ATF. The man's wife was the sole witness to the incident. Nothing definitive in the investigation implicated which man instigated the fight. It became he said vs. he said.

Racist comments peppered the woman's eyewitness account of the events. White lawmakers put pressure on the white District Attorney, and finally, Preston met his fate at the hands of an all-white jury.

While Greyhorse did his time in jail, the couple arrived home one night to find unwanted visitors in their house. Preston's accuser and his wife were transported out to the desert. Staked to the ground, branding iron "IP" burns soon covered their bodies. The woman left a note. She stated that she had lied to the Tribal Police about the incident. Someone had slit her throat and her severed tongue was found in the campfire that heated the metal irons.

The FBI, ATF, and Tribal Police searched the couple's house for clues to the perpetrators while a gun and money left untouched in a cabinet. Prison provided a solid alibi for Preston Greyhorse and not a single witness came forward. No arrests were made. The case went permanently cold. The only thing of interest, found taken from the murdered couple, was a copper penny collection. Preston received a cancer diagnosis after his release from prison. His life ended a short time later in front of an evening campfire with what appeared to be a self-inflicted gunshot to the head.

Some said suicide while others said murder. Coroner ruled inconclusive.

Preston's brother Peyton, father to Parker, Paul, and Peter, led Indian Posse next. Sadly, one day, Peyton, a dedicated Indian judicial activist left home and never returned. Preston's inconclusive death report and Peyton's missing case file sat next to each other in Samuel Bear's filing cabinet, collecting dust.

53

Parker Greyhorse took control of Indian Posse next and shaped its destiny, including its numerous confrontations with Federal, State, and Indian law enforcement agencies. Looking back on its history, the only significant event Treehorn remembered during that time was the day they buried Preston Greyhorse, Samuel earned his promotion to Navajo Nation Police Chief.

Treehorn stopped at his Gallup FBI office to change his shirt and text a short message to his fellow agent, Raven Shelly. Two years younger, the pair partnered on multiple cases when Treehorn took the lead and Raven did the research. They became a solid investigative pair for the district, under the supervision of Eli Henderson.

Next, the agent drove the one-hour trip on the I-40 to Cibola County Correctional Center, a medium-security facility with both federal and state inmates. Capacity at near eleven hundred, the federal government also housed illegal and undocumented Mexican felons. Many of those, Treehorn found maintained their hometown connections to the Mesa Cartel, a deadly criminal organization from Northern Mexico.

Piles of documented cases detailing the long-term partnership of Indian Posse and the Mesa Cartel filled the filing cabinet of lead DEA agent Matias Quintero. His investigation files showed their marijuana distribution network from Mexico to the United States, although they maintained a lower priority status since heroin and fentanyl-related arrests commandeered the DEA's attention.

The two-story cement and barbed-wire structure rose from the desert floor. The motion-detected security lights brightened the area as Treehorn's vehicle entered and parked in the empty visitor lot. No amount of light could bring warmth to this facility, or warm the chill Treehorn felt crawl up his spine.

The agent entered the lobby where one glass barrier and a steel, locked door combined and separated all visitors from the correctional staff.

The white guard took one look at the man's attire of jeans, t-shirt, and a lightweight windbreaker and sneered, "No visitors allowed this late on Sunday."

Treehorn opened his identification. "F...."

"I don't give a shit who you are. No visitors this late. Do you *understand* English?"

Treehorn squinted at the man's sweaty, white face and without blinking examined the man's name tag: "L. Henson". He reached for his phone as he clenched his jaw.

A female operator answered, "Cibola County Correctional Center. How may I direct your call?"

"Assistant Warden Jennifer Buchanan."

"Your name?" the operator asked.

Treehorn leaned forward to make sure the occupants in the room would hear his voice through the six-inch wired security window, "FBI Special Agent John Treehorn."

A Hispanic guard behind Henson glanced around the man's shoulder at the Fed, and over to the correctional officer. He recognized the agent's name and moved strategically to watch the coming storm. His dumb, white co-worker didn't have a clue who he had just offended.

"I'll try her office. If she's not there, I'll place you on hold while I locate her."

A few seconds of silence was greeted by a no-nonsense voice, "Jennifer Buchanan."

"John Treehorn."

"Did you get held up?"

"Yes, by an overweight paleface by the name of Henson."

"I'll be right out."

Treehorn slipped his phone into the rear pocket of his jeans and made sure the movement exposed his gun and gold badge for Henson to observe.

The guard raised his middle finger and pointed toward the exit.

The Navajo agent curled his lip in contempt.

"Henson!"

The sweaty officer snapped to attention.

"Let the Federal Agent in!"

Henson hit the release button for the main door.

Treehorn entered and promptly unsnapped his service weapon from its worn leather belt.

"Gentleman, let me introduce you to FBI Special Agent John Treehorn who's definitely one of the most disliked men inside these four walls."

Treehorn glanced at Henson and said sarcastically, "I wouldn't go that far."

"I would. Make a note, men, this agent is to have 24/7 access here until further notice."

"Morales, secure the agent's gun and phone."

The guard accepted Treehorn's items and shook his hand.

"Eric Morales. Nice to meet you."

Treehorn nodded once.

"Henson, I need a replacement for Rockwell tonight and you just volunteered."

The guard clenched his jaw and nodded once.

Treehorn said nothing as the white man's karma arrived.

"Morales, tell the staff to secure the inmates in their cells. Let me know when that's completed."

"Yes, ma'am."

"John, let's wait in my office."

After the door closed behind their boss and the agent, Henson turned to Morales, "Feds don't show up here wearing jeans and a t-shirt. What makes him so special?"

"The Assistant Warden wasn't joking when she said the inmates disliked him. He's probably arrested all of the more violent offenders here. She doesn't want a riot on her hands when the inmates see him."

"We've had arresting LEOs here before with no lock down."

"He's the agent who walked Parker Greyhorse in here without handcuffs."

"That's against protocol."

"I know and it's still talked about. Did you know the Feds removed Greyhorse from central holding twenty-four hours prior to his arrival here? I guess they had a serious meet-and-greet with him."

"No, I didn't know. You think he gave up any information?"

"Does he appear to be the type to discuss his activities?"

"No."

"Do you know what Fed took him into custody?"

Henson suspected.

"John Treehorn," Morales said, shutting his co-worker down before leaving to comply with his boss's order.

The agent followed Jennifer into a basic administration office. Diplomas, achievements, and a graduation photograph from the FBI Academy lined the light blue wall.

"Do you miss it?"

"What? Being an agent?"

Treehorn examined her graduation image.

"Yes."

She pointed to another photo next to it explaining, "I married a widower last year and became a mother to his two young sons."

"Congratulations."

"A bullet ended my FBI career and the direction of my life's plans. We can't change the past. We can only forge ahead to the future."

She glanced one last time at both pictures.

"This is true."

The assistant warden examined her ex-co-worker. Half-Navajo, she knew he was thirty-five, the same age as her, same degree, and same status once held as a Special Agent. A status she retired when a bullet shattered her pelvis.

Treehorn remembered the day she surrendered her badge.

She remembered he held her while she sobbed.

Treehorn knew leaving the FBI had pained her more than the lead that pierced her body.

Jennifer stared intently at the handsome, resilient Navajo agent. She had envied his deceased wife, someone who had been loved and touched by him. She doubted whether the solitary man had truly allowed anyone in, since.

"Yes, we move forward."

"Greyhorse."

"Parker Greyhorse, leader of Indian Posse. The only inmate in here who no one dares to touch. And when I say no one, I mean staff included."

"What's his current status?"

"Three years left on his time. Not a single incident report recorded since his incarceration."

"How many Indian Posse members are here?"

"We have 1,100 inmates and 25 with the "IP" brand on their wrists. Parker and those other 24 control this place. He's aided by the Mexicans connected to the Mesa Cartel."

"Any recent problems?"

"No, but any prisoner stupid enough to screw with them pays the price."

"They're loyal. I'll give them that."

"I saw something on my first day here: an attack on José Gutierrez, a Posse member. He had a release date set for the following week."

"What happened?" The agent knew how the scenario would unfold.

"You would think the IP member would have walked away from a confrontation when freedom was so close within his grasp."

"And?" Treehorn wanted the identities of the parties involved.

"A group of MS-13s decided to corner a young IP member by the name of George Lopez. José stepped into the fray, choked the attacker, and broke his neck."

"José and Lopez?"

"Fifteen added to his sentence. Lopez's release date scheduled in a few months."

"And MS-13?"

"Parker Greyhorse had a little talk with their leader. Los Zetas haven't looked sideways at an IP member since. Loyalty, these men never give it up. It's like the brand they carry on their bodies. It's engraved on their souls. No one leaves Indian Posse."

"No one leaves them without Parker Greyhorse's permission."

"Exactly."

"What happened to Paul Greyhorse?" The assistant warden needed the details for the file.

"Shot dead. It appeared to be a gun deal gone south but even that's questionable right now."

"Do we need to keep this place on lock down for the safety of the inmates and guards until you have some definitive answers?"

"I can't make that recommendation, but I'll keep you posted as a professional courtesy if I believe anything may be of concern connected here."

The telephone beeped. Jennifer picked it up and listened.

"Thanks, Morales."

Treehorn glanced at the FBI photograph one last time. He rubbed his watch face, his father's gift to him the day he became an agent. The words that were spoken by the FBI director: 'Fidelity, Bravery, and Integrity'. No loyalty. He knew that wasn't true.

"They're ready for you. Greyhorse is in cell number 151."

Senior correctional officers lined the corridor. Their battalions readied for an offensive if Parker Greyhorse became a security threat. Sweat poured from Henson's face and darkened his shirt armpits as he stood at the rear of the pack. Their stance and demeanor made it clear the sole inmate intimidated them—but did not faze Treehorn.

The agent passed Henson without a glance, entered the general population wing, and walked toward Parker's closed cell door.

Inmates sensed the outsider among them.

The officers heard the routine prison noises change…to an uproar.

The inmates pressed their faces against the unbreakable glass in their steel doors in an attempt to catch a glimpse of the visitor who had entered their domain. The din started slow and worked up to pandemonium as they recognized Treehorn. The prisoners pounded their anger and hatred as they found anything in their cell they could use to make noise.

Morales watched in sick fascination as this single agent caused such an uproar.

The agent ignored them all, except one.

Assistant Warden Jennifer Buchanan stayed back and supervised. She watched with envy as the Fed's gold badge gleamed in the overhead lights. His long, denim-clad legs covered the distance within seconds across the cell block. She cracked a smile over the comparison between her stressed-out staff and the agent who stayed calm and on task. A different breed among men.

Treehorn looked neither left nor right as he walked directly to the cell. His face was reflected on the eight-by-twelve-inch, wired, encased safety glass in the gray metal door. He glanced inside, then ordered Morales, "Open it."

The guard unlocked it and swung it to a fully flat position against the wall. On a normal day, you'd hear the metal clang, but the uproar from the other prisoners masked any secondary sound.

Treehorn motioned for Morales to back away.

The guard looked at the assistant warden for confirmation.

Jennifer's voice carried the perimeter, "Everyone back."

She knew the inmate heard her terse statement. It may have earned her a future favor.

Morales stepped back while the other guards tightened their grip on their batons.

Treehorn stayed outside of the six-foot by eight-foot cell. Austerity would be overrated here. The gray cinder blocks, flat in color, matched the dull, dirty cement floor. The stainless steel toilet and attached sink, a different shade of gray, stood necessarily at one end. A threadbare blanket covered a single cot. Someone had removed the standard desk. A bible sat atop an envelope box on the floor. Cruel and undeserving punishment for any man regardless of what judgment had been levied against him.

Treehorn thought of the classic idiom as he stood outside the prison cell: *Better the devil you know than the devil you don't.*

Who was the devil here?

Parker Greyhorse, Navajo, and the same age as Agent Treehorn. Thirty-five. Over the years some psychiatrists had diagnosed him as a classic sociopath while others had deemed him a psychopath. Treehorn knew otherwise. Some thought they were brothers. In a previous lifetime, they may have been. Both were six feet tall, lean, with just enough muscles to win a fight.

Treehorn said nothing as the inmate's back faced him. The prisoner stared out at the barren landscape of his steel-barred window.

"How?" Parker's voice could barely be heard over the clamor.

"Bullet to the heart, then one to his head," Treehorn answered succinctly.

"Did he suffer at the end?"

"He accepted his fate."

"Peter?"

"Word's been sent."

"I knew you wouldn't be here if it had been my baby brother," Parker stated calmly over the noise, then turned and faced the man that had delivered him here for his imprisonment.

Treehorn's full body muscles involuntarily clenched as he stared at Indian Posse's leader. The inmate's face had aged slightly since their last encounter, a year earlier, but it was Parker's black, fathomless eyes that had showed the test of time. They lacked all emotion.

Each man sized the other up. Head to toe.

Treehorn examined the inmate. His long, black hair was restrained in a ponytail by a thin piece of leather, he wore the standard prison attire of a gray shirt and pants with a pair of black sneakers. His surname was printed on the flap of his right shirt pocket, while his prison identification number was sewn on the other. No watch or leather band. His only allowed jewelry, a silver wedding band.

Parker observed FBI Special Agent John Treehorn. His short, black hair cut to FBI standards, his heterochromic eyes of brown-blue showed his mixed heritage of half-Navajo, half-white, while his tanned body was outfitted casually in jeans and a t-shirt. His gold badge peaked out from beneath his windbreaker. He came directly from the crime scene on a day off. The red dust on his boots proved that, and finally the FBI watch he wore to tell time and his loyalty.

Parker raised his right hand. The one that carried his Indian Posse "IP" brand on the top of his wrist. He looked outside his door over Treehorn's shoulder and hand-signaled the inmate across from his cell.

Treehorn didn't glance left or right as each prisoner motioned the opposite prisoner, who in turn gestured to the next until the noise level decreased to a routine level.

The security staff watched the measurable progressive event.

The Fed took two steps into the prison cell.

"He didn't die alone."

"Bart Baker."

Treehorn wondered whether Parker guessed.

"What was the deal?"

The inmate knew the agent would figure out any details in time.

"Bart, his old lover…" Parker said, glancing at Treehorn's body, "…planned to hook up with some beers over a campfire upon his release from the Texas penitentiary. A weapons deal appeared. Paul said it felt wrong but he'd go through with it. The timing seemed... *calculated.*"

"Who brokered the deal?"

"Some Mexican half-breed out of Brownsville."

"You got a name?"

"Not one I'm willing to share."

Parker ambled forward into Treehorn's space. The agent didn't move a hair.

The inmate's breath blew against Treehorn's face, "I can give it to you for a price."

"You'll give it to me if you want Paul's killer caught."

"I already knew who, before you arrived."

Treehorn's only movement, his eyes squinted straight to Parker's, "Give it to me."

Parker reached out and caressed the top of Treehorn's wrist near his watch. He then stepped back with a leer on his face and closed his eyes to hold onto the memory.

If he had kept his eyes open, he would have seen Treehorn's clenched fist swing.

All Parker felt was the painful impact of the man's fist when it struck his jaw, causing his head to snap back and his body to stagger further away from the agent's personal space.

Treehorn raised his other hand to prevent the guards from rushing the prison cell.

"Back off!"

The officers looked to their boss for confirmation.

"Do what he says."

Jennifer watched as her ex-coworker appeared to lose his cool, something she had never witnessed in all the years she had worked with him. Her officers focused on the inmate while she focused on the Fed.

The guards retreated, the tension in their bodies displaying their displeasure. They wanted a reason to beat down this inmate. Everyone believed Parker controlled the Fed, except her. The assistant warden watched as the two strong men faced a confrontation that may have been long overdue.

Greyhorse straightened and flexed his jaw.

"Never lay your hands on a Federal agent." Treehorn snapped, relaxing his clenched fist.

Parker rubbed and moved his jaw, somewhat surprised that it wasn't broken. His lips lifted into a smile, but the emotion didn't reach his eyes.

"You'll pay for that one day soon, my friend."

And having a personality disorder that he did, in the blink of an eye he changed the subject, "Do you think Deputy Daniel Tsosie is up there laughing at me?"

Treehorn showed no reaction as the conversation diverted from his active murder investigation to his most challenging cold case.

"His investigation jailed me from the grave. He couldn't nail me when he was alive, but a roadblock set up by the NNP on their dead deputy's birthday caught me driving a vehicle with its trunk full of pot."

"You've lost your criminal touch."

Treehorn never speculated on the number of crimes the Indian Posse leader committed, but he knew without a doubt this man controlled his organization from this prison cell.

"I've had some time to think about that." Parker didn't elaborate on the details.

Treehorn asked the one thing Parker didn't expect, "How's the wife?"

"She hasn't visited me once since I've been here," Parker's humorous tone turned threatening, "Stay away from her."

"If she's part of this investigation then I'll interview her."

"She's not."

Treehorn doubted that.

"Tell me who killed Paul, so I can bring them to justice."

"You needn't bother," Parker sneered.

"It's my job. I'll make them pay with a prison cell just like this. Your reach isn't as long as you think."

"My arms are plenty long."

"Were you the target and Paul the scapegoat?"

"I don't believe my brother's activities had anything to do with his death."

"How do you know?"

"Because he never left a witness."

"Bart?"

"Trouble followed Mr. Baker like a shadow and cloak of deceit. As soon as I kicked him out of Indian Posse his usefulness to me became very limited."

"Why did you contact him after he left IP?" Treehorn caught Parker's slip.

The inmate hesitated as he clenched his fists.

"Some old business needed closure."

Treehorn clenched his jaw and felt the tic develop in his cheek.

"You may one day, if you're lucky, identify the killer but you'll never find him."

"Let me do my job."

Parker turned away from the agent and returned to stare out the bar-covered window.

"What do you see when you look out into the darkness?"

"Darkness."

Treehorn played the game, too. He also knew at that moment Parker wouldn't be of any further help to him.

"One day that'll change. I'll see you around, my friend. We'll be rattling some bones, soon."

"I'll see you in three years when you're released."

The agent missed Parker's smirk as he said, "It'll be sooner than later."

Treehorn eyed the other man's back.

"Do you want to make a bet on that?"

The agent's words echoed inside the cell as he walked out.

Parker chuckled.

Treehorn would lose that bet.

Jennifer observed the agent's face as he exited the cell. She recognized the demeanor: a man focused on his investigation.

Treehorn pulled the assistant warden aside.

"Can you email me a copy of his telephone records and recordings for the last month?"

"I'll have to separate a lot of calls. I should have it to you by morning. Why?"

"He knew his brother was dead before I got here and that's an amazing feat since Paul died late last night."

"You think the killer called him?"

"Someone did. Hopefully, it'll provide us with a solid lead."

Jennifer nodded.

"Nice swing."

"You missed the landing?"

"Yes, and so will my report. Can you keep me posted on the investigation if anything pertains here? We'll keep this place on lock down until morning for the safety of my staff and the inmates. It'll give everyone time to cool down."

"That's probably a good idea."

Treehorn walked out of the prison with more information than when he entered, but he questioned whether it would bring Paul and Bart's killing team to justice.

Henson examined Parker Greyhorse's visitor's log toward the end of his double shift. Only two visitors during the man's incarceration: an Indian lawyer named Delroy Byrd from Chinle, Arizona and a man named Benito Del Toro from Tucson. When the guard exited the facility at sunrise, he made a call from his car phone as he sat in the staff parking lot.

An older man answered on his speaker phone with a

simple, "Yes?"

"Parker Greyhorse had a visitor today."

"Who?"

"FBI Special Agent John Treehorn."

The sound of papers rustling irritated the guard while he waited impatiently for the man's measured response.

"I'm reading the *Indian Times* article this morning on Paul Greyhorse's death."

Henson became impatient.

"What do you want me to do?"

"Greyhorse is a problem. Are you working right now?"

"I just finished but I return for the evening shift."

"Make sure Parker Greyhorse leaves that prison in a body bag tonight."

"How much?"

One man calculated the other man's worth.

"A hundred-thousand-dollar contribution to your retirement fund. Find two inmates who will soon be up for parole. Tell them I know someone that'll make it happen."

"How do you want it to go down?"

The older man thought maliciously about how he wanted this Greyhorse's brother's life to end. Suffering would be required.

"What are my options?"

"Knife, but it's messy with no guarantee. Fentanyl would have less risk."

"Do the drug. That Indian prick is known to avoid narcotics. This time I want him dead and no longer a problem."

This time.

Henson heard the slip of the tongue.

The old man's anger increased, "I want him to suffer and you tell him his father-in-law did it. I want it to be the last thing he hears before he's sent straight to hell."

Henson wondered what Parker did to this man to make him so hate-filled crazy.

"I'll smuggle the drug in a plastic-filled syringe. I can hide the metal tip in the hidden compartment of my lunch pail. It will contain enough Fentanyl to drop a horse."

"Do it and I'll make sure I piss on his grave the first chance I get."

Ninety minutes later, northwest of Cibola and north of Gallup, Treehorn arrived at his mother's home on the reservation. The glow of lights welcomed him from the long day, as exhaustion settled deep into his bones. This case already felt black as the night.

Anna Treehorn welcomed her only son with open arms.

"I was here three days ago."

He welcomed the hug.

"I know but I love the feel of my only child in my arms."

She saw the tiredness etched on his face.

"Let me grab a quick shower."

"Are you hungry?"

"No, just thirsty."

Treehorn grabbed a beer on the way to his bedroom.

When he returned to the living room, a fire was crackling and his mother had prickly pear cobbler with vanilla ice cream waiting. It was his favorite dessert. He grabbed another beer and settled into the comfortable sofa while Anna sipped her rum.

"How bad?"

"Paul Greyhorse and Bart Baker, an ex-Indian Posse member. Both took a bullet to the head."

"Criminal was their middle names."

"I know."

"And Parker?"

"Visited him at Cibola."

77

Anna poured herself another straight rum, neat. A little larger than the first.

"Has he changed?"

"Not in the least. He said he knows who killed his brother."

Anna pursed her lips.

"You think there's more to this case than two dead members of Indian Posse?"

Treehorn nodded.

"He made an offhand remark about Daniel Tsosie."

"That devil never acts without a purpose."

"I need to find out his endgame and put a stop to it."

Anna knew from over twenty years of experience in dealing with Indian Posse, it wasn't going to end well for her son when Parker Greyhorse was involved in the investigation.

Chapter Four:

Calling Shady Lynch

FBI Field Office, Gallup, New Mexico

Treehorn arrived bright and early to start his day.

Mary Sweetwater, the office administrator, greeted him as he entered the building.

"The bulletin board is set up in Raven's office and I'll get you some fruit and sandwiches when you're hungry. He's probably drinking the coffee I made for you."

Treehorn had been telling Mary for years it wasn't her job to wait on him but she never once listened.

The agent entered his co-worker's office, which they shared whenever they worked cases together on the Navajo Indian Reservation.

FBI Special Agent Raven Shelly—33 years old, Navajo, married, father of two, and Treehorn's faithful wing man—watched from his desk as the coffee pot brewed its second carafe of the day.

"Finish the first one already?"

Raven smiled.

Treehorn observed the bulletin board positioned at waist level instead of its normal height. The adjustment became apparent when his fellow agent limped around it and his left strapped foot came into view.

"What happened?"

"Sprained left ankle. I fell in the living room."

Treehorn looked at his co-worker's injury and observed his flushed face.

"What *actually* happened?"

Raven whispered so no one would overhear, "I was chasing Dana when I tripped on one of the kids' toys."

"She'll now find comfort in your arms."

"Nothing wrong with that…"

The two men chuckled.

"Since when did murder become a funny matter?" came a third voice.

"Never, sir," Treehorn replied first.

Eli Henderson, District Supervisor, entered the office and closed the door. His hard-earned promotion had become overshadowed when his supervisor, Lyman Begay, committed suicide under suspicious circumstances. A cold case to this day.

"I read your report on the Greyhorse and Baker murders."

Treehorn and Raven waited for their long-winded boss to continue.

Eli grabbed a clean cup and filled it with the freshly brewed coffee.

"Indian Posse. Greyhorse's Gang. I lost track of the number of years. Sometimes, I wonder whatever happened to Peyton Greyhorse. As always, we've assumed he came to an early demise because of his activism. Father to three sons. The middle one, Paul, your murder victim. Will we ever know the truth? Only if the Spirits rattled his bones."

Treehorn and Raven remained silent. They both knew the man would get to the point on Indian time.

"Indian Posse, or more precisely Parker Greyhorse, has been the bane of law enforcement for years. I don't need to tell either one of you what you already know. He maintains leadership even while incarcerated at Cibola. Heaven help us when he's released and bound by no constraints."

The agents knew this to be true and waited for Eli's point in the conversation.

"Treehorn, I'm asking that you don't leave broken pieces of this investigation scattered across the Rez when you return to Washington."

The penny dropped.

"Leave only footprints."

Raven couldn't keep his glib comment to himself.

Eli continued to chew his territorial bone, "I'm telling you every agency and agent here will deal with Indian Posse after your departure, including Raven."

Treehorn's jaw clenched tighter. He nodded once to show that he understood what was expected of him.

"I don't want another dead LEO at the hands of Indian Posse."

"We have no proof one of their members killed Daniel Tsosie."

"And we have no proof that one didn't." Driving home his point, Eli continued, "You've never solved the deputy's case. I don't want another file sitting next to it gathering dust. Understood?"

Raven spoke before Treehorn, "The case had zero leads from day one. It could have simply been a crime of opportunity."

Eli turned on Raven, "That's where you're wrong. We all know Parker Greyhorse knows what happened that night."

"I was there when Treehorn interviewed him. He denied all knowledge," Raven said, defending his fellow agent.

"There's not been a single lead since that interview. I know because I've checked on a regular basis."

Treehorn defended his investigation but Eli appeared to have an ax to grind.

"How many times have you gone back to re-interview Posse members after Daniel's body was found miles from his car, dumped in the desert?"

Treehorn knew the exact number but refused to provide the answer.

"Why didn't you put pressure on Parker when he was arrested for the marijuana?"

"I questioned him when I transported him to Cibola. He gave me nothing."

"He wasn't going to give you shit on his way to prison."

"I think solving the cop's death has never been a priority for you for some reason you've failed to disclose."

Raven glanced at Treehorn's desk. Tsosie's file sat on the corner in a red envelope where it had been since the deputy's death. The agent hadn't dismissed it for a single day.

Eli shook his head.

"I don't know what it is with you, Treehorn, but Parker Greyhorse has always been two steps ahead of you.

He'll deal with his brother's killer when he's released from Cibola. We both know that. Every man has a weakness. Find his, and do what it takes to break him. Then make sure you pick up the pieces when you return to DC."

"Understood."

"Solve Daniel Tsosie's death or I'll speak to Mancuso about having you permanently reassigned elsewhere. Do I make myself clear?"

Both agents knew when to keep their mouths shut.

"What is it with you two that you can never tell the whole story?"

Eli looked at Raven's strapped foot and said, "A kid's toy? I could have come up with a better one than that. Thanks for the coffee."

No one spoke as Eli topped off his cup, opened the door, and walked out.

Neither Treehorn nor Raven mentioned the warning that came with their jobs. They both knew what was at stake in every investigation. Cases never ended with just a conviction.

"This is what we know. We have two murdered men. One was an active member and one was an ex-member of Indian Posse. One body was intentionally moved to get the

Feds' attention. We have a cache of ATF weapons that Finch confiscated. Said it was a gun deal with a Mexican from Brownsville. Parker Greyhorse knew Paul was dead before I showed up."

"Cibola is sending the phone records and audio recordings. Find out who called him last night and notified him of his brother's death. He mentioned Daniel Tsosie and the night he was arrested at the roadblock. Pull Parker's arrest file and court documents. Pull Daniel Tsosie's complete file. And last, he said his wife wasn't involved," Treehorn summarized the case.

"Which means she *was* involved. I'll check and see if Gina Greyhorse has any records on file."

"Let's get to work on what we can while we wait for the phone records to arrive."

"I'll watch for them."

Posted on the bulletin board first was the standard Navajo Indian Reservation map with the Four Corners Monument and Paul's cabin near Shiprock circled.

The driver's license image enlargement covered the top of the board with basic information:

Paul Greyhorse, Shiprock, New Mexico, age 33, single, Navajo. Indian Posse member.

Bart J. Baker, Gallup, New Mexico, age 38, single, Navajo/White. Ex-Indian Posse. Brownsville, Texas and Fort Stockton Prison, and supervised by Texas Parole. Drug possession and assault. Guilty plea. Half-brother of Theo Nez, Navajo.

Parker Greyhorse, Window Rock, Arizona, age 35, married, Navajo. Indian Posse Leader. Drug possession, Cibola.

Face #1 - Shooter - Four Corners Monument, Male Footprint

Face #2 - Shooter - Four Corners Monument, Male Footprint

The wall-mounted television, muted, flashed a media loop of updated arrests and law enforcement activity from the federal agencies, which both men occasionally glanced at.

Raven recognized a man, "Hey, there's Fink."

"Turn it up."

Treehorn's curiosity about the man's activity determined his decision to watch.

"Indian Times, Jori Lansing reporting. Today, Southern District ATF Assistant Director, Colin Finch, and DEA Senior Agent, Matias Quintero, released a joint statement regarding a border weapons-and-drug bust that occurred last Monday."

86

The video showed men dressed in black fatigues with bulletproof vests labeled "ATF" and "DEA". The next images focused on the post-law enforcement confrontation: the tailgate of the green military jeep, shrink-wrapped kilos of cocaine, piles of bound cash, and a container of weapons were neatly stacked for the cameras, while white, bloodied sheets covered the two bodies that lay slumped on the single truck seat. Two bullet holes were visible in the windshield but not a single bullet hole appeared on the SUV's exterior.

"ATF Colin Finch reported that in the southern New Mexico town of Socorro, 10 million dollars' worth of drugs were confiscated along with one million dollars cash, and a cache of illegal weapons. Two Mexicans who illegally transported the haul exchanged gunfire and died during the raid."

"Finch sure gets around," Raven said, muting the television.

"Yes, he does."

"That will make Hector look good for his re-election campaign."

Treehorn took the remote from Raven's hand and backed up the video to examine the weapons box.

"Something catch your attention?" Raven asked.

87

Treehorn took out his phone and snapped a picture of the container.

"The case Finch removed from Bart Baker's SUV yesterday appeared very similar. Can you contact *Indian Times* and get a copy of their video footage?"

"Sure."

Treehorn located Bart Baker's parole information online, dialed the Texas Department of Criminal Justice Parole Division, and pressed the speakerphone, "Is Parole Officer David Lincoln available?"

A Southern-accented voice answered, "Lincoln here."

"FBI Special Agent John Treehorn, Gallup, New Mexico."

"Badge and contact number?"

Treehorn provided it.

"Who offended you?"

"Bart J. Baker."

Computer clicks sounded over the telephone.

"Jeez, the ink isn't even dry on his paperwork. Can I assume he's not in the State of Texas?"

"You assume correctly."

"Where is he?"

"Dead on a slab in the Farmington morgue."

"Well, that just decreased my caseload."

Raven chuckled.

Treehorn didn't.

"Anything in his history that's not in the file?"

"Long rap sheet of dealing with narcotics. He's an ex-member of Indian Posse. We get a few of those assholes in here once in a while."

Treehorn met Raven's eyes.

"Baker's last drug charge got him caught dealing on the Kickapoo Indian Reservation. They literally kicked the poo out of him."

Treehorn didn't find any of this a laughing matter.

The parole officer coughed.

"The Indians roughed him up pretty bad, tied the drugs to his body, and left him to the elements. Lucky for Bart, a Border Patrol Agent found him but he didn't learn his lesson. A few weeks later he assaulted an ATF agent. A real piece of work. What's his cause of death?"

"Someone used him for target practice."

"I'll need a copy of the death certificate for the file," said Lincoln.

"I'll need a copy of his file for the investigation."

"No problem, Agent Treehorn. I'll send it to Gallup today, but I recommend that you read it cover to cover. It details his history, names associates, and another little tidbit."

"What's that?"

"A sealed court proceeding requested by the ATF. No one in this office could access it but someone wanted it never to see the light of day. You may have better luck."

"Can you make sure all of his visitor and telephone logs from day one of his incarceration locations are included?"

"Sure. No problem."

"Thanks."

Raven looked at Treehorn after he terminated the call.

"Sealed record?"

"Sealed by the ATF."

Mary Sweetwater's speakerphone interrupted Treehorn's train of thought, "Greyhorse's medical examiner, line one."

"Thanks, Mary." Treehorn clicked the speakerphone, "Hey, beautiful."

"Wow, Treehorn, I never knew you felt that way," Dr. Gallagher mocked the agent, as Raven spat coffee out of his mouth and onto his shirt and tie.

"I'm—sorry," Treehorn stammered, grinding his

molars.

"Results for Paul Greyhorse's and Bart Baker's autopsies," The ME continued, not missing a beat.

"Go ahead."

"What you see is what you got. Paul Greyhorse, first shot, the rifle to his femoral artery. Second shot, the revolver to his heart became the kill shot. He was dead when the third shot entered his skull. He would have died from the first bullet if left unattended. What was left of his blood pooled in his lower extremities before his body was dragged to the Four Corners Monument."

"And Bart Baker?"

"First rifle shot was to the femur then the pelvis. Either shot would have ended his life too. He was alive when the revolver's bullets struck his leg and hands. The .45 slug to his head signed the man's death certificate. I still think it was overkill. In conclusion, the rifle disabled the men and the revolver killed each, just in case you find two men arguing about their criminal charge."

"Drugs and alcohol?"

"Positive for THC and alcohol. You'll be sent the other results. You guessed correctly to Reynolds, both men were HIV positive and their bodies responded well to the new meds. They would have led a productive life of crime if a bullet hadn't stopped them."

"Where are the bullets you removed?"

"Su Hawkins stayed next to my side while I extracted all of them from both men. She said she didn't trust ATF Finch not to come in and steal them. Aren't we on the same team?"

"I thought so at one time. Anything else?"

"Mancuso sent Dr. Reynolds to conduct the autopsies on the two Mexicans who Finch is flashing on TV from Socorro."

"Thanks, Doc."

"Oh, one last thing. *You have a nice ass.*"

"Consider us even," Treehorn snapped.

Dr. Gallagher laughed as he ended the call.

Treehorn didn't.

Raven recognized his co-worker's intuitive look as he examined the bulletin board. They both suspected the murders appeared to cover up something, "Finch?"

"Find Quintero and tell him that I'm looking for him."

Treehorn texted Samantha, "*Send me the preliminary report on the two Socorro victims when completed.*"

"*Why?*"

"*Finch.*"

The agent dialed the ballistics department.

"Hawkins."

"Treehorn, any results?"

"No."

"You're slipping."

"I have a life outside of the FBI and I'm clever enough to secure any bullets when Finch is around."

"Smart idea in this case."

"Mancuso emailed me. An agent with ATF connections would be coming to secure the guns. I'm testing the slugs and guns we've recovered. I haven't run the serial numbers yet because I don't want to red-flag Fink and have him arrive to remove them, again."

Treehorn suspected that could happen.

"Greyhorse's permit?"

"The .45 you recovered matched his permit filed with the Navajo tribe. We know Baker's parole prevented him from carrying."

"Okay, keep me posted."

"What else would I do?" Su joked.

"Today." Treehorn parried back.

"I'll see what I can do, sir."

Next Treehorn dialed the Crime Scene Laboratory

lead technician.

"Irene Logan."

"Treehorn here. What's the preliminary?"

Papers shuffled.

"We've prioritized five specific locations. The monument, campfire, SUV, the knoll from where the rifle appeared to have been fired, and a second hill where we found additional footprints."

"Did you find anything out of the ordinary?"

"No. It appeared the two victims met there, partied together, were shot from the distance, then were shot close up, and lastly, one victim was dragged to the monument."

"What about the primary hill?"

"Samuel tracked it."

"And?"

"We have two sets of footprints from the rifle shooter's location. Sizes 11 and 13."

"And on the other hill?"

"Another size 13. Different sole treads on all three pair of shoes."

"Where did they walk?"

"Samuel tracked the two from the hill to the campfire. Size 11 and 13 shot the men. Those were obvious."

"And the other size 13?"

"He came off the other hill and dragged Paul Greyhorse to the monument."

"The FBI would then become involved."

"You may have a witness to the murders."

"I don't believe the third man's involved in the shooting."

"How do you figure?"

Treehorn theorized, "This man waited until the two men departed. Gallagher stated that Greyhorse's blood pooled in his lower body. That takes a little time. The man then came off his vantage site and dragged the body to the monument. What else?"

"Samuel submitted the two bags of evidence you requested, then found a third. I'll run the DNA."

"Thanks, Irene. Keep me posted on the results."

"Samuel found something on the second hill. He's delivering it to you personally."

"What?"

"The man left you a gift."

At that moment, NNP Chief Samuel Bear entered Raven's office, said "Good morning," and walked straight to the coffee pot to fill his "Samuel" cup.

Treehorn handed him the keys to the NNP vehicle as

he took his first sip.

"Thanks for the loaner. I filled the tank and spare can for you."

"Anytime. Did Parker give up anything?"

"He mentioned Daniel Tsosie's roadblock the day he was arrested."

"You mean the one time we actually caught him committing a crime?"

Sarcasm covered Samuel's bitterness.

Treehorn opened the red envelope on his desk labeled *"Daniel Tsosie – FBI – Confidential"*.

He glanced at the deputy's summary, his age, then at Samuel. His stoic demeanor showed no emotion as he removed the man's image.

Glancing at Treehorn, Raven observed the split second of hurt visible in his co-worker's eyes before he turned toward the bulletin board.

Treehorn pinned the deceased officer's uniformed photo right between Parker's dated arrest mugshot and Paul Greyhorse's picture.

Raven's fingers worked his keyboard as he said, sadly, out loud, "Tsosie, a young Navajo cut down in his prime, age 33, my age when he died, and the same age as Paul."

Treehorn repeated Parker's conversation in his head while he filled his coffee cup. One man's truth became another man's lie. When he faced Samuel, he felt composed.

"Logan said you found something on the second hill?"

"You have a witness."

Samuel removed a tiny evidence bag from his pocket and handed it to Treehorn. It contained a single penny.

"I found it placed on a stone as it waited to be discovered."

Treehorn's eyes met Samuel's.

"It's an Indian Posse penny."

The Police Chief stressed, "Yes, it is, and the lab lifted a print from it."

Raven understood this created a problem because every officer in the room knew the owner of the penny signed his death certificate by not intervening and preventing the death of a fellow Indian Posse member. His curiosity made him question, "Whose name is on the penny?"

Treehorn rubbed its smooth surface.

"Someone who didn't want to be identified. They removed it by sanding it smooth."

Samuel glanced at the coin adding, "That makes it a

traitor who hides in plain sight." He glanced at the images on the bulletin board, "Bart Baker and his half-brother, Theo Nez, both ex-members of Indian Posse. Those traitors hid in plain sight, too."

"Do you think they had anything to do with Deputy Tsosie's death?"

Samuel and Raven both looked surprised at Treehorn's question.

"A hiker found Deputy Tsosie's body in a desert dry wash. Doc Gallagher calculated he'd been there for at least 48 hours. Theo Nez died before the body was discovered," Samuel said.

"It could explain why we never heard anything," Raven surmised.

Treehorn speculated, "Nez *could have* shot Daniel Tsosie."

"Too bad he's six foot under or I would ask him," a woman's voice spoke from the doorway. Agent Melanie Hopper entered Raven's office with a fellow agent.

Treehorn and Samuel raised their heads in greeting while Raven spoke for all of them, "Assigned here?"

Melanie nodded.

"Yes. Special Agents John Treehorn and Raven Shelly, NNP Chief Samuel Bear. Agent Kendrick Moore,

FBI liaison with Treasury and DEA."

The agents shook the hand of the late-twenties, sharply dressed, African-American agent.

"Mancuso informed us we're at your beck and call until further notice."

"I see you haven't lost the flippant attitude."

Mel chuckled, "Someone will have to knock it out of me."

"Probably," Treehorn snapped.

"How are you, Samuel?" Mel asked, shaking his hand.

"Good. Are you staying out of trouble?"

Mel laughed, "No."

Examining the bulletin board and the usual suspects Kendrick said, "Mancuso said you asked for a Treasury connection."

Treehorn pulled out an evidence box from beneath his desk. He removed two labeled evidence bags. One contained a set of saddlebags, the other cash. He handed both of them to the newly arrived agent.

"There's $200,000 here. I want you to work with Treasury, then DEA, and finally ATF to find out where this money originated from. CSU needs to examine it before you take possession."

"I'll do my best."

"Watch your partner's back while you're at it."

"Where'd you find the money?"

Samuel watched as the agents transferred the evidence.

"Paul's painted pony at his Shiprock cabin."

Raven's computer dinged and he examined the email header.

"Cibola sent two telephone recordings from the last 48 hours."

"Samuel, stay and listen."

Treehorn updated the LEOs, "Parker Greyhorse, Indian Posse leader. He knew his brother was dead before I arrived at Cibola yesterday. The only person who could have called him was either the killer or someone who knew the killer."

Raven's fingers moved across the keyboard, "One incoming, Sunday, 3am and the other outgoing at 8am."

Treehorn ordered, "Put them on speaker so we can hear them."

A sympathetic man's voice offered his condolences, *"Parker Greyhorse, this is the Whispering Winds Crematorium. I'm sorry to inform you that your brother, Paul, has died."*

Parker whispered, *"I'm going to kill you when I get out."*

The man's reply spewed anger, *"A Colt .45 did it if you're wondering, not my gun of choice."*

The phone headset slammed down.

Treehorn instructed, "Play it again."

Raven clicked his keyboard and everyone listened closely.

Samuel voiced the obvious, "Parker knew him."

"He's also the sniper..." Treehorn countered, "...because the third man wouldn't have been close enough to determine the gun's caliber."

"Let's hear the second," Treehorn ordered.

Raven activated the audio and his eyes rounded as soon as the caller identified himself after the phone rang once.

"Shady Lynch."

Treehorn's fists clenched in anger.

"Parker here."

"Hey, what's up?"

"How's Uncle Hector doing?"

"He's working hard on his paperwork. Have you seen my nosy mojito lately?"

"Yes, I have and you better watch for him."

"He'll be searching for Paul's guiding spirit."

"He's at peace. How are my horses?"

"I'm taking real good care of them," Lynch assured him.

"Have you located my stray?"

"Yes, he's playing on the pond."

"You visiting soon?"

"I'll be seeing you on Monday."

"Don't forget to give the little mojito a kiss for me."

Parker laughed, "Oh, definitely."

Samuel's knuckles whitened as he grasped his black holster belt. He recognized the men's voices on the second recording. "It's going to be an Indian Posse afternoon."

Treehorn didn't respond to the comment. Instead, he removed a Glock from his desk safe and secured it to his belt. He then slammed the drawer, causing everyone to jump.

"What does that mean?" Mel asked Samuel.

"They show up in the morning and Treehorn spends the afternoon with them."

Samuel's face pinched in disgust.

Treehorn focused on the younger agents, "Kendrick, deliver the money to CSU and follow up with it when they've released it."

Kendrick nodded.

"Mel, check that crematorium. Do your job. Find out who made that call."

Melanie nodded at Treehorn's snip.

Raven watched his fellow agent's unusually angry behavior as he shoved his phone and keys in his pockets. "Cibola?"

"Cibola. Send those recordings to my phone."

Treehorn stormed out, leaving everyone on edge, except Mary Sweetwater.

All eyes went to the office administrator who did a little happy dance next to a chalkboard where Treehorn's lead investigator closure case number held a '60'. She erased that and wrote '61'.

Raven winked at her.

"What just happened?" Melanie asked flippantly.

Raven and Samuel looked at each other.

Neither one answered.

"Well?" Mel demanded.

Samuel relented, "There are only two men in this

world that make Treehorn very angry: One is Shady Lynch and the other is Parker Greyhorse."

"Who's Shady Lynch?"

Raven and Samuel looked at each other.

The agent joked, "A man with a perpetual bloody nose."

"That makes no sense."

"He's a spook."

Samuel knew the man's arrival spelled trouble.

Mary added her two cents, "Dirty rotten rat."

Melanie pointed to the case closure figure, "Why did his number increase?"

Mary dusted the chalk off her hands explaining, "Greyhorse and Lynch already know this case is solved. Now, they'll make Treehorn jump through every Indian hoop to its ending."

"Why?"

"Because that's what they're good at."

"And us?"

Raven remained silent. He knew how this would conclude.

"We're all in this dance together," Samuel replied, anger pinching his face.

One would think everyone would be happy the case is

solved, except the person who paid the piper for the tune.

Everyone in the room focused on Parker Greyhorse except Melanie, who studied the board where Theo Nez's image appeared to watch her. She would bet that the ex-Indian Posse member's spirit still danced among the living.

Treehorn quickly checked the supplies in his SUV. No agent traveled the Rez or the surrounding area in their vehicle, at hundreds of miles on command, without being adequately stocked with an FBI armament, clothes, and prepping supplies. He set his phone in its dash holder, looped both audio recordings and hit 'Play'. The agent's anger increased with every mile he drove from Gallup to Cibola as the speakers emanated the men's conversations. His flashing red and blue lights couldn't get him there fast enough as he sped down the highway.

Today, the parking lot overflowed with automobiles of staff, civilians, and visitors. Once again Treehorn entered the glass-enclosed security office and presented his identification to the correctional officer, J.J. Waterson.

"FBI Special Agent John Treehorn to see Assistant Warden Jennifer Buchanan and inmate Parker Greyhorse."

"That may be a problem. Is she expecting you?"

"No. Why is that a problem?"

"Let me see if she's available and she can answer your question."

The guard called her and received a quick response.

"Come on in," he said, hitting the buzzer and door release, "Sign-in sheet. Weapon and phone in the locker. You know the drill."

Treehorn readily complied.

"Follow me. They're waiting for you."

The agent wondered who "they" were.

Treehorn found the answer when he entered the office of Prison Superintendent Miles Lawson, a 60-year-old lifelong cantankerous correctional state employee who generally tolerated the Special Agent's professional visits.

Waterson whispered to Treehorn as he left him at the door, "Good luck."

Miles waved Treehorn into his domain. "Have a seat. We're just discussing you."

Assistant Warden Jennifer Buchanan sat in one of the two chairs positioned in front of the boss's desk while Treehorn sat in the other.

"Come to pay Parker Greyhorse another visit?"

"That was the plan."

"It's amazing, Treehorn. In all of my years, I've never

106

seen what I saw this morning."

Treehorn glanced at Jennifer whose eyes remained on her boss, but her middle finger tapped her leg. FBI code for *you're so screwed.*

"Eight am this morning the New Mexico Lt. Governor Maxwell walked into this office. He held a commutation for Parker Greyhorse."

"He's released?"

"The governor's office sent a vehicle, too."

"That was kind of them."

Miles slammed his palm down on his desk.

"I was here the day you brought Greyhorse in. My guards just about pissed their pants. I don't know whether they were more scared of you or Parker. Whose idea was it for him not to wear handcuffs?"

Treehorn knew the superintendent's tirade was only just getting started.

"I'm going to miss him. He's a brilliant sociopath and I enjoyed my conversations with him. I felt like I was his private psychiatrist."

Treehorn knew sociopath wasn't Parker's diagnosis and would lay money the man in charge had no clue as to how he'd been manipulated.

"I have to deal with the fallout here. Buchanan will

keep the facility on lock down for a few days to keep staff and the prisoners safe from attacking each other. Do you know what the irony is…" Anger denoted each word, "… *FBI Special Agent Treehorn*?"

"What?"

"Greyhorse was contained here. Now that he's released you and I both know he's going to make the person responsible for his incarceration pay…probably with their life."

"I don't doubt that."

"I have one question for you before I kick your ass out of here. I knew something was wrong the minute I read Greyhorse's conviction. Why didn't you do something about it?"

"His plea bargain was signed and sealed before the FBI even knew of his arrest."

"Then you boys slipped up on that one."

"I interviewed him twenty-four hours before his incarceration here."

"You got nothing. Do want to know why I'm thoroughly upset?"

Treehorn let the warden use him as his whipping boy.

"Parker Greyhorse made a few unkindly comments to my staff on the way out. He told them he made a list of every officer that had mistreated him and his gang. He would make them pay regardless of how long it took."

"I guess you should have given them their due respect."

Treehorn didn't take kindly to any prisoner being mistreated especially based on their skin color.

The warden's face flushed red and his eyes squinted at the Fed. "Get out!"

"May I see his cell? I can put in a good word with Parker for you when I catch up with him today. You know, out of professional courtesy, and such."

Warden Lawson considered his options and ordered his second-in-command, "Jennifer, please accompany the federal agent to Greyhorse's cell, then be as so kind to escort him off the premises."

Treehorn followed Jennifer out of the office.

"Greyhorse isn't the only problem here. I'm not going to apologize for his behavior."

"I didn't ask for one. Are you going to ask?" Treehorn chose his words carefully.

"I read Greyhorse's file. He pled guilty to the charge. You can take me out of the FBI, but you can't take the FBI out of me."

"I never questioned the charge."

109

"That's not the thorough professional FBI agent I knew." Jennifer noticed the man's reserved demeanor. "So, was it personal?"

"Like I said, Parker and his lawyer negotiated a deal faster than it took the ink to dry."

"Wasn't that alone suspicious?"

"Parker refused to discuss the matter before I delivered him here."

"So, what did the Feds question him about?" Treehorn refused to answer. The agents never disclosed their information unless someone needed to know, and she didn't.

Their arrival at Parker's cell prevented Treehorn from answering. Once again, the agent observed the bible, and this time, its lone placement on the pillow. He opened it and flipped the pages. "May I take this?"

Jennifer nodded. "I have something for you in my office."

Treehorn followed her out of curiosity.

She opened a cabinet and handed him a box. "Here's every letter Greyhorse sent to you. Someone marked, "*Return to Sender.*" I guess you didn't want to read them."

Treehorn placed the bible inside the shoe box of letters.

"Do you know what I found interesting about Greyhorse's plea bargain and court file?"

Treehorn refused to guess.

"Greyhorse pled guilty to the federal charge as long as its prison time ran concurrent and first with his state time. His federal sentence ended last week. It was as if he knew he would receive a commutation from the governor of New Mexico."

Treehorn needed to re-read that file and call Washington.

He dialed his office administrator, Abby. "Treehorn here."

"How's my favorite agent?"

"Busy hunting a shot in the dark. I have something in my desk that I need sent."

"What is it?"

"In my bottom drawer, there's a box labeled Nettie Tsosie."

"Did you find her son's killer?"

Abby delivered each of Nettie's letters to Treehorn's mailbox weekly. She knew he treated everyone with due respect and promised, one day, he'd find the man's killer.

"I'm on the case. Can you send me the whole box today?"

"I'll do it right now."

"Thanks, Abby. Is Mancuso available?"

"I'll check and good luck."

Chapter Five:

Two Bets For My Man

The telephone rang once. "Leo Mancuso."

"Treehorn."

"I figured you'd be calling after I got off the telephone with ATF Director Spencer."

"Who won the yelling match?"

"I would tell you never to draw your weapon on Finch again, but it gave me a bit of pleasure hearing Spencer scream like a whiny, little bitch. What's our status?"

"We may have a witness at the murder site. Parker Greyhorse has been released from Cibola, and Shady Lynch is in the area."

Mancuso processed the information, "Finch?"

"Yes, Finch took the cache of weapons, we recovered the $200,000 in transaction funds, and someone telephoned Greyhorse and informed him that his brother was dead before I arrived at the prison."

"How in the hell did Greyhorse get released?"

"Commutation from the Governor."

"What's Shady Lynch doing in the area?"

"I'll let you know when I run into him. He contacted Greyhorse."

"Is this day going to get any worse?"

"Two things: Greyhorse will be gunning for two people. He knows who killed his brother and then he'll go after the person responsible for putting him in prison."

"I told you to get ahead of this. First Greyhorse and now Finch kicked your ass. Why did Finch make a weapons deal at Four Corners?"

"Greyhorse and Baker worked a gun deal."

"Are you going to investigate it?"

"What do you mean? If it's part of the murder, yes."

"Come on, Treehorn, you're not stupid. You and Finch have circled each other for years. The whispers have grown. Finch is dirty. Why do you think he hates your guts?"

"Because I've sensed it since day one."

"Exactly."

"What are my orders?"

"Do your job. Bring him down. You have three things on your side."

"What?"

"I have your back and you have the law."

Treehorn felt the hair on his neck rise as he asked, "The third?"

"Parker Greyhorse."

"What does he have that we need?"

"When did you and Finch develop a dislike for each other?"

"During the murder investigations of Theo Nez and Deputy Tsosie. Finch took the gun and bullets from one and wanted the bullets from the other, but Samuel Bear and I held our ground and refused to surrender them."

"What connected the two cases?"

"Parker Greyhorse and Indian Posse."

"We both suspected at the time that he held the answers to both murders."

"He won't give up anything without a price."

"Find out Shady's and Greyhorse's agendas. Work the case and do what you have failed to do at this point: bring a cop-killer to justice."

"What if the cost is too high to pay even for us?"

"When has that ever stopped you? Find their weakness and exploit the hell out of it."

"And Finch?"

"If the money is a dead end...." Mancuso started.

"…then follow what you have. The guns," the agent finished.

"Which one?" his boss demanded.

Treehorn's lip curled as he said, "All of them."

Mancuso now had a bone to pick with CIA Assistant Director James Dieter as he dialed the agency's number. "Leo Mancuso here."

"Hey, Leo, how's it hanging over at the Hoover building?"

"What's Shady Lynch doing in New Mexico?"

Mancuso couldn't tolerate the man's evasive bullshit.

"That little scrapper does get around. First, he's on your side then he switches to ours."

"Treehorn's in New Mexico. The state's not big enough for both of them."

"Want to wager?"

"Okay. My man against yours. A favor, and the Hawaii condo for a week."

"Deal. My man against yours. A favor, and Jackson Hole house for a week?"

"Deal. What's Shady doing in New Mexico?"

"He's on vacation. You know the CIA doesn't operate on American soil."

"You and I both know Shady works the US/Mexico border as if it's an invisible line."

"I didn't hear you say that, but this time he's on your side."

"What side is that?"

"He's hunting a badge."

"Does this badge have a name?"

"Yes, not one the CIA's willing to share but I'll tell you what he did. He interfered with a brokered deal and two Mexican agents turned up dead. We're a loyal bunch to a fault."

"Depends on the day of the week, *'And ye shall know the truth and the truth shall make you free, '*" Mancuso said, quoting the CIA motto.

Dieter laughed, "Exactly."

Treehorn's supervisor pursed his lips as he terminated the call.

Mancuso opened his safe and removed the cream vellum business card with its telephone number written in solid gold. The assistant FBI director dialed the number which rang once and activated a recorded message, *"Hey, Leo, leave me a message."* Mancuso's jaw clenched upon hearing his name, "Treehorn's coming for you."

Mancuso's cell phone pinged. A straightforward message appeared from a Department of Defense secured server, *"Peter Greyhorse - AWOL. Consider him armed and dangerous."* Leo shook his head. The nation lost a great soldier today.

Mancuso's message light on his desk phone flashed red. *"Good Morning, Leo. D.A. Susie Shipley. We intercepted a wiretap this morning. An unidentified man arranged a HIT today with Cibola guard Louis Henson against Parker Greyhorse. Sending FBI agents to Cibola. Grand jury indicted Henson on hate crimes with his white supremacy group White Riders."*

Leo replied from his smartphone, *"Greyhorse released from Cibola. Send me that recording. Treehorn's on the case."*

As the agent drove toward the Rez in search of Parker Greyhorse, two black SUVs with tinted windows entered the Cibola Prison parking lot. The four suits exited the vehicles, gold badges, and guns secured beneath their dark suits.

Assistant Warden Jennifer Buchanan stood at the security door awaiting their arrival.

Jackson Freeman, the lead FBI agent, handed the woman a copy of the arrest warrant.

"Have a seat, gentlemen."

She glanced at the wristwatch her mother gifted her the day she graduated from the FBI academy. It read 2:30pm.

The ex-Fed gave the men a knowing smile and said, "He'll be with you shortly."

Henson and Morales reported to Cibola prison fifteen minutes later for their shift.

The four, armed FBI agents stood and watched their approach.

"Hey, Morales, can you take my lunch pail to my locker? I forgot something in my vehicle."

Morales glanced at the four gold badges who focused on Henson. "Carry your own shit!"

Henson knew his career as a guard was over when the agent stepped toward him and said, "Louis Henson, FBI…" and promptly relieved him of his lunch pail. "…we'll take your last 'meal.'"

Another agent lifted his handcuffs.

"Louis Henson, you're under arrest. Turn around."

"What's the charge?"

119

Henson knew his involvement in the White Riders would catch up with him one day so he'd kept meticulous records on their activities.

"Conspiracy to commit murder."

Agent Freeman removed his Miranda Warning card and began reading Henson his rights: *"You have the right to remain silent. Anything you say can and will be used against you in a court of law. You have the right to an attorney. If you cannot afford an attorney, one will be provided for you. Do you understand the rights I have just read to you? With these rights in mind, do you wish to speak to me?"*

Henson's face paled as he choked his response, "No."

Parker Greyhorse once told him his white-ass karma would catch up with him. The guard wondered how the betrayal occurred as the handcuffs snapped tightly around his wrists. He couldn't make a deal with the Federal District Attorney Susie Shipley to save his skin, because he hadn't a clue who'd hired him to kill Greyhorse. A telephone number, a lucrative deal, and subsequent cash transactions deposited anonymously into his bank account had been orchestrated from day one of the Indian Posse leader's incarceration. He knew the father-in-law was an alias code. Spy on the inmate and make the man's life miserable.

Henson managed that with minimal effort.

The African-American FBI Agent, Jackson Freeman, glanced at Henson in his rear-view mirror, "I have a question for you. You're not at liberty to answer, but by any chance, do you happen to know who Parker Greyhorse calls 'friend'?"

The two FBI agents assigned to the Albuquerque office glanced at each other and chuckled. Apparently, *they* knew the answer.

Treehorn stopped once en route to fill his gas tank and used the facilities to change into casual clothes. When he returned to his SUV, he opened Parker's bible and examined the single photograph hidden within the pages. Three teenage boys smiled at the camera. An Indian, a half-breed, and a pale face. He would hunt Parker Greyhorse down even if it took all day and night.

Agents Melanie Hopper and Kendrick Moore arrived at the Whispering Winds Crematorium in Albuquerque. The compound appeared to take pride in death and the afterlife. Beautifully aged, metal signs pointed to a cemetery, crematorium, and an outdoor marble-covered mausoleum. The agents entered the reception area. Signs pointed down a stone walkway where crypts and a columbarium for inurnments lined its walls.

A shifty, young man appeared from an office as soon as the agents arrived at the doorway.

"FBI Agents Melanie Hopper and Kendrick Moore. Your name?" Mel presented her identification.

The man answered, "Andrew Shattuck."

Melanie checked the spelling, "S-H-A-T-T-U-C-K?"

The kid nodded as a sweaty sheen developed on his pimply face.

"We're investigating a telephone call that originated here, Sunday morning, at 3am. Were you here at that time?"

The kid nodded but didn't elaborate.

"What were you doing here after hours?"

"When we have late-night cremations, someone stays to monitor just in case of power outages."

Melanie looked at the kid and asked, "Sunday morning?"

"I completed my paperwork in the office and jammed to some tunes."

"And?"

"This man scared the death out of me. He pounded on the door to get my attention."

"What'd you think he was a ghost?"

"When you work in this place around dead bodies all the time your imagination runs wild. Like one night, a flash exploded in the hallway."

"And?" Mel's curiosity diverted from the interrogation.

"Well, not a single light bulb needed to be replaced, so where did the light come from?"

"Kid, can you describe the guy?" Kendrick brought the attention back to the case.

"White dude, mid-forties, wore aviator sunglasses and a hoodie. He told me to keep my face down."

"So, a man showed up and asked to use the phone?"

"Yep."

Mel stepped a foot closer to the kid and asked, "What was the deal?"

The kid's eyes shifted.

"He walked in and offered me five Franklins to use the phone. I waited outside the office and kept my ear buds in so I wouldn't hear the conversation."

"And you kept your head lowered?"

"Until he finished his short call. I glanced up and saw him wipe down the phone with the corner of his jacket. How cool was that?"

The two agents didn't react.

"It was too good of a deal, huh?"

The agents' heads nodded once.

Kendrick removed an evidence bag from his pocket.

"The money?"

"Well, there's a little problem with that."

"Why, did you buy pot?" Mel grilled.

"No, that's illegal, *in this state*. I bought a new phone to talk to chicks."

"How much is left?"

"One Ben-n-n," the kid stuttered as he reached for his wallet. He opened it and a joint fell out from next to a condom.

"Stop right there," ordered Agent Hopper.

The kid froze like a deer caught in an automobile's headlights.

Mel snapped on a pair of latex gloves explaining, "I need the gloves for a cavity search."

The kid's eyes rounded.

"Joking. Hand me the wallet. I'll remove the money."

The kid gave a nervous laugh and handed over the nice leather. Then, he casually bent over and pocketed his joint from the floor.

"What do you want to do with your life?"

Mel eyed the kid while she placed the bill into an

evidence bag that Kendrick held.

"I want to be a pilot."

"Then I suggest you stop smoking dope."

"Oh, that's cool. I'm going to fly helicopters for the drug cartels."

Mel handed the kid his receipt.

"Ten years from now, we'll be arresting your ass."

The kid smiled.

"What happened after the guy wiped the phone?"

"Max, the janitor, came around the corner and told me no late-night visitors allowed."

"And?"

"He opened the office door and ordered the man to leave. The guy lowered his head and walked out. That's it."

Mel looked at the kid and said, "No, that's not *it*."

"I'm telling the truth."

"Can you point to the location where the guy knocked on the door to get your attention?"

The kid pointed to the glass. A smudge mark dirtied the window.

Mel smiled as she examined the evidence.

"Andrew, where's your toolbox?"

"Why?"

"We need a hammer and a screwdriver."

"Why?"

"We're taking the door with us."

"We are?" Kendrick eyed his partner.

"Yes, we are."

"Why don't we just call CSU to come and collect the evidence from it?"

"We're taking it to the lab tonight."

The agent questioned his co-worker's dedication.

"How many merit awards do you have?"

"I'm working on my first," Kendrick whispered.

"I have two because I go above and beyond the call of the badge. *Master Treehorn* taught me that."

"Master?"

"You'll understand it one day."

Kendrick removed his suit jacket and tie.

"Okay, grasshopper. Andrew, did you find the tools she needs? We'll drive the door to the lab."

"Hopefully the lab can identify prints or DNA on these items tonight because we need the results by the time we have the morning round-up at Gallup."

"Round-up?" Kendrick raised his eyebrows.

"Treehorn meets with the staff to discuss the findings so we're all updated at the same time and place in the investigation."

Chapter Six:

BAR NONE, An Indian Posse Establishment

Treehorn's phone pinged as his tires skidded to a stop in the dusty parking lot of BAR NONE. The gray, weathered building's exterior looked no different and it appeared no one had made an effort to change it with a whitewash paint job. Even the red Navajo dust would have been an improvement on the structure.

The agent examined Mancuso's message, *"Peter Greyhorse - AWOL, Shady's hunting a badge, and someone hired a hit on Parker Greyhorse this morning. Sending wiretap recording."*

Treehorn didn't budge from his SUV as he stared at the key fob in his hand. He could return to Washington tomorrow with the knowledge that Parker and Shady would take care of the killer. He knew they'd do it, without a doubt, the second he heard their recorded voices. His fingers turned white as they clenched the steering wheel. If he walked away, he wasn't doing his job. He knew he'd see this through to the end even if both men dragged him through the mud to its ending. Treehorn's grip relaxed on the wheel. He would keep his promise to Samuel and find

Deputy Tsosie's killer. Parker needed something from him and that would be the first payment in the negotiation.

Ike Johnson, the establishment's bouncer, sat on the porch in his comfortable chair under the building's sign, "NO LEOs ALLOWED", and watched the Fed's arrival. He looked at his trainee, Reggie Dunham.

"I bet you a hundred bucks you can't stop him from entering."

"Two hundred and you have a deal," the cocky rookie countered.

"Deal." Ike said, standing up to watch the song and dance, "He's all yours."

Treehorn exited the black SUV, locked it, and dropped the fob into his pocket. His long, white t-shirt shirt hid his badge, handcuffs, and pistol secured to his black leather belt. The agent approached the porch and saw the aggressive Indian staking a claim to the front screen door entrance.

"Trainee?" the agent asked, glancing at the older bouncer.

Ike gave one nod as he tapped his crooked nose. The appendage that Treehorn's fist had smashed into and broken a long time ago.

The agent looked at the trainee and asked, "What's your name?"

"None of your damn business."

Treehorn glanced beyond the arrogant youth's shoulder and then eyed the older man.

"Parker inside?"

Ike nodded once.

Treehorn gave the kid a chance, "Step aside, None of your damn business."

Ike chuckled.

"Name's Reggie and you don't belong here."

The kid remembered the stories told by the Indian Posse members of the day the agent and Ike went a single round, with his mentor losing. He raised his arms into a boxer's stance and prepared for a punch from the Fed.

Treehorn flexed his shoulders then charged the young man like a linebacker who needed two feet to the goal line.

As the pair smashed through the screen door, Treehorn lifted the lightweight and carried him toward the antique saloon bar, while the kid tried to make a dent on the agent's back with his fists. The kid's ribs impacted the corner of the bar and his howl of pain confirmed he had sustained either a broken or cracked rib. Treehorn dropped the kid like a sack of potatoes who now withered in severe pain on the floor.

"Ike!" Parker yelled.

"Yeah, boss."

The bouncer hesitated before approaching the Indian Posse's leader.

"Did you bet money against a member?"

Ike's eyes shifted from Treehorn to Parker. A bad sign.

"Two Franklins."

Treehorn's lip curled.

Parker reached out his open palm.

Ike handed over the money then Parker's fist swung and knocked the man on his ass.

"You *never* bet against an Indian Posse member unless it meets with my approval. Now take the kid to the medical center and babysit him."

Parker turned and kicked the kid in the ribs, who now howled in pain.

"You can take down any man if you know their weakness. Learn!"

The Indian nodded while he drooled on the floor.

Treehorn and Parker stepped around the kid as Ike assisted him up off the floor.

"Beer?"

"On duty."

Glancing around the quiet establishment Treehorn asked, "Where is everyone?"

"Out on Indian Posse business."

Criminal business.

"We received a call from a woman asking for our help. Her man slapped her around so some members went out to slap him around."

"You think that will change him?"

"He'll be given a choice." Parker left the rest unspoken.

"Where's Nola?"

Parker looked at the empty space behind the bar where the bartender usually stood silently working and explained, "She took a couple days off. Court case." He shoved the $200 into her tip jar. Today, Parker did her job: a beer and a water.

"How'd you get out of jail?"

"Would you believe, I had a *'get out of jail'* card waiting for me?"

Treehorn raised his eyebrow, "Who killed Paul and Bart?"

"They're being taken care of."

131

"They?"

Parker let that one slip.

"Your coroner dug out two different slug types, right? And, you already suspected there were two shooters."

"Let me do my job."

"You're doing your job."

"Tell me who they are so I can bring them to justice."

"How you and I define justice differs slightly, my friend."

"Tell me and I'll do everything to make sure they spend their life in prison."

"What would you give me if I whispered his name in your ear?"

"Nothing."

"What would it take for that *nothing* to change to *something*?"

"I don't have anything to negotiate."

Parker placed his hand on Treehorn's arm, once again leaned into his space and whispered seductively, "Cross the line and I'll give you the killer's name…"

"I'll be gone from here in a week regardless of whether this murder is solved or not."

"Cross the line and I'll tell you about Daniel Tsosie's killer."

"You don't know it."

Parker smiled but his eyes stayed flat black.

"Samuel can finally lay his deputy to rest."

Treehorn tolerated the man's touch on his arm.

"I'll tell you so you can close the file that's sat on your desk all these years."

Treehorn shook Parker's hand off him.

"If you had the killer's name, you would have given it to me a long time ago."

"You need to learn the art of negotiation."

"You mean manipulation?"

"Same thing." Parker raised his beer to the agent. "You just have a moral compass."

"You do not."

"You care about every victim."

"You don't care about *any* of them."

"I cared about you."

Treehorn closed his eyes.

"I cared about you, Parker. Friends care."

"I loved you."

"Parker..."

"You were there for me in my time of need."

"Everyone was."

"Not everyone."

The men finished their drinks as they remembered troubled times.

Parker reflected, "I miss Skyler and the laughs we had."

"I do, too, but the years have passed, and we've become adults."

"Without Skyler to guide us."

"You, me, and Shady."

"I still question Shady's definition of adulthood."

Treehorn chuckled. "True. You two *have* tested my patience."

"We've always done that."

"Because you two have always seemed on one side of the fence while I was on the other."

"I envied you and Skyler."

"Why?"

Parker leaned into Treehorn's space and whispered the answer.

Treehorn pushed him away.

"I see you've moved your wedding ring to your right hand."

"I see you're not wearing yours."

"Have you met someone?"

"Have you forgotten yours?"

"Who is it?"

"Sam, not your business."

"Is he Native?"

"Not discussing it."

"You swing for the other team finally?"

"No. Her name's Samantha."

Treehorn's thirst continued even after he downed his water.

"I've always admired that about you, my friend. Our sexualities never affected our friendship. Peter's straight as an arrow. Paul, he was queer as a two-headed penny. And, I was lucky enough to get the best of both worlds. And, you stayed friends with all of us."

"I didn't have sex with any of you, though."

Parker laughed, "I know."

Treehorn relaxed enough to chuckle, too.

"Do you think we would have turned out differently if our fathers had stayed?"

"I don't know. You had each other. I envied that with you and your brothers since I was an only child."

"So, now you're no longer alone. Is this woman as special as Skyler?"

"Not up for discussion."

"Be careful, Treehorn, when you hold something dear, you become vulnerable."

"Speaking of the vulnerable, where's Shady?"

"Haven't a clue."

"What have you two planned?"

Parker looked at Treehorn and stayed silent.

"This is why my patience runs thin around you two. I'm an FBI Agent. I want the murderer caught, convicted, and justice served."

"I want that, too. What are you going to do when you find Shady?"

"Either break his nose or bloody it."

Parker and Treehorn both laughed because they knew the history.

Treehorn could picture the white freckle-faced teenager from memory as he recalled, "He made the mistake of trying to kiss Skyler."

"She broke his nose the first time with one serious punch," Parker remembered, picturing her as a long-black-haired, brown-eyed Indian teenager, pulling back her fist and punching a scrawny pimple-faced white kid in the nose.

"When I arrived home, she was waiting to tell me he made a pass at her, then she broke his nose. I saw red."

"I shouted, '*Run, Shady, as if your life depended on it!*'"

Treehorn laughed as he recalled how his tanned fist struck the scrawny kid.

"I chased him down and broke his bandage-covered nose again."

"Do you recall the number of times over the years that you've bloodied or broken his nose?"

Treehorn remembered as the years passed.

"I broke it only two more times. On the day he graduated from the FBI Academy and then, again, on his thirtieth birthday."

Shady at 16 wearing a baseball cap as he received a fist to his nose. Bloodied.

Shady at 17 wearing a beer cap as he received a fist to his nose. Bloodied.

Shady at 18 wearing a white shirt and tie as he received a fist to his nose. Bloodied.

Shady at 19 eating cake as he received a fist to his nose. Bloodied.

Shady at 20 wearing a University of Arizona jersey as he received a fist to his nose. Bloodied.

Shady at 21 wearing a green turtleneck as he received a fist to his nose. Bloodied.

Shady at 22 wearing a long-sleeve black football jersey as he received a fist to his nose. Bloodied.

Shady at 23 wearing a graduation cap and gown as he received a fist to his nose. Bloodied.

Shady at 24 wearing an FBI-monogrammed t-shirt as he received a fist to his nose. Two punches, left and right fist. Bloodied then a broken nose.

Shady at 25 wearing a khaki shirt in the jungle as he received a fist to his nose. Bloodied.

Shady at 26 wearing a sombrero as he received a fist to his nose. Bloodied.

Shady at 27 wearing black and green camouflage face paint as he received a fist to his nose. Bloodied.

Shady at 28 wearing a mask during Mardi Gras as he received a fist to his nose. Bloodied.

Shady at 29 smoking a joint as he received a fist to his nose. Bloodied.

Shady at 30 wearing a heavy ski jacket on a mattress as he received a fist to his nose. Definitely broken.

Shady at 31 eating a corn dog on a stick as he received a fist to his nose. Bloodied.

Shady at 32 wearing a filthy, grease-covered shirt as

he received a fist to his nose. Bloodied.

Shady at 33 sitting on the hood of a Jeep as he received a fist to his nose. Bloodied.

Shady at 34 wearing sunblock on his face as he received a fist to his nose. Bloodied.

Shady Lynch's birthday is this week. Gift: a bloody nose.

"Broken three times, bloodied too many," Treehorn chuckled.

"What happened the two other times?"

"He did something he shouldn't have," Treehorn replied, his smile disappearing.

"Are you going to enlighten me?"

"No."

"You ever wonder why he returned?"

"We all do. We're friends. It's that simple."

Parker drank his beer, wondering how wise it would be to update Treehorn on the current events.

"What are you and Shady into?"

"Are you asking as a friend or agent?"

"Agent."

Parker would have answered if he had replied 'friend'.

"Still on the fence, Treehorn? In the white man's land,

you're looking in, and on the Rez, you're looking out.
Never truly fitting into either."

"There's no fence when I wear my badge."

Treehorn stood up, went behind the bar, and removed
another water and beer from the cooler.

"What's Nola's court case?"

"The little pissant that touched her walked out of jail
this week."

"What were Paul and Bart into?"

Treehorn wouldn't stop his questions until someone
was held responsible for the loss of these men's lives.

"I'll tell you something about their deaths if you tell
me something."

Treehorn thought about his limited options and
nodded once.

"Bart picked up the guns in El Paso and transported
them to Paul who held the money to pay for them. Bart's
plan required that he return to Texas to pay the guy. ATF
would nab the illegal dealer. Now tell me, what's wrong
with that picture?"

"Why go to such lengths? Give the money to Bart to
make the transaction and have the ATF arrest him
immediately."

"Exactly."

The two men's eyes met in silent communication.

"Tell me why you walked away after my attack," Parker whispered.

"I gave you a night at the hospital. It was all I could give. I realized that day I wasn't cut from the same cloth as you and Shady. Probably I'd always known it, the feeling of being on one side of the law while you two were on the other side," Treehorn clarified.

"I needed you."

"I know."

"You walked away."

"I returned to Quantico, my job. I promised you that I would deal with your attackers when I wore my badge."

"Shady took care of one of them." Parker finished his beer and slammed it down onto the counter. "He didn't need a badge. He had a knife."

"Have you ever identified the other man?"

"Yes, fate played its hand. I recognized him the night of the roadblock arrest."

"Give me his name and I'll put my handcuffs on him."

"Why should you arrest him when I have the option of staking him to the ground?"

"Because I'm the law."

"White man's law."

Parker pushed the empty bottle aside while Treehorn threw his water bottle into the recycle bin.

"Someone hired a hit on you this morning at Cibola."

Parker's eyes clashed with Treehorn's.

"Hope they got a refund."

"Who's gunning for you?"

"I would say the same person who's always wanted me dead."

"Who?"

Treehorn watched as Parker changed. The Indian Posse leader's face shut down, telling the agent nothing more would be forthcoming.

"Watch your back and tell Shady I'm looking for him."

"I'll be sure to do that. You've seen how fast that little freckle can appear and disappear."

Parker watched Treehorn's long legs as he walked away from him, again, and headed toward the broken front door.

Unfortunately for Shady Lynch, he decided to make his entrance at the same time. He lacked the timing to get out of the way of Treehorn's right swing. The impact with his nose caused his body to fall back and land against the wall of Indian Posse pennies, where he found no way of avoiding Treehorn's next maneuver of clutching him around the neck and holding him hostage.

Shady removed his dark handkerchief, never white because that would be a sign of surrender—something he wasn't well versed at—and used it to absorb his blood.

"My mojito! I don't think it's broken this time."

Treehorn clenched his fist and pulled back his arm, readied to deliver a second blow.

"Who's the badge? What's your agenda?"

There were no preliminaries when he dealt with the sneak.

"Nice to see you with Parker. Is there a bed in the rear of this place that I didn't know about? You know I don't kiss and tell."

Both men heard the distinct click of a switchblade. Shady used his free hand to wipe his bloody nose and because he had a death wish, he pressed it against Treehorn's pristine white t-shirt.

Parker approached the pair.

"Jeez, Shady, that's ballsy, bringing your knife to a fist fight."

Shady smiled, his pearly white teeth contrasted with the blood on his face.

"Better than a gun."

"Put the knife away before Treehorn shoots you with his."

"Put your hands up!" A DEA-labeled, bulletproof-vested man appeared and held a pistol aimed at Treehorn.

Shady slowly raised his arms. Bloody handkerchief in one, his knife in the other.

"You, drop the knife and you, step back from him."

The DEA agent's gun moved from man to man.

Treehorn gritted his teeth and squeezed Shady's neck tighter before he released him, slowly raising his hands as he stepped back.

A click sounded behind the DEA agent's shoulder.

"Nice picture. Holster your weapon, Rodriguez, he's on our side."

DEA Quintero holstered his own weapon and pocketed his phone.

"And the guy with the knife?"

"Shady Lynch. You have my permission to shoot him," Quintero joked.

Treehorn stepped between Shady and Rodriguez's barrel.

"You don't want his agency crawling up your ass."

Parker interrupted the men's pissing contest with, "If

you don't have a warrant get off the premises."

Rodriguez holstered his weapon and proceeded to do a fake pat-down of his pockets.

"I have it somewhere."

"You got a warrant?" Treehorn snapped, his face flushed angrily.

Rodriguez gave him the *"Are you serious?"* expression.

Quintero stepped back from the doorway as Treehorn grabbed the DEA agent, shoved him through the door, and sent him flying off the porch where the man landed on the red-soiled parking lot.

"What the hell?" The young officer stood and readied himself for a fight.

Treehorn raised his shirt and presented his gun and badge.

"FBI Special Agent John Treehorn. You don't enter these premises without a warrant. Do you understand?"

"What are you, a lawyer?" the man snapped, attempting to dust off the red dirt from his uniform.

Quintero chuckled and shook his head.

"Come to think of it —*Yes, I am.*" Each word was stressed by Treehorn.

Quintero pointed the younger agent to their SUV. He

understood the silent command.

Rodriguez gave Treehorn the finger as he walked away.

Treehorn's lip curled.

Parker arrived at the porch and handed the two agents bottled waters. "Take them to go."

Quintero accepted the water.

"Heard you got out today. Planning on staying out of trouble?"

Parker looked at Treehorn and said, "I plan on getting laid."

Treehorn grabbed the water as he quipped, "Good luck with that."

Quintero spoke to Parker's back, "You're lucky you're bisexual. If one sex turns you down, you can go for the other."

Parker answered Quintero's comment by giving him the finger.

The DEA officer chuckled.

The FBI agent didn't.

"Job getting to you, Treehorn? You seem a little *tense.*"

"I have the Greyhorse-Baker case."

Treehorn watched as Parker disappeared from sight

back inside *BAR NONE*.

"Never enough answers."

"That's the nature of the beast. Raven said you had some questions about Socorro."

"Tell me about it."

"That was a shit show. Finch invited us to the photo shoot. The plan: ATF's credited with removing weapons off the street, DEA received the drugs, and the New Mexico governor made to look good with both deeds and a couple million in cash for the police coffers."

"What happened?"

"Finch happened. It was supposed to be a meet-and-greet, not shoot and kill."

"Explain?"

"The two dead Mexicans didn't belong to a cartel, but I'm thinking Mexican CIA agents who gathered information against the Mesa Cartel for the transaction. Finch denied shooting them but when we arrived the two dead men were still warm, and supposedly everything in the van remained untouched."

"Supposedly? Whose drugs, money, and weapons?"

"The cocaine belonged to the Gutierrez Cartel, not the Mesa Cartel. An offer, maybe, to make someone look good. You know how favors work. The thing is I took a couple samples to test. The drugs were shit but provided a worthy photo shoot."

"The weapons?"

"They belonged to the ATF. One hundred guns were being returned to be destroyed."

"A hundred? Baker's weapons locker in his vehicle contained the same number."

"Coincidence?"

Quintero raised his eyebrows. The agent knew of Treehorn's long-standing stance.

"Never believed in them. And the cash?"

"There's the million-dollar question. You know what's missing?"

"What?"

"A million dollars. Someone will pay with their life and then some for that."

Treehorn eyed the entrance of the *BAR NONE* establishment where two men tried to reinstall the broken screen.

"Have you let your patrols know Parker's out?"

"Why? Nothing's changed. We knew he ran his operation from Cibola."

Treehorn's black mood increased as he looked at the establishment.

"When Parker and Shady get together I know we'll all be kept busy."

"Parker does *some* good in delivering marijuana to the sick."

"Illegal but true."

"Better than the narcotics poisoning our kids."

"Again, illegal but true."

"Shady keeps the agencies hopping. Has anyone ever determined his agenda?"

"Depends on the day of the week but this time someone crossed a serious line."

Treehorn clenched his jaw as several cars departed in different directions from the rear parking lot. He ground his molars because he knew Shady rode away in one of them.

"Old case. Whose car was Parker driving when he was arrested?"

"Randy Bonito's."

"How did you know the answer so quickly?"

Quintero grimaced, "You don't forget some cases."

"Was Parker set up?"

"I believe so."

Treehorn needed to re-examine Greyhorse's file.

"Who did it?"

Quintero shrugged his shoulders, "Whispers, Bonito appeared to be caught in Finch's cross hairs with a car full of weapons and pot he transported from Brownsville. I think it was a put-up show for something else."

"You think Parker became the set-up and fall guy?"

"Maybe. Now that Parker's out we'll see how the penny drops."

"Where's Randy Bonito now?"

"Probably shitting his pants if he's heard Parker was released early."

"Do you know what happens to an Indian Posse member who's disloyal?"

"They don't live to regret it."

"I thought the Feds interviewed Parker before his prison term."

"I had him for 24 hours. He only told me what I didn't want to hear."

"Every man has a weakness, Treehorn. Find Parker's and exploit it."

Treehorn wondered how Quintero would have reacted if he told the DEA agent that *HE* was Parker's weakness. He felt no further ahead in this investigation. Shady's running told the agent all he needed to know. Parker and Shady were up to their eyeballs in this case, and neither one would be forthcoming with any information until he found more answers.

The agent sped down the highway toward his mother's home. He needed a shower, a clean shirt, and a comfortable bed. His phone rang as he left the pavement for the red dirt road to Tohatchi.

"Treehorn."

"Hello, Mr. Special Agent Man."

Treehorn visibly relaxed as he said softly, "It's good to hear your voice, Samantha."

"Can we talk?"

"Yes. Are you still in Socorro?"

"I finished the two autopsies."

"And?"

"The two men, José Vargas and Juan Garcia, were raised in a Reynosa orphanage. They took good care of themselves. Diet, dental, all in good health. Their records are connected to an El Capitán of the Mesa Cartel named Benito Del Toro."

Treehorn clenched the steering wheel.

"Go on."

"Interesting fellow. His records were sealed by Leo Mancuso and a recently redacted name of an FBI agent. Do you know anything about that?"

"If I did, I couldn't tell you."

"That didn't answer my question."

"Samantha, you know our relationship may interfere in investigations."

"Now, that *did* answer my question."

Treehorn pinched the bridge of his nose.

"Remember Dennis Donovan?"

"Yes."

The Fed recalled the dirty FBI agent who died while in an FBI holding cell in Williston, North Dakota. The investigation remained open on Treehorn's caseload until he located Hanna Redstone's twins. He didn't give up on any victim regardless of how long it took for justice.

"Small world. Whoever assassinated Donovan also killed these men in Socorro."

"Are you 100% positive?"

"Treehorn, are you questioning my work?"

"I question *everyone's* work."

Samantha chuckled.

"A sniper shot the two men with an M-16 rifle while the vehicle traveled down the road. Blood splatter in the truck proved that. A shooter then walked up to the men and put two 9mm bullets in each of their skulls. The handgun's ballistics matched the slugs removed from Donovan."

"What about the rifle?"

"There's no ballistic history. That's a dead-end."

"What else?"

"The cocaine sample showed its poor quality. It would have caused more problems on the street than its value."

"You have the information on the drug quantity, cash, and weapons, right?"

"Yes. Is there anything else?"

"I've missed you."

"I've missed you, too. I'm sorry I haven't called."

"Hard case?"

"Yes."

"I'm returning to Washington tonight."

"Samantha, when I return to DC, I may be in a bad mood for a long time. I want you to know it has nothing to do with you."

"Okay."

"It has *nothing* to do with you. It's this case," Treehorn reiterated.

"I'll try to understand," Samantha whispered.

"I'll tell you the story of Parker Greyhorse when the time is right."

"All right. Be safe."

"You too. Call me when you arrive in Washington."

"I will and good luck finding the connection between the cases."

As Treehorn drove his vehicle over the pothole-laden road to his mother's home, he knew Shady Lynch and the Mesa Cartel connected these cases. When he caught up with the little nose-bleeder, he'd pound the truth out of him.

Chapter Seven:
Mrs. Parker, I presume?

Treehorn entered the front door of his mother's house and set Parker's letters on the coffee table. He washed his hands in an attempt to rid himself of the taint that he felt now covered him. Sleep wouldn't be his companion tonight, so he made a fresh pot of coffee. His mother's soft steps reminded him he wasn't alone.

"Hungry?"

Food, the panacea of a long day.

The weariness etched on her son's face worried her, but the stain on his shirt caused anxiety.

"Is that *your* blood?"

"No."

He filled his cup and hers, too.

"Long day?"

As she sat on the sofa she noticed the box of envelopes.

"What's this?"

Her curiosity allowed her to check the contents. She noticed the chronological order of each. The first letter's flap had been re-taped, the postage stamped a year ago with

155

its FBI address crossed out and 'Return to Sender' written by her son's pen.

"Did you read any of them?"

"The first one, then I returned it."

"Where did you get these?"

"Cibola. They freed Parker this morning."

Anna sat aside her coffee and headed for the refrigerator.

"Do you want a beer?"

"No. There's more. Shady's in town."

Treehorn watched as his mother's expression darkened.

She grabbed two beers for herself, "Two devils dancing."

"They both know this case from the beginning to its conclusion."

"The only two men on this planet who can outstep, outmaneuver—and probably outrun you—too."

"They can't outrun me." Treehorn knew his ability. "They're hiding something."

"Don't we all? Let me guess, they don't want you to play in their sandbox?"

"That's the problem, they do. Parker knows who killed Paul *and* Daniel Tsosie. Shady's not talking, yet."

"Let me guess, both of them probably want something you have?"

"Probably, but I don't know what it is at this point."

"Find out their agendas and do what you do best."

"They don't play by any rules or laws for that matter."

"True and Leo Mancuso knows that."

"My loyalties lie with the FBI."

"Funny, when the FBI's motto is fidelity, bravery, and integrity. No loyalty."

Treehorn rubbed his watch and said, "I think it's a given."

"Samuel will understand if Tsosie's case remains unsolved."

"I made him a promise and it's my cold case, too."

"Then, make sure you carry your dance card."

Treehorn rubbed his weary eyes

"I need a shower to wash off this day."

Anna finished her first bottle as her son walked away. She thought of the times over the years that her son had spent with Parker Greyhorse and Shady Lynch. She always knew one day something would occur that would test their boundaries.

Treehorn's telephone pinged from Samuel as he re-entered the living room, newly showered and shaved, *"Randy Bonito's at TMC."*

The agent typed: *"ETA 30."*

Samuel replied: *"No hurry. I'll be here."*

Treehorn pocketed his phone.

"Samuel's at Tséhootsooi Medical Center with Randy Bonito."

"Is he dead or alive?" Anna raised her eyebrow.

"I didn't ask."

"You're a man of two worlds. You've dedicated your life speaking for the victims. Remember that tonight."

Treehorn grabbed his gun and FBI equipment and drove to the hospital.

Tséhootsooi Medical Center

When he arrived at the TMC parking lot, only Samuel's NNP vehicle sat in the dedicated spot for law enforcement.

Treehorn entered the emergency department and approached the staff with his identification open.

"FBI Special Agent John Treehorn. I'm meeting Navajo Nation Police Chief Samuel Bear regarding Randy Bonito."

As he spoke to the older woman, a younger woman dressed in a nurse's uniform caught his attention.

"Hello, Gina."

"He's in the morgue," Gina Greyhorse answered for the receptionist.

"You know this man?" the woman asked her co-worker.

"I wouldn't go that far, Debbie."

Treehorn didn't respond.

"Gina, do you mind showing him the way? I'm sorry, Agent Treehorn, the construction's made a mess of everything. It would be easier if she pointed you in the right direction."

Treehorn glanced at Gina. "I'd appreciate your help."

Gina pursed her lips and nodded her head in the direction of a clear plastic-covered hallway.

As soon as they distanced themselves far enough from the receptionist, Treehorn asked the woman, "Mrs. Parker, I presume?"

"Hello, Treehorn." Her voice lacked any resemblance of warmth.

"Where's your husband?"

"How should I know?"

"I assumed you would know his whereabouts since he

was released from Cibola this morning."

"I didn't know and I don't care to know."

Treehorn gave the green-eyed brunette a serious stare-down but she didn't flinch.

"Did he have anything to do with this?"

Gina ignored his question and said, "Down the hallway. Last door on the right."

"Tell your husband I'll be seeing him."

Gina sneered, "I'll be sure to do that."

She watched as his long legs carried him down the corridor. The nurse felt the color of her gray scrubs matched her dying spirit. She wondered what color women prisoners wore nowadays.

Treehorn entered the morgue and found Police Chief Samuel Bear standing silently beside a sheet-covered body on a gurney.

"What happened?"

"I responded to a male being dumped in the ER parking lot. The death comes as no surprise. It's Randy Bonito, age 29."

The corpse's arm lay outlined beneath the white hospital sheet that covered the rest of his body.

"Indian Posse member and another dead Navajo."

160

Samuel lifted the sheet.

"Ex."

A fresh flesh-burnt circle covered Bonito's old Indian Posse "IP" brand.

Treehorn's stomach heaved as the smell of scorched skin competed with the morgue's disinfectant smell.

"Cause of death?"

Treehorn's question became rhetorical as Samuel flicked the sheet off the upper half of the body.

"IP" hot branding iron marks scorched the man's body. They started at his neck and disappeared beneath the sheet.

"He's covered to his toes."

The agent frowned at the severity of the torture.

"The mark of a traitor." Treehorn observed Bonito's blood-covered face. "His tongue?"

"Cut out," Samuel said with a grimace.

Treehorn snapped a picture and forwarded it to Leo Mancuso with an attached message, *"Randy Bonito, DOA, Ex-Indian Posse Member."*

"You know Greyhorse did this?" Samuel said, covering the deceased to his neck with the sheet.

"What was the time of death?"

"Approximately 4pm."

161

Treehorn nodded once.

"The NNP can only cover so much of the Rez and Diné have refused to report these crimes. But this…" Samuel points to the corpse, "is wrong. Greyhorse isn't like us. We follow the law."

"White man's laws." Treehorn knew the difference with his badge.

"Greyhorse deserved to be in prison."

Treehorn looked at his friend and fellow officer as he said sadly, "You've always believed Parker contributed to Daniel Tsosie's death. I chose to follow the facts."

"Parker refused to provide an alibi during the time of my deputy's death."

"Doesn't prove he killed him."

"Doesn't prove that he didn't."

Treehorn refused to inform Samuel that he knew Parker's exact location and activities during that time frame.

"Has Randy's next-of-kin been notified?"

The agent tensed as a man's voice answered from the doorway.

"Yes, I have," Parker Greyhorse said as he ambled into the morgue.

Samuel mocked, "You're Bonito's contact?"

162

"Indian Posse members are loyal and family, plus Randy's an orphan." Parker eyed Treehorn. "Hello, again."

The agent passed on the greeting and went straight to the interrogation, "What got him killed?"

Parker smiled and Treehorn observed that once again the smile didn't reach the man's eyes.

"He wasn't loyal and forgot the family."

Samuel lacked subtlety as he snapped, "Did you do this?"

Parker countered, "I heard Daniel Tsosie was another dirty cop."

Samuel charged Parker.

"Why, you…"

Treehorn stepped between the two.

"…pig!"

Parker's body slammed against Treehorn's back while his arms tried to strike Samuel.

Treehorn pushed Samuel back with his arms while he used his body to push Parker back.

"Stop it, you two."

Parker looked at Samuel with disgust over Treehorn's shoulder. "If Samuel ever turns up dead with a bullet, I'll be your first suspect."

Samuel countered, "It'll be a double homicide."

"Stop it," Treehorn shouted.

Parker glanced once at Bonito's exposed head and then ignored the body. He placed his hand on Treehorn's shoulder who immediately shrugged it off.

"After you left me earlier…"

Samuel snorted.

"…I got thinking about our conversation. Can I have a minute?"

Treehorn questioned the Indian Posse leader's sincere expression and checked the time on his FBI watch as he replied, "I'll give you *one* minute."

The Police Chief wondered whether the Fed had misplaced his objectivity.

"Don't waste your time with him."

"Samuel. Please."

Treehorn felt his exhaustion weighing him down. Having to deal with these two men didn't help the situation. One would think that they're related the way they're at each other's throats.

"I'll wait here." The Police Chief unsnapped the leather that restrained his holstered pistol as he said sarcastically, "Give me a reason to fire my weapon."

Treehorn shook his head at Samuel.

As Parker and Treehorn walked toward the morgue's

164

office, the agent's phone rang.

"Wait inside." He pointed toward the empty grieving room. "I have to take this."

Parker sauntered toward the office.

The agent relaxed his clenched jaw as he answered his phone, "Treehorn."

"Mancuso. I told you to get ahead of this."

"Out of my control."

"Greyhorse is running this shit show."

"I know and that's what will solve this case."

"I doubt that. Do I need to assign a different lead agent?" Mancuso demanded.

"No, sir, but there's going to be casualties. I'm on this to the end."

"Does Greyhorse have knowledge?"

Treehorn eyed Parker as he waited in the office. "Yes."

"How bad is this going to get?"

"Real bad."

"Have you seen Peter Greyhorse?"

"No," Treehorn said, closing his eyes and pinching his nose.

"Good luck because now you have another trained killer in your midst and the Military Police are en route to hunt him down."

Mancuso abruptly terminated the call.

Treehorn wondered, who was the other trained killer?

Parker held the door for Treehorn to enter.

Samuel's eyes begged Treehorn not to acquiesce to the Indian Posse leader's demands.

Treehorn walked ahead and never looked back.

Parker closed the door and lowered the window shade.

Treehorn didn't know what the ruthless leader of Indian Posse wanted, but he kept his surprise to himself when Parker spoke.

"I can tell you how to solve Deputy Daniel Tsosie's murder."

Treehorn wondered why after this many years. "What do you want in return?"

Parker provided Treehorn with his three demands. "The first two now and the last when Samuel can bury his deputy with honors."

Treehorn's seven generations of ancestors would be proud. He stood stoic and didn't flinch as he listened to Parker's voice weave his tale. It wasn't what he expected. Treehorn watched as the hands on his watch traveled for fifteen seconds. That's how long it took him to contemplate his options and lose a little piece of himself.

"Yes, I give you my word."

Parker nodded once. "Ask me any question and I'll tell you no lie."

"Who killed Daniel Tsosie?" Treehorn wouldn't waste this opportunity.

"Neither I nor Paul were there but my brother told me that the gun that killed Deputy Dan was the same weapon that killed Theo Nez. Find the gun and you'll find the killer."

Parker pulled out his phone and the two men completed their business.

"Why did you get into Randy Bonito's car that night?"

Surprise flashed across Parker's face. "I needed to be someplace."

As Treehorn met Parker's eyes, he knew he'd only been given half of the answer. He yanked open the door and found the Police Chief hadn't budged.

Parker said with a smirk, "Sammy, you'll never find Daniel Tsosie's killer. How many years has it been?"

Greyhorse took his right middle finger and rubbed the corners of his mouth as if he had tasted something good, while the "IP" brand on his wrist pointed toward the police chief.

The flush rose on Samuel's face. It took all of his willpower not to smash his clenched fist into Parker's face. The man's only saving grace, the Indian Posse leader turned, gave him the finger, and walked away.

"See you around, Treehorn, don't forget our agreement."

Treehorn thought of his deal with Parker and tasted the bile rising in his throat.

"What did he want?" Samuel demanded.

Treehorn answered with a question, "How many times did you and I look the other way before I earned my badge because we believed what they did was justified?"

Samuel grabbed the Fed's arm and repeated, "What did he want?"

Treehorn avoided eye contact. "He gave me a lead on Tsosie's murder."

Samuel saw the angry flush cover Treehorn's face as he snapped, "At what cost?"

Treehorn met Samuel's eyes.

"A cost I willingly paid." The agent jerked his arm out of Samuel's grasp and ordered, "Send over Daniel Tsosie's file updates and his bullet first thing in the morning."

As Samuel watched his friend disappear down the

darkened hallway, he realized two realities had emerged from the meeting with Parker Greyhorse: the first, his deputy's murder might finally be solved so the man could be laid to rest with the dignity and honor he deserved. The second, Treehorn—for the first time ever—had lied to him.

As Treehorn drove through the night, he knew he needed to re-examine Parker Greyhorse's file from the night he drove Randy Bonito's car into a roadblock. What made the Indian Posse leader get into another person's car and drive it? Parker said he found the second man who attacked him that night. Was that the answer or was something more sinister at play? Treehorn's thoughts kept returning to Finch because everything in this case returned to the dirty ATF agent.

Lights illuminated Anna's home when Treehorn pulled into the driveway. He took the time to text Raven with the updates, *"Randy Bonito, DOA at TMC. Pull Theo Nez's file. Office AM. Tell Hawkins and Logan, 9am briefing for Greyhorse's, Tsosie's, and Nez's cases. Parker gave up details."*

When Treehorn entered the home, he found Anna

staring at the fire. Several of Parker Greyhorse's letters lay opened on the coffee table next to her revolver.

Treehorn didn't comment as he walked to the refrigerator and grabbed a cold beer. He remembered reading the first letter from Parker. He returned it and every one after that.

"Why didn't you tell me?"

"What? Ramblings from an inmate with too much time on his hands."

"These aren't that," Anna defended, "He reached out to you."

"He had counselors at Cibola."

"You've never walked away from a victim."

"It wasn't professional."

"Personal?" Anna looked at her son and found nothing forthcoming.

"This case has always been your destiny."

Treehorn didn't question his mother's belief.

"Daniel Tsosie waits for you."

Treehorn didn't deny that.

"Why wouldn't you help Parker?"

"Professionally or personally?"

"Why did you never question Greyhorse's roadblock charge? I heard the gossip."

Treehorn evaded his mother's eyes. "You never questioned me on it a year ago, why now?"

Anna found her son's evasiveness intriguing. "You never believed his guilt."

"No."

"Why didn't you do something about it?"

Treehorn thought long and hard, "If I assisted in his release, then he'd have been in a position to continue to dole out his brand of justice."

"Is that what bothered you, his following Indian Law?"

"He refused to discuss the arrest."

"Really? I think you walked away because you knew Parker would deal with the individual and you wouldn't be here to deal with him personally."

"I'm here to solve the murder."

"If you think that, then you're sadly mistaken. We know Parker didn't kill Tsosie."

"How do you know?"

"Because you were with him that night."

Treehorn's face flushed.

"I don't wish to discuss it."

"You're a good man, John. Don't be ashamed of helping him or was he helping you?"

Treehorn focused on the present, "I'm being manipulated."

"That's Parker and Shady's true natures. When will you learn?"

"Randy Bonito's dead in the morgue."

"Did Parker do it?"

"Not the direct attack. Parker, Shady, and I were at Bar None at the time of his death."

"Now, there's a perfect alibi."

Treehorn finished his beer. "Why do you have your gun out?"

"The horses were nervous and I was going to check on them."

"I'll do it."

"And these?" Anna pointed to the letters.

Treehorn avoided his mother's eyes, "Burn the box. Save the bible."

He grabbed a flashlight and headed to the barn.

The horses, Scout and Colter refused to enter the barn but stood in the corner of their corral, an indication that something was amiss. Treehorn held his revolver and shut off the flashlight. He knew the layout of the property and buildings with his eyes closed. A stranger didn't.

The man whistled as Treehorn entered the barn, not to warn him but because he had nothing better to do but wait.

The agent thought of leaving him for the night but knew that wouldn't solve a thing.

"Are we playing nice?" Treehorn waited for a response before he pressed a release button.

"Do I have a choice?"

"No."

"Nice addition, Treehorn. I didn't see it."

The agent pressed the hidden button and the floor's trapdoor released and opened downwards. On the suspended netting lay Peter Greyhorse with his military fatigues, black face paint, short cropped black hair, and brown eyes. At age 28, he was the youngest of Peyton Greyhorse's three sons.

"I thought you Army Rangers had your act together."

"We do but when I looked inside your mom's house and saw her with a gun, I figured it was best to stay hidden out here. Nice handiwork by the way. Who would have thought someone would have built a little hideaway beneath the floor?"

"Obviously not you."

The agent threw the military man a rope to climb out. Treehorn avoided the backpack that flew past his head.

"Nice touch when the net resets the trapdoor."

"I thought so. Anyone know you're here?"

"No, and I need to keep it that way."

Peter stood two inches shorter than Treehorn, but an estimated thirty pounds heavier with his defined muscles.

"I came to make someone pay."

"At the cost of your career?"

"I'm not worried about that. Who killed Paul?"

"Parker knows. The military police will be swarming this area by morning. They'll go to every connection in your file and they won't stop until they have you in handcuffs."

Peter ignored the sermon, "Where's Parker?"

Treehorn's face showed disgust as he replied, "BAR NONE. Released from Cibola this morning, but you already knew that."

"Just checking to see if you did."

"You better find a rock to hide under."

Peter's cold, flat eyes of a trained military killer told Treehorn of the coming storm.

"Neither Parker nor I will be stopped until Paul's killer is ground into dust beneath our feet."

"You'll be in the brig."

"We'll see."

Chapter Eight:

Who's Benito Del Toro?

In the morning, Treehorn went to the barn to check on his visitor and found him gone. He kept the coffee travel mug and didn't worry about being an accessory to Peter's criminal behavior. When he arrived at the office, well before starting time, he found Raven sitting at his computer with his left ankle still wrapped and propped on a chair.

"Peter Greyhorse showed up last night."

"We'll never identify the killer—much less find a body—if the Greyhorse brothers get to him first."

Mary Sweetwater rolled in a second bulletin board as Treehorn poured his first cup of coffee from the pot.

"I figured you'd need another bulletin board as the bodies have started to pile up," she said.

"Thanks, Mary."

"Did you sleep last night?" The woman never minced her words.

"I slept enough."

Mary grumbled as she stomped away. Her way of showing Treehorn she cared.

175

Raven handed his co-worker Greyhorse's arrest and court records.

"I read them last night. Parker's first arrest occurred when he was picked in a police lineup, but the charges were ultimately dropped by the local DA when Parker provided a videotape and receipts that proved he was a hundred miles away during the time of the incident."

Treehorn noted the date.

"The second: Randy Bonito's roadblock."

Both agents found it amazing that this was only the man's second arrest. They knew his long history of felonious behavior. No one pressed charges against the Indian Posse leader.

Treehorn began reading the summary.

"Parker drove Randy Bonito's car to the roadblock. The NNP K-9 reacted so the officers had justifiable cause to search the vehicle. The police found marijuana and $5,000 in cash in the trunk. Parker said he had permission to drive the car, but maintained he had no knowledge of the trunk's contents."

"The officer in charge of the roadblock: NNP Chief Samuel Bear."

"The District Judge, Wade Johnston, denied the defendant bail."

"Bonito provided a sworn statement against the Indian Posse leader that stated Parker made plans to distribute the drugs. The file contained no supported verification or proof of the intent. Bonito feared for his life because of his affidavit. The judge felt Parker's undocumented history contributed to him being a flight risk and a threat to the witness, thus he denied him bail."

"The Indian Posse leader made a deal with District Attorney Susie Shipley instead of facing trial and a possible longer sentence under a white man's jury."

Raven knew how the system treated his tribe.

"He wasn't stupid, and the odds were stacked against him in the court of law. He knew he would be convicted, not for the criminal charge, but for the color of his skin."

"Nowhere in the record did it address how the drugs originated in Randy Bonito's car or why Parker drove the vehicle that night," Raven said, pointing out the slip-up in Parker's modus operandi.

"Parker pled guilty to possession. His savvy lawyer, Delroy Byrd, and District Attorney Shipley agreed his federal time would be done first and concurrent with his state time. Parker's federal prison sentence finished last week, then the New Mexico governor commuted his remaining state time."

Something that couldn't have been done earlier under sentencing guidelines unless you were the President of the United States. Parker possessed the Indian Posse playbook and Treehorn knew he turned it one page at a time.

He kept asking himself, *What is Parker's and Shady's endgame?*

"I agree with Quintero. It looked like a setup. The question at the time was: who was gunning for him?"

Treehorn returned the files to Raven who handed him papers for the bulletin board.

"Gina Greyhorse, age 24, Mrs. Parker Greyhorse, mother to Zane Greyhorse. No criminal history at the federal or state level. Nurse at Tséhootsooi Medical Center. Parker may actually have been telling the truth for once when he said his wife wasn't involved."

"Maybe."

Raven handed Treehorn the image of the penny Samuel found on the hillside near the Four Corners Monument murders.

"The fingerprint is in CODIS." *Combined DNA Index System.*

Treehorn pinned it to the bulletin board and waited for the name.

178

Raven watched his co-worker for a reaction as he asked, "Who's Benito Del Toro?"

Treehorn clenched his jaw and didn't answer.

Raven caught his co-workers reaction.

"I can't access the file because it's sealed by FBI Assistant Director Leo Mancuso and FBI Special Agent John Treehorn."

"Above your pay grade."

"The individual may have witnessed the murders."

"Possible or he was there *after* the crimes."

"Are you going to ask *him*?"

Ignoring the slip Treehorn replied, "Let's label the individual '*Witness #1*' for now."

Raven nodded, tossing Treehorn a marker to tag the image.

Samuel walked into the office carrying a file box as Treehorn labeled the penny print.

"Did you get a fingerprint off it?"

"Yes."

"Who?"

Raven answered before Treehorn could, "The record was sealed by Leo Mancuso."

Samuel looked from Raven to Treehorn.

"Will your boss unseal it?"

Treehorn shrugged his shoulders.

"We don't know if the individual was a party to the crime."

Samuel silently questioned Treehorn's judgment call as he said, "I brought copies of Daniel Tsosie's files and the bullet with its casing."

Treehorn refilled his own coffee and handed Samuel a fresh cup.

"Thanks."

Samuel gave his friend a single reserved nod, showing not all was forgiven from the previous night.

"Gallagher sent over Randy Bonito's autopsy results."

Raven handed the image and single page to Treehorn.

"Cause of death was exsanguination. He bled out. A sharp blade severed his femoral artery. "IP" brandings done pre- and post-mortem. Tongue was cut out while alive. Time of death, approximately 4pm."

"Arrest Parker Greyhorse. We know any witness who says he was with him at that time is a liar."

"He didn't do this," Treehorn stated matter-of-factly.

"What proof do you have?" Samuel countered.

"I was with him."

"Seriously? Or are you protecting him?"

"I'll pretend I didn't hear you say that."

Raven interjected, "Parker may not have *killed* him, but he could have participated in the kidnapping and/or torturing the man."

"Or the Indian Posse members did it to pay for their loyalty. We can all agree Bonito became a target if he set up Parker."

"Who set up Bonito in the first place?" Raven asked.

Treehorn and Samuel answered at the same time, "Finch."

"Samuel, can you send over Bonito's file on Parker's arrest?"

"Why?"

"I want to see the bigger picture."

"Where do you want me to start?" Raven asked, eyeing his co-worker and police chief.

"We need to find the smoking gun to see if there's a connection to these cases."

"How far back do we go?"

"Daniel Tsosie?" Treehorn suggested, raising his eyebrow at the police chief.

"I want to see a summary of the deputy's cases. Can you provide that, Samuel?"

"Sure."

"And Nez, too."

"Theo?"

"Yes, he's connected to these cases and you're welcome to stay while we discuss them."

"Only if Raven makes another pot of coffee."

"Deal."

A few minutes to nine, Su Hawkins, FBI Ballistics Specialist, and Irene Logan, CSU technician, entered Raven's office while Samuel stood at the back of the room with his box. Agents Melanie Hopper and Kendrick Moore joined them a few minutes later. Then Mary Sweetwater entered, holding several papers and her notepad.

Treehorn started, "Last night Indian Posse member Randy Bonito turned up at the morgue."

Mary posted his driver's license and morgue image on the bulletin board.

The agent continued, "Deputy Daniel Tsosie, age 33. His body was found after Theo Nez's death but coroner determined that he had been killed approximately 48 hours prior."

Raven typed on his keyboard and the deputy's image appeared.

"He was shot while changing a tire on his patrol car. Two slugs to the head, then his body dumped in the desert several miles away. A sheepherder found the body."

Raven loaded an image of the patrol car, trunk open, spare tire out, and two yellow triangles on the ground labeled #1 and #2.

CSU Logan added, "We found the two casings next to the vehicle. They matched the bullets."

On the monitor, Raven opened an image that showed an enlarged photo of the NNP logo from the driver's door.

Logan continued, "The blood splatter and gunshot residue had a distinct outline that showed Deputy Tsosie was shot as he sat on the ground, leaning against the driver's door. Then, it appeared someone intentionally moved his body and shot him a second time. Why, we don't know, but the coroner's report determined the first shot was fatal. The second shot was either overkill or someone wanting to make it look like there were two shooters."

Treehorn's eyes met Melanie's. Her face showed no emotion during the presentation.

Raven loaded an image of a Colt .45 six-shooter revolver with an enameled inlay that spelled the letters 'DWJ'.

183

Then Treehorn began, "Last night, Parker Greyhorse informed me that the gun that killed Deputy Daniel Tsosie was the same gun that shot Theo Nez."

The agent looked at Samuel's angry face, and then at Melanie's troubled features.

"Let's determine whether that is true and if it is, why hasn't it been flagged in the system."

Nez's driver's license image appeared on the wall monitor.

Su presented her facts, "Theo's ballistics results are on file because I did them. I'll re-examine them and compare them with the Tsosie slugs."

Treehorn opened his locked safe and removed two evidence bags with one slug and one casing. Both were labeled with "Daniel Tsosie" and his case number. The agent transferred them to Su.

Samuel reached into his box and removed two more evidence bags that matched the Feds'. One slug and one casing. He signed the transfer document and Su handed him a receipt.

"I'll take good care of them," she promised.

"Just find his killer," Samuel requested.

Su commented, "Fact: we know the 'DWJ' revolver

did indeed kill Theo Nez."

Logan added, "We found seven DNA samples on it. The first is Beth Hopper."

Raven typed and the woman's image appeared on the screen.

"Any relation?" Agent Moore asked Melanie, nodding toward the image.

She didn't have time to respond before Treehorn spoke.

"The second DNA sample belongs to Melanie Hopper, age 16."

Raising his eyebrows at his co-worker Agent Moore said, "You've been holding out."

"The third sample is Theo Nez's and the fourth is Bart Baker's. Theo's half-brother and recently deceased murder victim. Both ex-Indian Posse members."

Raven repositioned Nez's image next to Baker's.

Treehorn pinned a female cutout and two male cutouts on the bulletin board.

"The fifth DNA sample is an unidentified white female. Number six and seven are two unidentified white males. The female and male #7 are father and daughter."

"I'll rerun them through the database to see if we have

any updated information," Raven offered.

Treehorn nodded.

"Su, what's the updated ballistics on Paul Greyhorse and Bart Baker?"

"The rifle fired a .30 caliber Winchester Mag approximately 600 feet from the hill to the campfire, then another 25 feet to the SUV. First shot hit Greyhorse who didn't move from his location. Second shot struck Baker next to the boulder. He crawled to the SUV where the third bullet blew the tire and the fourth struck him in the hip. A true marksman. Four casings with copper recovered and documented. No DNA or prints recovered. Rifle ownership unknown but there's a ballistic match in the system for two other shootings."

Raven posted the data on the monitor as he clarified, "Thirty-two-year-old Navajo male, Jeremy Begay. Shot in the hip as he stepped out of a woman's house in Shiprock. Unidentified shooter. No arrests."

"The second?"

Everyone watched the screen.

"Thirty-six-year-old Navajo male, Del Chambers, took one to the chest while driving south on Route 371 from Farmington. The FBI field office there covered it.

Unidentified shooter, single incident, non-targeted, and no arrests."

"Any connections?"

Raven checked his computer.

"Begay denied knowing Chambers in the follow-up notes. No connections found with family or friends. Begay, one arrest for assault and served time. Chambers, no criminal history."

"What's the current addresses?"

"Begay resides in Standing Rock and Chamber's widow resides in Crownpoint."

"Crime scene unit," Treehorn looked at CSU Irene Logan.

"There were two sets of men's footprints leading from the hill where the rifle shots were first taken. Size 11 and 13 shoes there. One a fatigue-style boot and the other more expensive. I've researched the manufacturers. The men came off the hill and walked to the two bodies. At no time did they walk to the Four Corners Monument."

"The third person participated at the active crime scene. We'll call him *Mr. Pennyman*."

Logan glanced at Treehorn because she knew the

man's secret identity: Benito Del Toro.

She continued, "His size 13 boot-style shoe, a very expensive and comfortable boot manufactured by the Monticello Leather Works, traveled down the hill from where he left the penny. He walked to the body of Paul Greyhorse, located at the campfire, then dragged the deceased to the Four Corners Monument. His footprints stepped on top of the two other boot prints."

Treehorn looked at Melanie.

"He's white."

"Indians don't touch dead bodies."

Melanie, a Navajo, knew that to be true.

"What does the crime scene tell us about the rifle and handgun?" Treehorn asked, eyeing the group of professionals.

Raven spoke up first after hearing Dr. Gallagher's insight, "The sniper wasn't the killer. He disabled the men so the Colt revolver shooter could hunt the men down and kill them."

Treehorn added, "Hunting wounded prey isn't much of a hunt. And, we know there's a difference in a man's mentality when he shoots someone at a distance or kills them up close. What else?"

Melanie speculated, "Baker appeared to be the target based on the number of non-lethal shots on his body. The killer had an ax to grind with him."

Samuel questioned, "You think Greyhorse just happened to be in the wrong location?"

"No. The money in his saddlebags placed him there."

Treehorn couldn't accept innocence on Paul's part in the illegal transaction.

Melanie continued, "The sniper was most likely militarily trained for that skill level."

Treehorn touched his nose and pointed to his co-worker.

"I agree, grasshopper. Raven, check the long-distance shooting ranges for anyone that has practiced with .30 caliber shells, although it'll probably be a dead-end because they won't disclose the information. Start pulling military personnel, snipers, and marksmen in the four-state area as well as rifle ownership. Re-examine Baker's history prior to his incarceration and his prison file. See if anyone may have wanted him dead."

"Agent Hopper, Baker possessed a 9mm pistol. Ask the owner in Albuquerque how their gun came to be on a dead felon."

Su Hawkins handed Melanie the profile.

Treehorn continued, "Parker Greyhorse received a telephone call from the Whispering Winds Crematorium early Sunday morning that informed him his brother had died."

Raven activated the recording.

"Parker Greyhorse, this is the Whispering Winds Crematorium. I'm sorry to inform you that your brother, Paul, has died."

Parker whispered, *"I'm going to kill you when I get out."*

The man's reply spewed anger, *"A Colt .45 did it, if you're wondering, not my gun of choice."*

A phone headset slammed down.

"He knew the caller and I would guess it's the voice of the sniper. Also, sounds personal so maybe both shooters had issues with the individuals."

Raven wrote down more information for his notes.

"What did you and Kendrick find out at the crematorium?" Treehorn asked, eyeing the two agents.

"A white male, mid 40's, entered the premises at approximately 3am and requested to use the telephone. The man paid the kid behind the counter $500 to look the other way. After completing his call, the man wiped down the phone but forgot that he left his DNA on the money and the glass door."

"When will the lab have the results?"

Melanie raised a document like a conjuring magician.

"These results?"

Raven gave her two thumbs up.

Treehorn's eyes flicked from Raven to Melanie.

Melanie continued, "The money gave us a partial print but not enough to identify the suspect. The hand smudge on the glass gave us a DNA match."

"Who?" Treehorn spun his finger as if to say *Hurry up!*

Melanie pointed to the suspect on the bulletin board.

"Male #6. He's a match for the sample taken from Nez's gun."

"How's that possible?" Raven wondered.

"Figure it out," Treehorn ordered.

"Logan, is CSU finished with the two hundred thousand dollars found in the saddlebags?"

"We should be, shortly. We're copying the serial

numbers. We've found some trace materials so we're being our usual meticulous selves."

"Send the serial numbers and file to Kendrick when you're finished."

Logan gave Treehorn a hand salute.

"Agent Kendrick, follow that money. I want to know where the cash originated."

Kendrick nodded.

"Melanie, what business did male #6 have at the crematorium?"

"No idea."

"Find out. No one enters a business in the middle of the night just to use their phone."

Melanie knew she'd screwed up.

Raven countered, "Cibola's staff would only connect a legitimate business call to a prisoner in the middle of the night if it was identified on a caller ID."

Melanie winked at Raven as a thank you.

Treehorn caught it.

"Agents Hopper and Moore, don't forget to follow up on the legal owner of Bart's 9mm."

Melanie learned her lesson as Treehorn repeated the order on the gun. His form of punishment to his junior agents.

Kendrick tapped his middle finger on his thigh. He caught it too.

"As for Nez, I want the Colt .45 from his murder re-examined. Hopper and Moore, if you can find the time, pay the ATF depository a visit. Sign it out with its two bullets and casings. I want the owner identified even if you have to crawl over Finch's dead body to find it."

Everyone looked at Treehorn to see if he was joking. His serious face implied otherwise.

"Finch took possession of the revolver a few hours after the Nez murder."

The senior agent glanced at Melanie as he continued, "Since we had a written confession in the case, we didn't need to take possession of the evidence. Parker Greyhorse stated the gun that killed Nez also killed NNP Deputy Tsosie. Let's see if that's true. Send the results to ballistics here."

Su glanced at the agent in charge. It appeared that she wanted to offer a comment but remained silent instead.

"Samuel Bear, do you have anything to add?"

The police chief pursed his lips and thought for a second.

As Treehorn saw the indecision on his friend's face, he wondered whether the police chief's hatred of Parker Greyhorse would interfere with their investigation.

Having made up his mind, Samuel slowly reached inside one of his boxes and removed a bloodied shirt.

"The night Parker Greyhorse was arrested driving Randy Bonito's automobile; he wore this shirt over a t-shirt. When the Feds took him away, this shirt was left in the NNP patrol vehicle. One of my deputies placed it in an evidence bag and filed it away."

Everyone pictured the sequence of events.

"Greyhorse arrived with a bloodied nose and a blackened eye. We documented everything and took pictures, too, so he wouldn't say one of my deputies beat the shit out of him. The only odd thing about the whole incident is that he denied being assaulted. If someone set Parker up that night, it just may be the person he had an altercation with before he got behind the wheel. Their DNA may be on his shirt."

"Thanks, Samuel."

After handing the evidence to CSU Logan and signing the transfer document, the police chief turned to Treehorn.

"I still believe Parker lied to you about the gun that killed Daniel Tsosie."

"I respect your position, Samuel, but as with every statement we've learned as law enforcement officers, the truth comes out in the end."

"Hopper, take the shirt with you to Albuquerque. See how fast the lab can conduct a DNA analysis on it."

"Will do."

Treehorn looked at his staff as he texted Su, *"Confidential: Send .38 and .357 with Hopper. Keep out of system."*

"Any questions?"

A few shook their heads while the others made notes.

"Good job, everyone. Send all updates to Raven."

The room quickly cleared out. Everyone knew they had a job that needed to be done.

Raven handed Treehorn a slim folder.

"These are the Begay and Chambers police reports and summaries. I'll have both files here by the time you return."

"Thanks, Raven. I want to know why two Navajos were used for target practice."

"We'll find the connection to Greyhorse and Baker. Bones are rattling…"

"…and the Spirits are speaking."

Treehorn grabbed his travel mug.

"Do you want to join me, Samuel?"

"Only if you have an extra travel mug."

Chapter Nine:

Follow the Guns

While Treehorn and Samuel headed northeast, Melanie and Kendrick drove to a little clapboard house weathered by the elements.

"What's here?"

"I need to dig something out of the tree," Melanie explained, grabbing an evidence kit out of the vehicle.

The two agents walked through the overgrown grass and scrubs to an old bristlecone pine. She pulled out a flashlight and examined the bark.

"Need help?"

"Hand me a flat screwdriver and needle nose pliers. Grab a couple evidence bags."

"Are you going to tell me what's in the tree?"

"Evidence."

Melanie dug into the wood and extracted two slugs which she dropped into a pair of evidence bags.

"What's so special about these?"

"These came from Theo Nez's gun. I know because I fired them into this tree when he left the weapon and ammo in my possession."

Melanie pointed to the house.

"That's my late grandmother's home. She left it to me. It's also where Theo Nez took his last breath."

A heavy-duty truck with a flat-bed trailer stopped and parked next to the agent's SUV.

"Agent Hopper?" A tall lanky man stepped from the vehicle.

Melanie nodded.

"CSU Carlyle. You wanted a tree cut down?"

Kendrick didn't question his co-worker's orders but watched and learned.

Melanie pointed to the pine tree where she just removed the two bullets.

"It's full of slugs from a murder weapon. Work with Su Hawkins to extract them carefully. Tell her they're from the Beth Hopper/Theo Nez file. She'll know what to do with them."

She handed him a slip of paper with the information.

"Will do," the technician tucked the paper into his pocket. Then he grabbed his chainsaw with its safety gear and went to work cutting down the tree.

"Do you want to drop those slugs off at ballistics before we hit the road?"

"No, I can examine them at the ATF lab and forward the results here."

"Well then, Albuquerque, here we come. Round two."

"No, let's take a little detour first."

"Where to?"

"BAR NONE."

"Why?"

"Let's see if Parker Greyhorse will tell us whose blood is on this shirt."

"He won't tell us."

"We'll see."

As they pulled up in front of the establishment Melanie said, "I want you to stay here."

"That's against protocol."

Kendrick looked around.

"I'll stay on the porch, how's that?"

"Deal."

The two agents walked to the entrance of the Indian Posse social club.

"Hi, Ike. Melanie Hopper."

"You've grown since the last time I saw you," Ike ignored Kendrick.

"Is Parker here?"

Ike chewed his toothpick and nodded his head towards the door.

"You can go in."

Melanie entered the establishment while Ike and Kendrick proceeded to have a staring contest. Silence came over the room as all eyes went to the agent with a gun and badge.

Melanie walked up to Parker Greyhorse, who sat in the corner with his back against the wall.

"Hello, Parker. FBI Agent Melanie Hopper. I'd like to ask you a couple questions."

"Treehorn's little prodigy...but before that...Theo Nez's," Parker smiled smugly.

"Yes and no. We have your bloody shirt from the night of the Randy Bonito roadblock."

Parker said nothing and his eyes showed no emotion.

"Whose blood is on the shirt?"

Parker examined her breasts and licked his lips.

Melanie felt dirty as his eyes lewdly traveled over her body.

"Was Theo your first?"

"I'm not going to answer such an inappropriate question."

"How about Treehorn?"

"Jealous?"

"Yes."

Melanie stared at the man who made criminality a career.

"You've wasted my time. He'll get to the bottom of this because it's his nature," Melanie turned away.

"Send me Treehorn's photo and I'll tell you whose blood is on the shirt."

"What's your number?"

Parker provided it.

Melanie typed into her phone. A couple seconds later Parker's phone dinged.

He didn't examine the image before he answered, "The blood's mine. I had a nosebleed."

"Liar!"

Parker grabbed a napkin, spat in it, and folded it neatly.

"There's my DNA. Test it," he challenged, handing her the wet napkin.

Melanie cringed as she pinched it.

"Thanks, I'll see if it matches the shirt's DNA."

She took out a plastic evidence bag from her pocket and deposited the sample into it.

The Indian Posse leader watched her ass as she walked out. Then he opened his phone to examine the contents. A picture of a weasel labeled "Parker" appeared and he laughed.

"Treehorn trained you well."

As the agents climbed into the SUV Melanie said, "Albuquerque, here we come."

Treehorn drove from Gallup north on the paved Route 491 to the red, dirt-covered road that crossed the reservation to the little community of Standing Rock. Its population didn't make the United States Census. No count, no funding.

Neither Treehorn nor Samuel broke the silence of their thoughts to discuss Parker Greyhorse. Both men knew this with heavy hearts.

Samuel stared out at the reservation as the desert landscape changed to stony outcroppings of sandstone. Indians living on a limited income and their faith dotted the highway.

The police chief accessed the NNP criminal database on the first man whose ballistics matched the Greyhorse/Baker shooting. Then, he broke the silence in the SUV.

"Jeremy Begay, age 32. Ex-electrician, single, no dependents. First arrest at age sixteen for assault. Served ninety days due to the circumstances. It appeared that he protected his girlfriend from an overly friendly male tourist. Then, a year ago, the NNP arrested him on a criminal complaint of sexual assault, and a charge of assault and battery against the boyfriend of the accuser in the case. The jury deliberated less than an hour and found him not guilty of the rape. The San Juan District Attorney, James Bedrow, dropped the assault and battery charges when new evidence came forth during the trial.

Treehorn and Samuel arrived at the single-wide trailer. An old, rundown picnic table sat in the red-dusted yard, not even a weed paid homage here.

Jeremy Begay waited for the officers on the dry cracked bench as they exited their vehicle.

Treehorn eyed the man who required the assistance of a cane to stand. He didn't move from his location but waited for the officers to come to him.

The Fed held out his hand for introductions, "FBI Special Agent John Treehorn."

"Jeremy Begay."

The police chief did the same, "NNP Chief Samuel Bear."

"You guys want a drink? I have coffee or water."

"No thanks."

"Have a seat. I can't stand long because of the damage."

The men sat on their own rickety bench.

"We're here to discuss your shooting incident."

"Did you find the guy?"

"No, but we have a ballistics report on a recent shooting that matches the bullet they extracted from you."

"Where do you want me to start?"

"How about the beginning?" Treehorn suggested.

Jeremy chuckled, then he began, "I was hired to do some electrical work in Shiprock. The job changed to shagging the white whore. Hot, little red-headed firecracker, if you know what I mean."

Samuel clenched his jaw as he focused on his notebook.

Treehorn pursed his lips.

"Stick to the facts, please."

"Anyways, we were having consensual sex. That was until the fiancée arrived. She said it was rape. Billygoat and I got into a little *altercation*. She called the NNP and told them I assaulted her and was killing him."

Samuel read the NNP police report then asked, "Billygoat?"

"Billy Gordon. Some white dude out of Texas. The NNP refused to listen to my side of the story." He glanced at Samuel, "What's new, right? White man's privilege while Indians bear the injustice."

"Go on."

"I went to jail, then to court. I showed the jury a few naked images she posed for me."

"Still could have been raped."

Jeremy looked at Samuel.

"Then wasn't I lucky I recorded our little sexcapade. The boyfriend and the jury got an earful. The jury found me 'not guilty' on the rape which I knew they would. I refused to plea bargain the assault charge since it was she who called me to her bed. Billygoat and I went round two at the courthouse. I informed him I had more pictures and names of some of the other men she screwed, and that they would be my witnesses for the assault trial. D.A. Bedrow recommended the charges be dropped and that we return to our lives."

"But, that's not what happened?"

"A month later, as I exited another little firecracker's

home in Shiprock, someone decided to use me for target practice. I took one in the hip. Long-range rifle. No witnesses, no footprints either. It was like I was shot by a ghost. Some incompetent Fed out of Farmington felt I was just in the wrong place at the wrong time."

"Did she have a partner who took offense?" Samuel questioned.

"No, this time I asked before we connected."

Samuel snickered.

Treehorn didn't.

"Do you know any Indian Posse members?"

"A few here and there but I don't belong to their gang if that's what you're asking."

"Did you know Paul Greyhorse or Bart Baker?"

Treehorn showed Jeremy their DMV images.

"Are those the two they found dead up at Four Corners? *Indian Times* did a story on them."

"Yes. Did you know them?"

"Nope."

"Paul was Parker Greyhorse's brother, leader of Indian Posse."

Treehorn showed the man Parker's image.

"Sorry."

"What about NNP Deputy Daniel Tsosie?"

"The dead policeman? Jeez, that was a long time ago." He shook his head as he added, "Never met him."

"How about Theo Nez? An ex-Indian Posse member." Treehorn showed his image.

"No, sorry. Did my shooter kill all of these men?"

"No. We're just looking for a connection. Do you have a military background?"

"I trained with the Army Corp of Engineers. That's where I learned my electrical trade."

"Any sniper training?"

Jeremy's eyebrows rose as he replied, "We used explosives and bulldozers."

"Is there anything you remember now that you didn't report earlier?"

"No. I have no idea why I was targeted. The Feds interviewed the little ass wipe who had me arrested. He didn't even know that I had been shot."

"Any guess on your part?"

"I was guilty of having consensual sex with a paleface girl."

Treehorn didn't question the man's choices, he merely said, "Here's my card if you remember anything."

Samuel voiced another theory as the officers walked to the SUV, "It may have been the same rifle but a different shooter."

"That won't help the investigation."

The agent called Raven on the vehicle's telephone, "Treehorn here. Any updates? We're heading to Crownpoint."

"None yet. Researching and pulling records."

"Thanks, Raven."

"He's been a good partner for you," Samuel said after Treehorn hung up.

"Yes, he has."

Once again both men preferred silence over any further discussion of the case on the sixteen-mile drive to Crownpoint. The sprawled-out community of approximately 2,400 residents held the Navajo Chapter, one of 110 governing agencies spread across the Reservation.

Samuel retrieved the police report and began to read, "Del Chambers, age 36, he took one gunshot to the chest as he was driving home from his employer, Los Alamos Gun Range. His widow, Marion Chambers, moved to

Crownpoint with her three children to be near her sister."

Treehorn pulled into the driveway of an older, ranch-style home with a fenced-in yard littered with dirt-covered kids' toys.

Treehorn knocked on the front entrance. The doorbell long broken and never repaired.

A Navajo woman answered the door. Marion Chambers, age 40, opened the door dressed in pajamas. The heady smell of alcohol hit the two officers in the face.

"Marion Chambers? I'm FBI Special Agent John Treehorn and this is Navajo Nation Police Chief Samuel Bear. We have questions regarding your late husband."

Marion opened the door wider and retreated into the house without a greeting.

The officers entered and found her pouring vodka and cranberry juice into a glass.

"I'd offer you one but then there would be less for me."

Treehorn glanced out of the living room window. Three young Navajo boys played in the rear yard.

"How old are your sons?"

A slight look of disgust registered on the woman's face as she glanced outside.

"Scott's twelve. He's the one standing alone. Allen's ten. He's the one with the toy gun, and David's nine. He's inside the playhouse."

She pointed to the furniture for her visitors as she sat in her chair with her drink.

Samuel moved aside some unfolded laundry while Treehorn moved a couple of stuffed animals from a chair.

Marion eyed the two officers with anger and snapped, "Why are you here?"

Treehorn led, "The ballistics from slugs recovered from two recently deceased men matched the bullet the coroner removed from your husband's chest."

"It's not going to bring my husband back, is it?"

Treehorn paused as he eyed the alcoholic whose sickness invaded her spirit while her children played, oblivious—or perhaps not so oblivious—to her illness.

"The police report states that your husband, Del, departed from his employer, then a few miles from that location a bullet struck and killed him."

"That's what the police told me."

"Was your husband involved in any illegal activity?"

"Guess it doesn't matter now."

Marion took a large swig of her drink, possibly for fortification.

"Del came home a week before he died and told me a couple of handguns turned up missing during his work hours at the shooting range. All hush-hush because they didn't want word getting out to the authorities."

Treehorn examined the police report.

"There's nothing documented in your husband's papers."

Marion laughed inappropriately and carried her glass into the kitchen for a refill from the gallon of vodka.

"My husband arrived home with a wad of cash and instructions to keep his mouth shut. Some rich, white dude lacking in brains left his car unlocked in the parking lot and someone stole a couple of guns from it."

Marion stared off into the distance as she tried to recall the incident.

"A 9mm like my daddy's and some fancy, engraved one. Del told me he remembered walking by the owner's car, but he didn't see any theft."

"Was the inlay on the gun, a word, numbers, initials?"

"Initials. D was one of the letters. The only reason I remember that was because of Del's name. Ask the shooting range. They should tell you."

"I'll check with them. What happened next?"

"A few days later, Del took a shot to his heart as he drove home. Police didn't find anything, but I knew it was connected to those two guns."

As Treehorn examined the date on the police report, Marion jerked her head toward the backyard.

"I've struggled for eight years to raise those three. Do you have any idea how hard it's been to raise them alone?"

Treehorn looked at the intoxicated woman and confronted her, "They need you. Get some help for your alcoholism. You can still be a good parent."

Marion pointed to the front door, fuming.

"Get out and don't come back."

Treehorn walked straight out. He knew an ATF incident report should have been filed, and still, he suspected one wouldn't be found.

Samuel eyed Treehorn as he asked, "Why were you so harsh on her? She's sick."

Treehorn stopped and faced Samuel.

"The gun that disappeared from that shooting range probably wasn't engraved, but inlaid."

Treehorn handed the FBI file to Samuel and continued, "Del Chambers' death occurred one week after Deputy Tsosie's. Eight years ago, Sammy. We saw that gun at Theo Nez's murder scene."

"You don't know a hundred percent if the stolen handgun is the same weapon."

"You don't know that it isn't."

"When your staff delivers the ballistic results, we'll know whether Parker lied to you about Tsosie and Nez being killed by the same weapon. It could be a different handgun with someone else's ego decorated on it."

Treehorn didn't comment. Instead, he pulled out his phone and texted Agent Hopper, *"Los Alamos Gun Range - a 9mm and a revolver stolen around Theo Nez's murder date. Check ATF records."*

Su Hawkins and CSU Ellis Carlyle worked together with saws, files, and picks as the pair carefully extracted seven .45 caliber slugs from the toughened pine. Agent Treehorn wanted the ballistics answered, *"Did the same gun kill Deputy Tsosie and Theo Nez?"*

Su would do her damnedest to find the answer. Agents and staff carried unsolved cases with them throughout their careers. When ATF Finch removed Nez's murder weapon and bullets from her possession eight years earlier, she sensed—as did Treehorn—that the weapon held a mystery, but neither of the men knew or suspected that *she held a clue.*

As Treehorn and Samuel drove the return trip to Gallup, Melanie and Kendrick arrived in Albuquerque.

The FBI lab accepted Parker Greyhorse's bloody shirt from his roadblock arrest and his spit sample. Melanie requested they notify Agent Shelly with the results.

Kendrick questioned the timing, "It would have saved us time and money if Police Chief Bear or the NNP deputies had asked Parker to identify the owner's blood."

"The police chief caught their man. Parker denied having been assaulted although his nose bled and his eye swelled shut. I read the county lockup medical report. The man didn't say one word while the doctor stitched him up."

"I'm impressed, little Miss Merit Award winner."

Melanie ignored Kendrick's poke and instead focused on Parker's modus operandi.

"He may not have known the attacker or he intentionally kept the man's identity from law enforcement."

"Why?"

"Oh, grasshopper, you have a lot to learn. You don't know Indian Posse. Parker Greyhorse, regardless of how long it takes, will hunt the individual down. That's his type of justice."

"Let the police do their job. Being a vigilante is still against the law."

"Treehorn taught me my first valuable lesson when I graduated from the FBI Academy. He said, *'Justice is inimitable and she'll never be denied.'*"

Next Agents Hopper and Moore drove to the Whispering Winds Crematorium. This time a security guard met them at the entrance.

"May I help you?"

"FBI Agents Melanie Hopper and Kendrick Moore. We're here to ask some follow-up questions in our investigation."

"Chris Abbott, Security. Anita Rowland and Marie Hayes, our administrators, are in the main office. They should be able to assist you."

"Have any reports of break-ins or strange events occurred here?"

"I read the incident report with the stranger asking to use the telephone. Odd, but not illegal."

"True."

"We've added extra security measures."

"Have you ever had any robberies, where someone's

buried with a family keepsake?"

Kendrick's eyes rounded as Melanie questioned the guard.

"None that I've heard of. We do have some rather peculiar individuals who come and prepare their funerary while they await their deaths."

"An example?"

"I can't give out the names of the owners, but when someone purchases a space, they've secured the right to visit it before their passing. People bring mementos, photos, and personal souvenirs. I knew one woman who brought her cremated cats in their wooden urns."

"Are the crypts secured?"

"Yes, each person brings their own lock. I have to return to my duties now, but Anita and Marie can help you."

"Thanks."

Kendrick waited until the guard walked out of earshot.

"Why those questions?"

"Why do you think a guy used this telephone in the middle of the night?"

"He saw the place was open and he didn't have a phone?"

"I think Raven was correct. The caller knew Cibola Prison wouldn't allow him to speak to Parker Greyhorse unless they verified the caller's location, Whispering Winds Crematorium, and from their recorded conversation, the men have an angry history."

Kendrick looked around.

"You think the man left something here?"

"Who would think to look at a crematorium for a murder weapon?"

"Treehorn's grasshopper."

"Exactly."

"I apologize for the earlier comment."

"We're good but don't do it again."

Kendrick smiled as he said, "Let's work on that next merit award."

"Deal."

Melanie knocked on the office's new door as the pair showed their identification, "FBI Agents Melanie Hopper and Kendrick Moore. We have a few more questions to ask in our investigation."

"Who would think someone using our telephone would require such an inquiry?"

"May I have your names for the record?"

"I'm Anita Rowland," a short, gray-haired, blue-eyed woman answered.

"I'm Marie Hayes," a taller brunette with green eyes replied.

"I'm sorry to inconvenience you but a killer entered these premises and used your telephone to terrorize a jailed inmate."

Kendrick watched the two women's eyes enlarge, then their expressions turn to remorse. Little grasshopper grew claws.

"We're sorry."

"No reason to be sorry. There's plenty of investigations where we can't give out details but this man's dangerous. Your guard stated you've increased security measures."

"Yes," Anita answered, "the incident helped with that."

"I see your establishment contains a chapel, crematorium, an outdoor mausoleum, and an inside inurnment with funerary crypts."

"Yes, we provide a full range of services."

Marie handed the agents a company brochure.

"Have any of your staff reported any other suspicious activity lately?"

"How do you define suspicious? Our grounds are open 24/7, so family members can grieve. Select buildings have varied hours due to burial requirements or regulations. We see a lot of behaviors in dealing with death."

"This is true for us, too."

"This building contains funerary recesses. Can you tell me about them?"

"They're purchased spaces that fit caskets. Some people have placed their urns inside with their personal possessions. They're obviously larger than a columbarium. Those compartments are sized smaller, usually two feet by two feet."

"Who can access the funerary recesses prior to death?"

"The legal owner can visit and place objects they hold dear to them. Those are the compartments with brass plates and black metal doors secured with private locks. Upon the loved one's death, the metal door is replaced with marble and permanently sealed with their possessions."

"Can we obtain a list of the funerary recesses?"

"Do you have a warrant?" Ms. Rowland asked.

"No, we don't."

"Sorry, we can't give out the ownership information, but you're welcome to tour the building. Some recesses have nameplates," Ms. Hayes explained.

"When can individuals access the crypts?"

"Anytime. Ownership isn't questioned because they own the lock to each and provide keys to who they wish to have access. We don't ask for identification. You're welcome to look around."

"May we take pictures?"

"Yes, you may."

"When's Andrew Shattuck's next shift?"

A pinched look appeared on both women's faces.

"He's scheduled for 9pm tonight. There are cremation services to be supervised."

"Thank you for answering our questions."

The agents walked out of the office and closed the newly installed door.

"Good try on the fishing expedition."

"No justification, no warrant, but we can document every funerary name and send them to Raven to run a background check."

Kendrick looked at the rows.

"Left-handed takes the left."

"Okay."

The pair documented the names from the metal plates. Melanie stopped in front of one labeled, "Betsy Justice." A wooden plaque, attached to the wall, held a single porcelain daffodil.

Anita whispered behind Melanie, "That's a sad case, a missing person. I believe her boyfriend bought this space so that they could spend eternity together."

The agent circled her name on the list.

"How long has she been missing?"

"Over 25 years."

"I'll examine her file. A fresh set of eyes on a cold case can't hurt."

"I'm sure the family would appreciate that. He still visits and I think a relative does, too, but I could be wrong."

"Sadly, when someone goes missing for that long, it usually turns out that it was foul play."

"Sometimes, bad news is better than no news at all."

"True, but some families long for closure."

Melanie and Kendrick documented fifty-one funerary recesses and forwarded the names to Raven. When the agents exited the crematorium, they didn't see Ronan photographing them with a long-range lens. They also

didn't realize that he had placed a GPS tracking device on
their SUV.

The photographer dialed his telephone.

"Finch."

"Ronan here. Two Feds just left the crematorium."

"What are you doing there?"

"What do you think?"

"Get away from there and stay away from there!"
Finch screamed, terminating the call without further
discussion.

Ronan's face pinched in anger as he watched the two
agents drive away.

"Where now, partner?" Kendrick asked.

"ATF."

As the two agents entered the building, Kendrick
received a text.

"The Socorro money's been released. They sent me a
file of serial numbers and they recovered a fingerprint from
it. I'll find a station to work at."

"I'll head to ballistics and have them run these tree
slugs against the Tsosie and Nez bullets. Greyhorse said the

same gun killed both men. If that's the case, then these bullets should match the ones on file."

Kendrick pulled Melanie aside and asked, "If that's the case, why haven't the slugs in the depository been red-flagged in the system. It's a cop-killer gun."

"What are you saying?"

"If Daniel Tsosie and Theo Nez were shot with the same gun, why hasn't it been identified before now?"

"You don't think there's a match?"

"I didn't say that."

Melanie eyed her partner.

"You think there's been a cover-up?"

"It would explain why Tsosie's case has been cold for eight years."

"The gun's been here in the depository. It should have been re-tested with the bullets."

"Why don't you take it with you to the ballistics lab and have it re-tested?"

"Treehorn's rubbed off on you."

"No, grasshopper, you have."

"Thanks, Kendrick."

"I'll follow the money."

"I'll follow the guns."

The high-tech ATF depository covered a complete building that contained the latest in computer data security and access. Melanie presented her identification to the sign-in agent, Michael Hollander, then she was able to walk the sections uninhibited. Computer screens lined the numbered corridors and after she typed the required case number of Theo Nez into the database, an evidence serial number appeared with its matching locker.

Once located, she typed in her security clearance. As the file information loaded on the screen, she remembered Kendrick's question. She hit "HISTORY" and examined it. The gun and bullets *"Evidence Deposit Date"* didn't immediately follow Theo Nez's death, but occurred four weeks later and was deposited by one person. No one accessed the locker since the original entry. Melanie hit "PRINT" and sent a copy of the locker report to her phone and email.

Inside, she found a white box labeled in large red letters 'GUN' and in smaller black type 'THEO NEZ' with his case number. Opening the container, a heavier-than-usual non-transparent plastic bag secured the Colt .45, and an adjacent compartment held clear twin evidence bags that contained two bullets. The agent removed the box, sealed the locker, and signed out of the terminal.

Melanie entered the lab and located her favorite technician, June Holden, a short pug-loving widow who dedicated her life to the study of ballistics. Pinned to the walls, her targets—with dead-center shots—showed her accomplishments at the shooting range.

"What do you have there, Mellie?"

Melanie pulled a plastic bag from her pocket.

"These two bullets I extracted from a bristlecone pine tree this morning."

She opened Theo Nez's gun box and pulled out the two bullets from inside.

"These bullets came out of Theo Nez's body. Tell me they're fired from the same weapon."

"Were they from the same box of bullets?"

"Yes."

"How do you know that?"

"Because I loaded the gun."

June set the four bullets into labeled dishes and proceeded to weigh each.

"Are you sure these are from the same box?"

"Yes, why?"

"Their weights are off. The two you gave me are 200 grains and the two from the box are 250."

"That's odd," Melanie's brow creased.

Treehorn and Samuel returned to the FBI Gallup office with more questions than answers.

"I left Deputy Tsosie's file for you in Raven's office. Send me the results of the ballistics when you receive them."

Treehorn frowned at his friend.

"Why don't you come in and see if any arrived?"

"Okay, if it'll solve Daniel's murder, then it's time well spent."

Mary Sweetwater greeted them upon their entrance at the office, "Are you guys thirsty?"

"Not for me. Sammy?"

"No thanks, Mary."

"Su wanted me to tell you she finished a report."

"Can you tell her to come to Raven's office when she's available?"

Mary smiled and nodded.

"I left you a sandwich and a cold drink in your refrigerator. Let me know if Raven touched it."

As the two men walked toward the rear office, Samuel asked, "Has Raven ever dared touch something Mary left for you?"

"Yes, but I've covered for him."

"She'll catch him one day."

"I know."

Treehorn's corner lip curled as the men entered the empty office.

Samuel broke the uncomfortable silence, "I still believe Parker lied to you."

"I don't."

"Why do you have so much faith in that cruel man?"

Su overheard the question as she entered the office, and knew by the angry flush on Treehorn's face that her arrival prevented him from answering.

"Do you want me to come back?"

"No."

"Do you want to discuss this privately?"

"No. Samuel needs to hear the results. It's his Deputy."

Su avoided eye contact with the men as she read the results, "Tsosie's and Nez's bullets in the system don't match."

Samuel's face flushed in anger as he mocked, "Parker Greyhorse pissed on you again, Treehorn. When are you ever going to learn?"

The police chief looked at his friend in disgust, walked out of the office, and slammed the door.

"Wow. I've never seen the police chief upset."

"We thought we'd find answers today."

Treehorn's telephone rang, "I need to listen to these updates from Washington, don't move."

ATF Lab

Continuing her examination of the four bullets, June used her compound microscope to examine their lands and grooves.

"Ready for the results?"

"Yes."

"These bullets weren't fired from the same gun."

"How is that possible when I have the gun right here and I shot those bullets?"

"Did you fire the bullets into Theo?"

Melanie didn't reply but opened the gun box.

"I want you to fire two bullets from this gun, then tell me what pair they match."

"It'll take a few minutes."

Melanie opened the evidence plastic and removed the Colt .45.

"Let's hold off on that. I need to borrow your terminal for a minute. I have another question that needs an answer."

June stepped aside.

The agent logged in and searched the ATF records for Los Alamos Gun Range. She clicked on incident reports, typed in the time parameters of Theo Nez's death, and keyed in 'theft'. Then she hit 'Enter' and waited. *'No Match'*. She re-entered 'theft', '9mm', and '.45 Colt' and hit 'Enter'. *'No Match'*. Then she clicked on 'Members'. The computer requested her security clearance and she entered it. The names appeared, with some she immediately recognized. She forwarded the list to her email.

"I need to telephone Agent Treehorn."

"Are we going to test the Colt?"

"No. The gun, itself, gave me my answer and it's a tale-teller."

Treehorn turned to his ballistics technician after his recorded, FBI call concluded.

Su Hawkins' eyes met Treehorn's as she said, "Parker *didn't* lie to you."

The agent squinted.

"Show me."

Su sat down at Raven's computer and signed in. As she typed, images of copper slugs with striations appeared on the wall monitor with each labeled, 'Greyhorse', Baker', and 'Tsosie'. "All the lands and grooves matched. These

229

men died by the same gun."

"Okay."

Su loaded another .45 caliber image next to the three.

"This is Nez's bullet on file at the ATF depository."

The lands and grooves didn't match.

Treehorn examined the screen and waited.

"CSU Carlyle dropped off a log from Beth Hopper's yard earlier. Agent Hopper verified that she fired Theo Nez's gun into the pine tree the day before he died."

"Those bullets should match Nez's slugs at the ATF depository."

"They don't."

Treehorn comprehended.

"Finch."

Su agreed, "Finch."

"You said, *"Parker didn't lie to you."*

Su opened her hand. Two clear evidence bags held two bullets.

"Whose bullets are those?"

"Theo Nez."

"I thought Finch removed the revolver and its bullets eight years ago."

"Not exactly."

"Explain."

"I fired two bullets from the revolver and labeled them 'T. Nez'. Finch never asked if they were from Theo's body."

Treehorn pictured the sequence of events.

"These two original bullets, then, should match the slugs removed from the tree."

"They do."

Su typed and two more slugs appeared next to the others labeled, 'TN-01 and TN-02'.

"They were fired from the same weapon that killed Tsosie, Greyhorse, and Baker."

"Parker Greyhorse told me the truth and someone tampered with the evidence."

"The bullets Finch has on file aren't from the same gun and definitely aren't fired from the gun that killed the four men."

The agent's telephone rang. Melanie's FBI Academy graduation picture appeared on his screen as she held her gold badge and a bouquet of daffodils.

"Treehorn."

"Mel here. I'm at the ATF ballistics lab. I have Nez's inlaid 'DWJ' Colt in my hand. Guess what?"

"It's not the same gun that killed him."

"How did you know?"

"The ballistics from the tree slugs don't match Nez's bullets in the depository, but they do match for the gun that killed Tsosie, Greyhorse, and Baker."

"Treehorn, someone went to a lot of trouble. They duplicated a gun with a mother-of-pearl inlay and destroyed evidence in a murder investigation."

"Yes. It's called tampering with evidence and obstruction of justice, for starters. Secure it."

"Yes. I searched for a theft report file for the Los Alamos Gun Range around Nez's murder date. There's no incident report filed on either the .45 or 9mm."

"Finch," Treehorn uttered.

"Guess who's a member of the club?"

"Finch. Grasshopper, follow those guns."

"Yes, sir," she said as she hung up the phone.

Melanie's and June's eyes met and they understood each other.

"June, I'll take the four bullets back, please. If anyone calls and asks why I was here, you tell them that you tested two bullets and determined, '*No Match.*'"

"What's going on?"

"Treehorn's hunting a dirty badge."

232

Melanie went straight to the ATF depository from the ballistics lab. Once again, she followed the required security protocols and re-deposited the gun box into Theo Nez's locker.

Michael Hollander examined Agent Hopper's two visits to the depository on his video security feed and telephoned the ATF Assistant Director.

"Finch."

"Hollander here. FBI Agent Hopper checked out and returned Nez's evidence gun from his safe."

"Secure that locker. Access is denied to anyone without my authorization. Understood?"

"Yes, sir."

Melanie opened her computer and started her research on the .45 and 9mm. She glanced at Kendrick who appeared totally engrossed with his money-tracking project.

"What are you doing?" ATF Colin Finch demanded as he stood in front of her desk.

Melanie's finger struck a blackout screen key as she raised her eyes to meet Finch's.

"I pulled up Theo Nez's ballistic profile and his evidence from the depository. I ran it against all the cop-killer bullets."

"Why are you in Nez's file?"

"Did you know he was Bart Baker's half-brother?"

"What did you find?"

"Nothing. Nez's bullets on file here are a *'No Match'* to any others. Gun's a dead-end."

"So why did you sign it out?"

"I just wanted to double-check everything for the record."

"That's smart. The gun shouldn't match because it's been here since Nez's murder, a crime confessed to, by your grandmother."

"You're right. The gun and bullets don't match to any others."

"Do something constructive. Find the two missing guns from Four Corners."

"Yes, I'll work on the guns," Melanie agreed as Finch walked away.

She opened her safe and inside two handguns, a .38 and .357, lay secured in a pair of evidence boxes. The agent picked up her phone and snapped an image of their make, model, and serial numbers written on the outside labels, then secured her locker. Her fingers flew across her keyboard, not for the weapons in her desk, but for the Colt .45 and Bart Baker's 9mm from Treehorn's crime scene.

234

Kendrick scouted the office area before whispering to Melanie, "Who's Benito Del Toro?"

"He's *El Capitán* of the Mesa Cartel and he visited Parker Greyhorse at Cibola."

"It's his print on the Socorro money."

"Well, the money did come from Mexico."

"No, it didn't."

"Where did it originate?"

"CIA and Andrew Shattuck's $100 bill came from the same sequenced lot."

"I'll notify Treehorn. Log off your computer so no one sees your work. I have Bart Baker's 9mm owner's information. Let's pay them a visit."

"Only if we stop for coffee first."

Melanie nodded as she took out her phone and texted Treehorn, *"Socorro money is CIA. Single fingerprint on it - Benito Del Toro. Whispering Winds $100 came from Socorro $$. Chasing guns.—Mel."*

Treehorn frowned as he read Melanie's text.

"Bad news?" Raven asked, seeing his concern.

"Socorro money is CIA with one fingerprint. The hundred dollar bill from the crematorium belongs to the funds."

235

"Whose fingerprint?"

"Benito Del Toro."

"Shady Lynch. The man with two names."

Treehorn's jaw clenched. *The man had a third, too.*

"There are only two men that cause a reaction from you: Parker and Shady."

"He's CIA."

"Really?" Raven chuckled.

He obtained Benito's identification within five minutes of hearing his name, but didn't disclose that to his co-worker.

"We're on the same team."

Treehorn didn't respond.

"I telephoned Mr. Lynch from the number Parker used at Cibola. They've recorded all phone numbers of incoming and outgoing calls."

Treehorn raised his eyebrow.

"There was no answer."

"Give it to me."

Raven forwarded it.

Treehorn dialed and the phone rang once, *"Hello, my mojito. Leave me a message."*

The agent's fingers whitened on his phone as he spoke, "Who killed Bart Baker and who's the badge you're hunting?"

Raven's curiosity grew as he asked, "Why do Shady and Parker play these games with you?"

Treehorn didn't answer nor did he expect a reply from his message but his phone beeped.

"Find the Colt. It'll give you the badge and his partner. Sniper owns 9mm."

Treehorn texted, *"You left a fingerprint on the Socorro money."*

"I know."

The Fed frowned, *"Where are you?"*

"Waiting for you."

Treehorn pocketed his phone.

"Raven, ballistics matched the Colt .45 to all four killings: Tsosie, Nez, Greyhorse, and Baker."

Raven whistled.

"So, Parker knew about both the Tsosie and the Nez cases all these years. Why didn't he tell you?"

Treehorn refused to speculate. Daniel Tsosie had worked Indian Posse crimes exclusively since joining the force. Parker could have assisted in the deputy's murder investigation at any time, and Treehorn knew the Indian Posse leader realized the irony. The agent also knew Parker had intentionally kept the information from the Navajo

Nation Police and Chief Samuel Bear out of spite.

Treehorn and Raven both understood the crime that occurred.

"Finch removed Theo Nez's gun from Su Hawkins' possession eight years ago and delivered it back to the original owner…"

"…who then used it to kill again."

"Finch knows their identity."

"We need to locate the Colt .45."

Chapter Ten:

An Unpaid Debt to Society

"You're going to need it, so I made you a fresh pot."

"Why's that?"

"I suspect you're going to have a long evening hunting down bad people who have done bad things."

Treehorn eyed Raven as he asked, "Where do we start?"

"Remember the container in Baker's SUV at Four Corners?"

"Yes."

"It's ATF. They purchased several of them. And they matched the containers from the Socorro bust."

Treehorn spat one word: "Finch."

"The DNA results from Parker's bloody shirt."

"Whose is it?"

Raven pointed to the bulletin board.

"Male #6. The same man who left DNA at the Whispering Winds Crematorium."

"And, the same man who telephoned Parker at Cibola."

"Yes."

Treehorn reached for the largest coffee cup.

"I pulled Jeremy Begay's and Del Chambers' criminal cases and they're connected."

"District Attorney James Bedrow?"

"Yes, but someone more influential."

"Who?"

"Judge Wade Johnston."

Treehorn's brow creased.

"The judge on Parker Greyhorse's court cases?"

Raven nodded.

"One and the same. They're in your inbox, along with Parker's complete court documents, county jail reports, and the Cibola file."

"I want Johnston's court case summaries pulled."

"Already submitted."

Treehorn's lip raised in approval.

Observing the tell, Raven said, "I re-ran the DNA from Nez's gun in the system."

"Updates?"

Raven handed his co-worker a marker for the bulletin board.

"The unidentified female now has a name thanks to her employer's mandatory database."

"Who is she?"

"Gina Greyhorse."

Treehorn clenched his jaw as he filled in her name on the profile.

"Do you have her history?"

Raven handed Treehorn a copy.

"Someone lied to you. Here's her marriage certificate."

Treehorn examined the legal document filed in Fort Benning, Georgia. Home of the United States Army Rangers.

Raven swore he heard Treehorn's teeth grind together.

"What else?"

"Zane Greyhorse's birth certificate."

Treehorn examined it then said, "Gina listed Parker as the father. We know that's not true."

Raven added, "There's more. Here's her birth certificate. Remember the DNA on Nez's gun that had a paternal match to hers? Look at the father named."

Treehorn's face flushed red with anger as he grasped her birth certificate.

"If it's accurate, you need to ask him how his DNA ended up on a murder weapon."

"Find him, Raven!"

"He won't take kindly to it."

"That's too bad."

"Parker and Shady knew the truth."

"Oh, definitely."

Treehorn texted Shady, *"Where are you?"*

The reply appeared within seconds, *"Where are you?"*

Treehorn responded only because Shady answered, *"Gallup."*

"Checking out cabin real estate. Find Colt's owner?"

"I'm on it."

Shady pocketed his phone with a smirk while his next-in-command drove their black SUV through the forest north of Albuquerque. Two similar vehicles followed closely behind carrying more agents dressed in camouflaged fatigues.

Two military police vehicles stood guard in front of Gina Greyhorse's house as Treehorn drove past. He'd question her when she finished her hospital shift.

Agents Hopper and Moore passed through a gated community entrance and pulled to the curb in front of the address of the gun owner.

Kendrick looked around at the expensive, neat houses.

242

"Nice vanilla neighborhood. How did this woman become involved in a gun deal gone bad at Four Corners?"

"Why do you assume she did? All we know is she's the registered owner of the 9mm handgun recovered from Bart Baker's bag."

Kendrick raised his eyebrow.

"Treehorn said if you assume one thing then one thing is all you'll see."

The agents approached a well-dressed woman as she unloaded groceries from a Land Cruiser.

"Jacqueline Kingsley?"

The woman looked suspiciously at the two agents and didn't respond.

"FBI Agents Hopper and Moore," Melanie said as they showed her their identification.

"What's this about?"

"We'd like to examine your 9mm pistol."

Kendrick showed the woman a photograph of the gun.

"That's not mine."

"Our records indicate you're the registered owner."

"I own a .38. It's in my purse. Do you want to see it?"

"This purse?" Melanie asked, pointing to a purse visible on the front car seat.

"Yes."

The woman reached for the purse but Melanie stopped her.

"Agent Moore will examine it."

Kendrick removed the gun from the purse. It's a .38."

"Do you have your pistol permit?"

"It's in my wallet inside the purse."

"Is this your only gun?"

"Yes."

Kendrick handed the woman her wallet and she removed her pistol permit.

"What's this about?"

Melanie examined the card. Only a single .38 caliber pistol was registered.

"The Alcohol, Tobacco, and Firearms records indicate that you're the owner of another handgun."

"No. This is the only weapon I've ever owned. How did this happen?"

"We'll contact the manufacturer and obtain the legal owner and then the ATF records can be corrected. We're sorry for the inconvenience."

Kendrick placed the gun inside the purse and handed it to the woman.

"Someone probably keyed in the wrong information, but it will be easily rectified."

"The woman glanced from one non-white agent to the other as she added sarcastically, "Probably some uneducated, underpaid lackey."

When the agents returned to the vehicle Kendrick added, "I think she wanted to say something else, but the color of our skin prevented it."

Melanie suspected that, too, but didn't comment.

Next, Melanie telephoned the Black Hills Firearms and Ammunition Company in Wyoming. The operator transferred her to the records department as soon as she identified herself as a federal agent.

"Mark Connelly."

"FBI Agent Melanie Hopper."

"Badge number and contact."

Melanie provided it.

"I have a 9mm in my possession and the information in the ATF database is incorrect. Who's the legal owner who first purchased it?"

"I would love to help you but our computer system took a hit when the wildfires blazed through eastern Wyoming last year."

"Did you have a backup?"

"We kept all original documentation on the weapons

manufactured in a separate, secured vault. What's wrong with the ATF?"

"There's an error in the ownership database. We're correcting it."

"Give me the make, model, and serial number. Someone will drive to the separate vault and pull the paperwork. We won't have an answer until tomorrow, though. Give me the number where you can be reached."

Melanie supplied all of the information.

"Anything else?"

"Do you happen to have a list of professional crafters who do inlay on pistol handles? I'm looking for someone who's been in the business for at least eight years."

"I have a list with names on it from several states. It lists their websites so that may help you narrow it down if you're looking for someone specific. I'll email it."

Melanie provided her address.

"Thanks for your help."

"We can research the list later at the hotel," Kendrick suggested.

"Good idea."

She texted Treehorn, *"9mm ownership records falsified. File update in a.m. —Mel."*

Treehorn responded with a handcuff emoji as soon as he parked his vehicle in his mother's driveway.

Anna found him two hours later, asleep on the sofa wearing a fresh t-shirt and jeans. His open laptop and a half-eaten sandwich sat on the coffee table. Sadness etched her eyes as she covered him with a light blanket while he found a few minutes of peaceful sleep. She glanced at Nettie Tsosie's letters—including the most recent—and Parker Greyhorse's letters, all secured together on the table. The bible, she found in her bookcase.

Anna had removed the picture of the three teens, Parker, Treehorn and Shady earlier from the bible. Now it sat in a simple wooden frame on her son's nightstand.

The smell of a home-cooked meal awoke him.

Anna had left him a note that said, "Dinner's in the oven. Meeting at the Chapter House."

Treehorn smiled at his mother's kindness, finishing the first bowl of stew while the coffee pot brewed.

Treehorn knew Gina Greyhorse possessed details about this case that she had never disclosed. He swore he'd find the answers even if he had to drag her into an interrogation room to obtain them. Fate intervened when his telephone rang and Leo Mancuso's screen image appeared.

"Treehorn."

"I received a call from Arizona Governor Sagerman. Brock Thompson's being transported via ambulance to the Tséhootsooi Medical Center Emergency Room. Get there, now. Find out if Indian Posse committed this attack. Text me an update later."

Brock Thompson. A story that headlined newspapers for months. A white boy who served ninety days for an assault charge and a judge who refused to comment on the case. The agent understood Mancuso's order because Thompson's assault victim was none other than Nola Jessop, Indian Posse's bartender at BAR NONE.

Melanie didn't use the ATF database to locate the owners of the two handguns recovered from the rear of Bart Baker's SUV. She telephoned the gun manufacturers directly with their serial numbers, so Finch wouldn't know that she kept the weapons in her safe.

Agents Hopper and Moore arrived at a cookie-cutter apartment complex in the southern section of Albuquerque and knocked on the apartment door of the previously registered gun owner.

Pablo Cortez, a forty-year-old Hispanic male, opened the door as far as the security chain allowed. By the looks of his dusty construction clothing, it appeared he'd just arrived home from his worksite.

"FBI Agents Melanie Hopper and Kendrick Moore," The agents presented their identification, "We're here to ask you about the .38 caliber handgun you once owned."

Cortez unlocked the security chain and stepped outside. "My wife had the gun in her hand one day threatening to shoot my privates when the police showed up during our argument. She safely surrendered the weapon to them on that day, my *'Johnson'* thanked her, and I agreed to keep it locked in its safe with only me having access to it."

"Where's the gun now?"

"Some prick from the ATF showed up the next day with a court order. I'd been given the option, surrender it or they would jail me. So, I turned it over."

"Did you have a hearing on the weapon?"

"No."

"Just out of curiosity, why did your wife threaten you?"

"She didn't appreciate the interest I'd taken in her sister. I thought it was best to surrender the weapon before she could fire it."

Cortez's eyes examined Melanie's body from head to toe and back again, then he winked.

Melanie's lips curled in distaste as she turned and walked away.

Kendrick shook his head.

"Thanks for your time and, by the way, my partner wouldn't miss if she shot you."

Melanie looked at Kendrick after he closed the vehicle door.

"Think I should train the wife to shoot?"

Kendrick silently agreed.

Melanie and Kendrick drove to a nice, neat ranch in eastern Albuquerque.

A man in his late fifties opened the door. His buzz cut and bearing defined ex-military.

"Sherwood Franks? FBI Agents Melanie Hopper and Kendrick Moore."

"What can I do for you?"

"We're here to ask you about a .357 you once owned."

"Come in."

Everyone settled into a tidy living room.

"Would you like something to drink?"

"No thanks."

"The gun. I arrived home one evening from the base. The driveway held several cop cars. My seventeen-year-old son decided to shoot the neighbor's dog with my gun because it came onto our property chasing a squirrel. Of course, the dog didn't know that he killed my son's pet. Dog survived. Neighbors paid their own vet bill after we threatened to have the dog euthanized."

Melanie examined the extensive antique pistol collection in the glass display case as the guy spoke.

Franks continued, "ATF showed up the next day with a court order. I'd been given the option, surrender the handgun or go to jail for my son shooting the weapon without a permit."

"What happened?"

"ATF took the gun "

"Did you have a hearing?"

"No. I didn't want the hassle, being an officer."

"What happened to your son?"

A look of pride appeared on the father's face.

"Interesting turn of events. My son's eighteenth birthday arrived. He got his hands on a small caliber rifle with a silencer and started to do clandestine missions in the area. Of course, the first victim became the neighbor's dog. Son created a system of alibis and he went to town shooting several dogs before suspicions turned towards him."

"What happened?"

"The lead officer in the investigation gave me some kindly advice. My kid would be arrested the next day unless he enlisted in one of the Armed Forces."

"Where did he go?"

"Marines. Graduated with honors from their scout sniper school."

He grinned from ear to ear. The agents didn't.

"We thank you for your time."

As the agents walked away, Kendrick whispered, "Oorah."

"Have you ever heard of someone surrendering their weapon when faced with a simple court order based on no judicial hearing?"

"What do you think the ATF is doing?"

"I think they're confiscating weapons, then selling them on the black market to Mexico."

"You assessed that based on two interviews?"

"No, I based it on the fact that these guns were found in an ATF owned container. Why weren't they destroyed?"

"You think they're running guns?"

"No one would suspect such an operation."

Melanie texted Treehorn, *".38 and .357 confiscated by court orders without hearings. I think ATF is running guns. Socorro. Good Night."*

Treehorn responded to the text after he parked his vehicle at the hospital, *"Follow up tomorrow."*

Vehicles from the NNP, New Mexico State Police, Navajo Major Crimes, and several other dark SUVs lined the hospital parking lot, including a pair of tan Military Police Humvees.

Treehorn exited his vehicle wearing his long-sleeved dark blue FBI t-shirt that covered his gun and badge. He passed the ambulance staff as they pushed their sanitized gurney back to their vehicle. The screams emanating from the emergency room were so horrifying that even the spirits ran for cover, Treehorn swallowed down the bile rising in his throat from the smell of death and decay permeating the area. He presented his identification and signed into the law enforcement log.

The doctors and nursing staff hurriedly entered and exited a trauma room while the group of policemen stood and watched with a sick fascination.

Treehorn spotted one person in the background who

253

would provide him with a quick answer.

"What are you doing here?"

Parker suddenly became the focus of several law enforcement officers.

"I brought the wife a snack."

Treehorn lifted his shirt, presenting his badge and revolver toward the law enforcement group of individuals who eyed him suspiciously.

Then he said, "She's *not* your wife."

Parker winked at Treehorn slyly.

"When did you finally realize it?"

"Today, when her DNA showed up on a murder weapon."

Surprise replaced the smirk on the man's face.

Treehorn realized Parker hadn't known.

"Gina isn't strong enough to kill anyone."

"Some people walk away and some people don't, but DNA doesn't lie."

Treehorn stopped Gina as she hurried past.

"What happened, Mrs. Greyhorse?"

Gina eyed Parker but answered Treehorn, "Someone took a knife to Brock Thompson."

"How bad?"

"Sliced the white boy's penis clean off."

Gina's lips pursed.

"Guess he'll never jerk off again," Parker joked as he bit into a juicy, red apple.

Gina met Treehorn's eyes, "He'll be lucky to take a piss with what's left." She then glanced at Parker and spat, "Leave and don't come back."

"Well, that was a quick divorce."

Treehorn questioned the location of Brock's victim.

"Where's Nola?"

"Babysitting Zane at her house," Gina replied, walking away from the pair.

"The kid's safe," Parker added, "I assigned Posse members to him as soon as the military police arrived on the Rez. Just in case they try something illegal."

A pin could be heard when Brock's screams abruptly stopped.

"About time they gave that poor boy some drugs."

"Pain?"

"Indescribable."

NNP Assistant Police Chief Tyler Tsosie, cousin to Daniel, walked up to the men.

"You got balls coming here, Parker, with a full room of LEOs who would shoot you on principle alone."

"Find your cousin's killer yet?"

Tyler's eyes darkened with hatred.

The agent expected the man to strike the Indian Posse leader. Instead, he turned toward the Fed and said, "One day, Treehorn, you'll have to explain to everyone why you've associated with this piece of shit."

Parker offered a response that everyone within earshot could hear: "We've heard you can't satisfy your young wife."

Treehorn stepped in front of Parker as Tyler charged. The agent pushed the man back before other officers joined the fray.

"Stop it, both of you."

Parker stepped back as he mocked, "Tell your old lady to stop sniffing around BAR NONE."

Tyler shoved Treehorn's hands off him as Parker chuckled and walked towards the exit.

"Tyler, he's helped us with Daniel's investigation."

"Won't bring my cousin back and won't stop Indian Posse's crimes," Tyler said sadly, turning away to join the other officers.

Treehorn watched the LEOs eyes follow Parker as he sauntered out. Their professional faces filled with hatred and disgust.

One young NNP officer started toward the exit and

Treehorn stepped in front of him.

"You're wasting your time with Greyhorse."

"Not your business."

"FBI Special Agent John Treehorn."

"Protecting your chummy friend?"

Treehorn silently stepped aside and gave the officer a hand motion to follow Parker. He knew the Indian Posse leader would teach the green officer a quick lesson.

Treehorn typed 'Brock Thompson' into his FBI database while he waited for an update from hospital personnel. The young man was arrested for the attempted assault of Nola behind a dumpster outside a shopping mall in Albuquerque. Some Indian boys drove by and heard her screams. They stopped the alleged assault. Brock was arrested and served three months reduced sentence. The public outcry didn't change the sentencing by the Albuquerque Judge Johnston.

The boy told investigators it was consensual and that when she screamed *"No!"* he backed off. Neither Nola nor Brock were undressed so the district attorney allowed the kid to plead down to a misdemeanor. His release came a week ago. The agent shut down his phone. Nothing in the record mentioned anything more about Nola, Indian Posse, or the fact that she was under their protection. Treehorn wondered why the kid had returned to the Chinle area. Was he looking for his next victim?

The group of emergency medical staff emerged from the trauma room pushing a gurney carrying a drug-induced, heavily bandaged young Thompson. IV bags swung from the holder. As the perp-turned-victim passed by, Treehorn saw a sterile dressing covering the man's forehead.

Leila Peterson, MD, approached the group of officers to provide her single report.

"Brock Thompson, 22 years old. Someone dumped his body south of Chinle but before they did, they injected him with a little heroin. Lucky for him the EMTs picked him up and injected him with Narcan, soon discovering that someone had severed the young man's penis and cauterized it."

The majority of the men cringed.

"They weren't finished. They sliced his scrotum and removed his testicles. They then took a hot branding iron and burned a reversed "R" into his forehead. He's in surgery now."

Treehorn spoke up, "What time frame?"

"His family saw him last night, so my best guess is

around five hours ago."

Treehorn searched and found Gina casually leaning against the wall as the doctor concluded her update.

"The person who did this had some medical training. They wanted this man to survive and suffer. Before you clear out, I have one question. Why hasn't law enforcement made an effort to stop this vigilante justice?"

The corner of Gina's mouth rose slightly as the doctor spoke. Then her eyes met Treehorn's and the smirk disappeared.

As Treehorn passed two nurses, he heard one say, "He got what he deserved."

The other, more serious, added, "He won't assault anyone else. That's a win for us."

As Treehorn walked out of the emergency room he texted Raven and Mancuso. *"Brock Thompson, castrated. Can't verify Indian Posse retaliation at this time. Heroin involved. I'll leave incident report for Eli Henderson."*

The green officer walked toward the ER as Treehorn walked to his SUV.

"The quickie finished so soon?"

"He's an asshole."

Treehorn snorted, "I warned you."

Parker casually leaned against the vehicle.

"I asked him for a hand job and he refused."

Treehorn closed his eyes and pinched his nose.

"He didn't grab the joke," Parker said, chuckling at his friend's discomfort.

"Few would. Where's Shady?"

"I would say working his agenda or sharpening his knife."

"That's what I'm afraid of."

"A room full of LEOs inside the ER and they don't understand the difference between Indian vs. white man's justice."

"Who knifed Thompson?"

"I don't know," Parker said, showing no signs of subterfuge.

"He had heroin in his system."

"I know."

"How?"

"EMTs. They said they administered Narcan and when the kid woke up, they regretted it because he wouldn't stop screaming."

"Is someone copying the Indian Posse playbook?"

"Could be, but why?"

"Do you think it's right or wrong what happened to that kid in there?"

Parker looked at his friend and then at his badge.

"The white man's court hurt that boy—and Nola."

"Who killed Randy Bonito?"

"Don't ask me, my friend."

"Someone will have to take responsibility for it."

"In due time."

"I can't let you take the law into your own hands again. Who put the bullets into Paul and Bart?"

Parker sidestepped the interrogation by asking, "Tsosie's and Nez's gun and bullets matched, didn't they?"

"Yes."

"Let's go and have a drink."

Treehorn wasn't thirsty for company.

"Where's Peter?"

Both men eyed the Military Police Humvees parked on the perimeter of the parking lot.

"Hunting Paul's killer."

"The military police will find him and take him into custody." Treehorn yelled, slamming his hands down on the hood of his vehicle. "Why didn't you let me do my job?" Frustrated at the loss of the young man's military potential.

"Peter's hunted and evaded the Taliban. Do you think a couple MPs are going to compete with that?"

"He destroyed his career. It's over."

"You *think*?"

"What's the end objective?"

"We're going to get our man."

"At what cost?"

"At any cost." Parker deflected, "Don't forget, Treehorn, you *owe* me."

"I haven't solved Tsosie's murder yet."

Parker smirked as he said, "You will soon, my friend, and then you'll pay up."

"Find a decoy for the Military Police without killing them."

"I'll get right on it."

"Gina finishes her shift in an hour. I'll be waiting at her house to hear the truth."

Parker gave a little French salute.

Treehorn telephoned Samantha as he drove toward Gallup.

"Hello," Samantha's sleepy voice whispered.

"Hi, beautiful."

"Hi."

"Are you awake?"

"No."

"I've missed you."

"Have you been sleeping?"

"Here and there."

Treehorn wanted to tell her about Parker.

"Samantha?"

No response. He listened as her breathing indicated that she had fallen back to sleep.

Kendrick looked at Melanie as she reclined against the pillow of her separate bed.

"Please tell me again why we had to share a room?"

"Did I ever tell you the story…?"

"…no. I don't want to hear it."

"I feel like someone's watching us."

Kendrick squinted at Melanie, respecting her intuition.

"Okay."

Ronan pressed his face against his rifle stock as he looked through his scope toward the single hotel room of the two federal agents.

He waited patiently. His target, Agent Hopper. His

Uncle Colin despised her since the ATF and FBI directors created a liaison officer between the two agencies. Colin kept assigning her to the most dangerous operations and she succeeded at each of them. This investigation put her in his cross hairs and it became the only way to terminate the interference.

Then, Agent Moore appeared again and did something unexpected. He closed the blackout curtains. Ronan smiled. Opportunity knocked. He could achieve his mission while the two slept.

Chapter Eleven:

Love to Hate

Treehorn showered and changed into his black tactical gear with his bulletproof FBI labeled vest. He prepped the vehicle and checked his pistols. Then he drove to Gina Greyhorse's street and parked between two cars approximately five hundred feet from her house. He shut off all the car's lights and pulled his binoculars from their case. The dashboard clock read 9pm.

A Military Police Humvee with two occupants was parked in front of her house. They made no attempt at subterfuge. They were there to locate and arrest Peter Greyhorse at any of his known associate's locations. They also didn't seem to notice or care about the two Indian Posse members hiding in the shadows.

Gina's car drove past his vehicle and she parked in her driveway.

Treehorn watched as she helped her young son out of the vehicle and into the house. Lights came on as someone traveled the length of the small two-bedroom home.

The Humvee's engine started and the men sped away with their emergency lights flashing.

Treehorn noticed no one moved a curtain to observe the outside activity.

The police radio activated, "All-Points Bulletin for Peter Greyhorse. Subject has been located at the BAR NONE establishment. Proceed with caution. Subject may be armed and dangerous."

Treehorn jogged down the street and knocked on Gina's front door.

She checked the window, recognized the agent, and hesitated before she opened the door.

"It's late, Treehorn. Zane's in bed and I'm tired."

"Where is he?"

"Who?"

"Don't play stupid. Where's your husband?"

"Which one?"

"The one you're married to."

"Oh, that one."

"Yes, the one that's destroyed his career to hunt down his brother's killer."

Treehorn pushed open the door and entered the living room.

"Please leave."

"I feel like I'm in everyone's dust trail in Paul's investigation."

"You can't lead the pack all the time."

"Peter and Parker know who killed their brother. Parker will finish the job if the Military Police apprehend Peter tonight. Why couldn't he have just stayed in the Middle East?"

"Those three brothers had a bond that couldn't be broken, regardless of what they did."

Treehorn's phone pinged. He removed it and read the APB update to Gina, "Peter's been apprehended at BAR NONE."

Four Military Police Humvees and twice as many NNP patrol cars surrounded the BAR NONE establishment. Their red and blue lights illuminated the area.

By the looks of the bloodied faces and bruised knuckles of both the Military Police and Indian Posse members, a free-for-all had ensued between the parties.

Several Indians' handcuffs shone in the flashing lights, as the police dragged them out of the bar and loaded them into their cruisers.

The last one emerged, a short-haired Native American in Special Forces fatigues whose sewn name tag read, "GREYHORSE."

His eyes swollen shut, his fatigues torn at the upper

267

arm to verify his tattoo, and a bloodied and broken nose—a testament to the fact that the Military Police didn't take kindly to deserters. They opened the rear door of the Humvee and threw him into its compartment.

It took the strength of three Indian Posse members to restrain Parker from killing the MPs.

Samuel leaned against his patrol car, supervising the round-up.

Parker spotted the police chief and gave him the finger.

Samuel chuckled as he climbed into his cruiser and waited for his officers.

Parker watched as the police vehicle red lights receded down the road and he took out his phone.

Treehorn and Gina both glanced at the landline phone when it rang once.

The corner of Treehorn's lip curled as he asked, "What can you tell me about Theo Nez?"

Gina's eyes shifted away from Treehorn.

"How about his half-brother, Bart Baker?"

The woman walked to her refrigerator and removed a beer. A little Dutch courage to survive the thought of prison.

"Why is your DNA on Daniel Tsosie's murder weapon?"

The beer that had just gone down now came back up, as Gina retched over her kitchen sink.

"Stop it." a man's voice growled from the hallway.

"Hello, Peter."

"Treehorn removed a document from his pocket and unfolded the paper labeled, *'Birth Certificate.'*

"Why do you have Parker listed as Zane's father when we both know that's not possible?"

Peter took the document from Treehorn and examined it.

"Gina wrote who she wanted to. Now unless you have an arrest warrant, I suggest you leave before you're charged with being an accessory."

Treehorn looked at the woman who leaned against the kitchen counter for support.

"How did your DNA get on a murder weapon?" he questioned.

"Don't answer that!" Peter ordered his wife.

"Where's Shady?"

"Haven't seen him."

"He was there the night your brother took a bullet. He

moved the body onto the monument to get my attention. He told you and Peter who killed Paul."

"We'll take care of the shooter when we locate him."

"Let me do my job. Tell me who killed them and why?"

Peter remained silent.

"So, who was wearing your uniform at the bar?"

"My friend, Connor."

"You'll have 24 to 48 hours max, until they figure it out."

"I predict longer by the beating he received and the fact that we have identical tattoos."

"I hope you and Parker paid him well."

"We did."

"Tell Shady I'm gunning for him."

"Find his agenda and you'll find him."

Treehorn knew this to be true as he exited the house.

After the agent departed, Peter looked at his wife as tears rolled down her face.

"How *did* your DNA end up on a murder weapon?"

Gina didn't answer but went instead to the bookshelf and removed a beautiful wooden box.

"Do you remember giving me this on my sixteenth

birthday?"

"Yes. I remember making it with my own hands."

"You said it would hold our lifetime of memories."

"I remember."

Gina removed two Polaroid pictures and handed the first one to Peter. The image showed her aiming a silver revolver with an inlaid grip at NNP Deputy Daniel Tsosie as he leaned against his patrol car with the NNP logo visible.

Peter's face tightened with anger as he examined the photo.

"What's the other one?"

She handed it to him.

"The one you signed when you deserted me."

The image showed a naked Gina in bed with a long-haired Indian male whose face was hidden from view. One word was written on the image: "WHORE".

Peter remembered writing on it the night he found her passed out on the bed alone, with the picture. He packed his bags and walked out.

"Sit down."

Gina's shaky legs held her until she sank into the sofa.

Peter examined the two images.

"I know we agreed never to speak of that night after

we reunited."

Gina couldn't face him, but he sat in front of her and placed his comforting hands on her thighs.

"I want you to tell me everything you remember from that night. Start at the beginning and don't leave out a single detail. Do you understand?"

Gina nodded as she recalled the events.

"I remember walking home and Deputy Tsosie stopped in his cruiser and asked if I wanted a ride home. I said, 'No.' We laughed at something, then he drove away. I could see my house in the distance when Theo and Bart came up beside me and forced me into their car. They held me down and forced me to drink water that they had drugged. I don't remember shooting Deputy Tsosie. I don't remember having sex. I just remember waking up naked and alone."

Her cries filled the living room. Peter cried, too.

"Baby, I'm so sorry."

"Bart told Paul some of the events from that night. Parker then visited Bart in Huntsville and learned the rest. Both of your brothers searched the reservation for you. When Paul realized you had already enlisted, he knew it was for the best. I think he knew more but took it with him to his grave."

"I remember carrying two pregnancy tests that night as I walked home. I don't remember using the test, only finding it *'negative'* in the morning. One of the men left me a note taped to the other package that said, *'Try again next month.'* I did and that's when I discovered I was pregnant. I've never found the courage to determine who fathered Zane."

"I'm Zane's father."

"Parker agreed to be listed as the father on the birth certificate. He offered my son protection and called me his wife. No one would touch us when we're under Indian Posse protection."

Peter carried a lifetime of regret.

Gina grasped his arm and begged, "I want you to promise me something. If I go to jail, you'll take care of Zane."

"Your DNA on the gun doesn't prove that you killed Deputy Tsosie."

"It doesn't prove that I didn't. Treehorn won't stop until he apprehends the cop killer. When he finds *that* gun, he'll arrest me."

"The gun's buried because the owner knows it killed a deputy. They don't want that exposed."

Peter stood up, went to a hidden compartment, stripped out of his clothes and dressed in his military black tactical gear. Then he grabbed a match next to the fireplace and torched the image of Gina in bed.

"You're no whore and I was wrong to ever write that."

The other image he placed inside his Velcro-sealed chest pocket.

He had his brother's killer to hunt down. Now he possessed the identity of the man who orchestrated everything long before the night two bullets struck an Indian's body.

When he finished dressing, he placed a gentle kiss on Gina's lips as he said, "I want to adopt Zane and put my name on his birth certificate when this is over."

Gina tried to smile.

"I want to renew our wedding vows but not at the little chapel at Fort Benning."

They looked into each other's eyes. She needed to prepare herself.

"You're going to kill him, aren't you?"

"I'm going to make him pay for how he's made us suffer, but first I'm going to pound the rest of the story out of Parker even if it takes all night."

Whispering Winds Crematorium

The security lights dimly lit the pathways around the mausoleum's perimeter. A shadow moved and the camera recorded it.

Melanie's telephone rang as the two agents finished their dinner.

"Hopper."

The kid whispered, "Andrew Shattuck, Whispering Winds Crematorium."

"What can I do for you?"

"Your 3am caller's back. I'm hiding in the office with the door locked."

"We're on our way."

"Please hurry. We only have a mall cop here."

Treehorn was traveling down the highway toward Anna's hogan when he remembered the single telephone ring at Gina's.

"Damn you, Parker," he said. *You're going to tell me the truth.*

He swung the wheel of the SUV and the vehicle slid across the gravel road in a perfect U-turn. Treehorn floored the pedal and the SUV shot forward.

275

The FBI vehicle with its flashing lights passed the convoy of NNP and military vehicles as they headed in the opposite direction.

Whispering Winds Crematorium

While Andrew Shattuck hid behind the filing cabinet, his *'mall cop'*—a retired United States Marine Corp sergeant, Desmond Vincent—scouted the perimeter of the mausoleum.

Ronan Ryan came out of the shadows and attacked him. A knock-down, drag-out fight ensued between the two trained military men as Andrew Shattuck panicked and dialed 911.

The agents' SUV slid to a stop in front of the crematorium and they jumped out and ran into the establishment.

They could hear sirens approaching a few blocks away, but they weren't waiting for back-up. If this was the same man they wanted him identified.

Melanie and Kendrick drew their weapons and entered the business in an FBI-trained formation.

"Let's check the funerary first."

Someone moaned as Melanie turned a corner. Out of

the shadows, Ronan suddenly appeared and closed in. Before she could react, he blocked her gun, and his fist connected with her jaw. Mel went down for the count.

Kendrick raised his gun but Ronan's kick sent it flying. The two went at it hand-to-hand and after a few, even hits between the men, Ronan knocked Kendrick unconscious, too.

Ronan pulled out his revolver to put a bullet into Melanie's head, but Desmond charged him from the pathway and knocked his gun out of his hand. The blood flowed from the ex-Marine's cut above his brow obscuring his view, so he missed the vicious uppercut that caused him to lose consciousness.

Ronan heard the footsteps of approaching officers and since his weapon couldn't be located, all he had time for in that split second remaining was to give Melanie one good, steel-toed kick to her ribs before disappearing into the shadows.

Luckily for her, the bulletproof vest took the majority of the boot's impact.

Ronan slid into the rear seat of his vehicle, its tinted windows effectively obscuring him from any officer's prying eyes. Once again, he'd wait for an opportunity to complete his mission.

Treehorn arrived in the parking lot of BAR NONE and found three automobiles. Everyone cleared out after the NNP and military raid.

No one stood guard at the front entrance.

As soon as Treehorn entered the building, he heard shouting from the rear of the establishment as Nola stood nervously behind the bar.

"Are you okay?"

Nola nodded and pointed to the rear office.

"I'm fine Treehorn, but you better get back there. Peter's killing Parker by the sounds of it."

Treehorn hurried to the door and opened it without knocking.

Broken furniture and crates littered the room.

Peter pounded Parker's face as he screamed, "Tell me what you know."

Treehorn grabbed Peter and hauled him off his older brother.

"He knows more than he's told either of us," Peter shouted.

"Obviously…" Treehorn's sarcasm wasn't lost on either of the men.

Parker stood and removed his torn shirt, using it to wipe the blood from his face.

Treehorn studied the old Indian Posse tattoo of horses that adorned Parker's chest. An artist had added feathers and a leather braid with initials that now connected the three animals.

Parker turned away as he grabbed a fresh t-shirt, covered his body, and said nothing.

The agent looked at both men, "I think it's time you two told me the truth."

Parker avoided eye contact with Treehorn as he walked out of the room.

"I need a drink."

The men relocated to a larger room and settled at a table. Nola delivered several beers for the brothers, a coffee carafe with a cup for Treehorn, and a first aid kit.

"I'm heading home," she placed more napkins on the table.

"Thanks, Nola."

"See you tomorrow."

The men waited until the door closed and they were alone.

Peter removed the Polaroid image from his pocket and tossed it in front of Treehorn.

The agent examined it without commenting and pushed it to Parker. Treehorn removed the two dusty letters addressed to the brothers left by Paul at his Shiprock hogan. He handed them to each of the men.

They opened and read the same message, *"I'm sorry."—Paul.*

Parker grabbed a napkin and wiped the blood from his mouth.

"Paul learned the details from that piece-of-shit Bart as he drove him to Texas so his lover could report for his prison term. Gina's father hired Nez and Baker to destroy Peter's relationship with Gina."

Parker chugged his beer for some liquid fortification.

"He absolutely hated the fact that an Indian—especially one named Greyhorse—was dating his daughter. Theo and Bart met him at the Los Alamos Gun Range. After the meeting, Bart, known for his sticky fingers, lifted two items: a 9mm pistol owned by the right-hand man and the other, a Colt .45 with a mother-of-pearl inlay owned by Gina's father. The judge and his fixer searched for Theo and Bart but the men couldn't be located. Bart told Paul that they found Gina walking near her home and pulled her into their vehicle. They had specific instructions to be followed. They held her down and drugged her."

Peter reached for another beer.

"As they drove away from her house, they came upon

Daniel Tsosie as he changed a flat tire. Paul told me Theo pulled out the Colt and shot the deputy. There's no witness to verify that. Bart then moved the body so the NNP logo showed in the image with the dead deputy. They then placed the gun in Gina's hand and instructed her to shoot Daniel, which she did while drugged. They were sick bastards. Bart loaded the body into their vehicle and moved it into the desert so there wouldn't be a connection to him when they found the corpse."

Treehorn poured another cup of coffee and listened without commenting.

"The two men took Gina home, stripped her, and Theo posed with her to make it look like they had sex. They didn't. They were told not to touch her. They left photos for Peter to find. Theo pissed on the pregnancy test and left a note for Gina telling her to take a test next month since that one was negative. How did she get pregnant? She was *already* pregnant with Zane. She just never had taken the second test until a month later. It was cruel. Zane's your kid. Paul sent a sample of his DNA for testing without her permission."

Peter's fist connected with Parker's face and knocked him out of the chair.

"Pound him after he tells us what he knows."

Parker placed the cold beer on his cheek as his eyes looked towards his brother for understanding.

"Paul and I searched for you the next morning after Gina called us, hysterical. You had disappeared and, later on, we found out you had enlisted. Everything was too late."

Peter shouted at Parker, "I wanted to marry her. I wanted her to bear my children. I wanted to be a cop here. *He* didn't destroy us. *I* did that by not trusting her."

Parker didn't deny that.

"I caught up with Theo and pounded some of the truth out of him, including the fact that he dealt in narcotics. I kicked him out of Indian Posse. He tried to get some local kids to deal, including the kid Melanie Hopper. Well, that didn't end well for Theo when his ending came at the hands of a woman and the Colt .45."

Peter grabbed another beer.

"A month later, Gina was disowned by her family for being pregnant by an Indian. We helped her every chance we got."

Peter broke down.

"All of this was instigated by Gina's father because he hated the fact that his daughter loved a Greyhorse?"

"I told Gina to put my name on the birth certificate.

He would be under Indian Posse protection."

"Is that why you were attacked one month after Gina gave birth to Zane?" Treehorn wondered what had instigated the attack years earlier.

Peter looked at his brother for confirmation.

"People believed I was the Greyhorse that fathered Zane. Since you weren't around, they figured they had the wrong Greyhorse."

"She believed she shot and killed Daniel Tsosie. Is that why she never came forward?"

Treehorn shared the deputy's autopsy results. "I'm sorry Gina's suffered all of these years. The coroner stated Daniel was dead before the second bullet struck his body."

"Paul told me after the officer's death that Theo kept the gun."

"Within 48 hours, the gun did indeed end Nez's life. ATF Finch took possession of it. We have proof that the same weapon ended Paul and Bart's lives too."

Treehorn eyed the brothers.

"The gun belongs to Gina's father…" Peter started.

"…who's Judge Dwayne Wade Johnston," Parker finished.

"My investigation is taking me to Albuquerque tomorrow. Peter, you need to stay hidden until I return. I'll ask Mancuso to try to work out a deal with your command. Ask for some leniency for your punishment."

"Don't worry about it, Treehorn. I'll take full responsibility for my actions."

"You should have contacted me and let me do my job."

The agent looked at the military-trained killer and his revenge-seeking brother. Treehorn knew they wouldn't stop until the end.

"Do you have a disposable phone?"

Peter nodded.

Treehorn handed him his own.

"Type in your number. I may need you in the near future."

Peter understood what Treehorn implied. He punched his number in and hit save.

A dark van arrived at the rear exit of BAR NONE a few minutes later... Peter's getaway plan.

Whispering Winds Crematorium

Andrew Shattuck telephoned 911 dispatch again and reported the attack on his security staff and the FBI agents. Within minutes, the place was crawling with EMTs, ambulances, law enforcement, and the head of the Albuquerque FBI office, Hélena Hernández.

Ronan Ryan hid in his tinted black SUV across from the crematorium watching the activity with his binoculars, as the police scanner provided updates. No one went near the FBI vehicle or his. His stolen license plates taken from another LEO's vehicle didn't warrant a second glance from police as they surveyed the surrounding area.

BAR NONE

Treehorn and Parker listened as the vehicle's engine faded away into the night.

"You could have told him the whole truth."

"It wouldn't change anything."

Treehorn took a long look at his friend. The extra lines that creased the 35-year-old man's face. The journeys he'd traveled. He sensed his friend never truly healed from his attack. At least, Treehorn remembered he arrived at the hospital and held him in his arms as he cried. He'd been there for him when it was important, Shady too.

Parker finished his beer and remained stoic.

"We have a recording from Cibola from the guard

Henson. Who's the other man?"

Treehorn activated the playback.

"Yes?"

"Parker Greyhorse had a visitor today."

"Who?"

"FBI Special Agent John Treehorn."

The agent fast-forwarded the recording.

"How do you want it to go down?"

"What are my options?"

"Knife but messy and no guarantee. Fentanyl would have less risk."

"Do the drug. That Indian prick is known to avoid narcotics. This time I want him dead and no longer a problem."

"I want him to suffer and you tell him his father-in-law did it. I want it to be the last thing he hears before he's sent straight to hell."

"I'll smuggle the drug in a plastic-filled syringe. I can hide the metal tip in the hidden compartment of my lunch pail. It'll contain enough Fentanyl to drop a horse."

"Do it and I'll make sure I piss on his grave the first chance I get when I'm near it."

Treehorn shut off the recording.

"Who is it?"

"My court date arrived for my sentencing hearing to Cibola. Guess who showed up? Gina and Zane. She sat behind me as the court bailiff read the charges. As I turned to tell her to leave, she grabbed me and kissed me in front of her father. His face flushed, then turned to anger when he saw Gina had printed an exact replica of his .45 with his initials on the grip, onto her t-shirt."

"What happened next?"

"Gina whispered, *'I'm sorry,'* grabbed Zane's hand, and walked out of the courtroom. That prick didn't even *look* at his grandson. The bailiff approached me as I was handcuffed and whispered in my ear, *'The judge said you'll never make it out of Cibola alive.'* Well, I fooled him. *Here I am.*"

"The FBI will prove that's him on the tape and he'll be arrested for conspiracy to commit murder."

"He's a judge. He'll find a way to bury any evidence you submit to the courts. No jury will convict him."

"I'm the FBI and I'll find evidence to nail him."

"He'll never wear a pair of handcuffs."

Parker refused to believe that possibility until he saw the judge doing a perp walk.

The LEOs stepped aside as FBI District Supervisor Hélena Hernández approached the two agents being treated by EMTs.

"Hélena Hernández. I'm in charge here. What are your names and who's your supervisor?"

"Melanie Hopper."

She spoke through the pain of a swollen jaw and a possible broken rib.

"Kendrick Moore."

He uttered his name through a bloodied nose.

"We're rovers sent by Leo Mancuso."

"Who's your field supervisor?"

"John Treehorn."

"Where is he?"

"Navajo Reservation."

"What are you doing in Albuquerque?"

"Following the guns connected to Treehorn's murder investigation that occurred at the Four Corners. The shooter came here the night of the murder."

"I know Special Agent Treehorn. I'll secure this place down until he arrives. Now go to the hospital and get checked out."

"Yes, ma'am."

"When did you notify Treehorn?"

Agents Hopper and Moore looked at each other.

"We'll call him from the hospital."

Hélena Hernández pointed her finger from one agent to the other as she said, "You two thought wrong."

BAR NONE

Treehorn knew Parker had been wronged. He reached over and placed his hand atop his friend's as he asked gently, "Why did you get behind the wheel of Randy Bonito's car that night?"

The corner of Parker's lip rose as he contemplated the answer.

"Tell me no lie."

"As I told you at the morgue, I had someplace to go. Finch told me you were shot while working a case on the Rez, that you were life-flighted to the medical center, and not expected to live."

"He lied."

"No shit, Sherlock. Samuel knew you were my friend and my weakness. I knew it was a setup when I arrived at the roadblock and the chief was waiting with handcuffs swinging in the wind."

"You're lucky it was only pot and a small amount of cash in the trunk."

"Randy came to the county lock-up and begged for my forgiveness. He confessed Finch caught him with dope and weapons. I was his *'Stay Out of Jail'* card. He checked the contents of the trunk to make sure Finch didn't conceal a body inside."

"No loyalty, no forgiveness."

Parker eyed his friend, "You going to take the matter up with Samuel?"

"You should have called *me* when you were arrested."

"Shady got me out on schedule."

"I'll remember to thank him."

"You do that."

Parker stood and kissed his friend's forehead.

"Thanks for caring, my friend. How will Samuel feel when he finds out I had nothing to do with Daniel Tsosie's death?"

The agent knew Samuel would find the needed closure in the burial of his deputy.

"Have you ever asked Samuel why he hates Indian Posse?"

The agent never had. He assumed it was related to the

crimes the gang committed that kept the Navajo Nation Police Department busy. Now, he wondered whether it was something more.

Did Samuel and Finch set up the Indian Posse leader on a bogus charge using Treehorn as bait? This thought left a bad feeling in the agent's gut that overshadowed the solving of Deputy Daniel Tsosie's murder.

Hélena Hernández, the tough-as-nails supervisor who respected Treehorn when he worked her jurisdiction, telephoned the agent.

"Treehorn."

"Hélena Hernández. Agents Hopper and Moore have been transported to the Albuquerque Medical Center's emergency room with non-threatening injuries."

"What happened?"

"They were attacked by an assailant at the Whispering Winds Crematorium. Anything I should know about?"

"I'm hunting two shooters and a dirty badge. We've had activity at that location. Can you lock it down until I arrive? I'm west of Gallup."

"I'll keep enough agents here to satisfy your standards."

"Thanks."

Parker listened to the one-sided conversation without remorse.

"I have to go."

"Have a safe trip and say hi to Shady for me."

Treehorn pursed his lips as he hurried out of the building and telephoned Raven.

"Mel and Kendrick are at Albuquerque Medical Center. How soon can you pack a bag and meet me at the office?"

"I'm already en route there."

"Mel called you." It was a statement.

"She didn't want you disappointed."

"I'll see you in thirty."

Chapter Twelve:
Hunting a Badge

Ronan followed the ambulances to the Albuquerque Medical Center, strategically parking his vehicle so he could have a clear shot at either entrance. He knew he couldn't return to the crematorium until the Feds cleared the area. By the number of vehicles surrounding it, that wouldn't be for another 24 to 48 hours.

As he sat in his darkened vehicle waiting for the kill shot, he knew he'd made a fatal error the night he used the crematorium telephone to call Parker Greyhorse at Cibola Prison.

Looking over at the curtain that separated her area in the emergency room from the other agent Melanie asked, "Hey, Kendrick, are you having fun yet?"

Her partner slid the curtain open between the two gurneys. His hand held an ice pack to his swollen jaw as he whispered, "You and I need to discuss how we define fun."

Outside of the curtain, the agents heard Hélena Hernández issuing orders.

"No one enters these areas, do you understand? You check every hospital ID against the staff list. You piss in a cup. Do you understand?"

"Yes, ma'am."

Melanie looked at Kendrick and said, "He's not done with us."

Entering the space Hernández heard her comment and added, "Probably not. I would order you home upon discharge but I know how Treehorn's trained you."

Neither agent argued a moot point.

"I have two agents outside and two on the perimeter. They'll stay until you're discharged."

"Thanks for your help."

Hernández pursed her lips as she said, "I'd love to stay and watch Treehorn chew your asses out but I have better things to do."

She turned and walked away.

Kendrick's eyebrows rose as he asked, "How bad can he be?"

His partner broke out in a sweat. The last time Treehorn reprimanded her, he demanded her badge. Melanie's sheer determination was the only thing that allowed her to remain an agent under Mancuso's authority.

Ronan watched through his scope as a Fed exited the hospital and drove away in a black SUV with the standard-issue government plates. He pissed in a cup and waited.

Treehorn arrived at the Gallup FBI office. He tossed Raven's and his own travel bags into his SUV.

Raven utilized his cane for mobility while he carried his laptop.

"Melanie and Kendrick are still in the ER."

Treehorn didn't respond.

"Don't be too hard on them."

Treehorn stayed silent.

"Are bad people doing bad things in Albuquerque?"

"It's where we'll arrest the dirty badge and murderer."

Treehorn updated Raven on his conversation with Parker and Peter.

Then, he quickly texted his mother to let her know he wouldn't be home.

Anna received the message and noticed the coffee table no longer held any letters. She replied, *"Be safe."*

Nettie Tsosie's and Parker Greyhorse's letters sat neatly tied with a string on the backseat of Treehorn's FBI vehicle.

Raven opened his laptop as co-worker drove out of the parking lot.

"Hopper and Moore sent me a list of fifty-one named crypts from the Whispering Winds Crematorium. I ran their names to see if there were any major hits. Betsy Justice has a funerary access there."

"Who's Betsy Justice?"

"She's Bethany Justice's sister."

"Raven," Treehorn repeated, his face tightening, "Who's Betsy Justice?"

"You know her brother-in-law."

Treehorn pressed his telephone contacts on his dashboard phone and said, "Mary Sweetwater."

Raven's eyes grew round.

"I'm going to let Mary know that you ate my sandwich. She'll get this message as soon as she arrives. After that, she'll plan her lifelong revenge."

Raven's 33-year-old face flushed and panicked as he pressed the phone's disconnect button.

"She would kill me. I'm your wingman. Why would you do that?"

"Because you're a pissant."

"Okay, I surrender."

Treehorn cracked a smile.

"It's Colin Finch."

Treehorn lost the smile and his knuckles turned white on the steering wheel.

"What's the issue with Finch's sister-in-law owning a burial site?"

"Well, Betsy Justice isn't buried there."

Treehorn rolled his finger in a circular motion at Raven.

"She disappeared thirty years ago at the age of seventeen. Interesting case. Boyfriend said he arrived for their date and she never showed. She's been declared missing ever since. Guess who the boyfriend is?"

"Raven…" The warning came swift.

"DW Johnston."

"Judge Johnston?"

"The same. His full birth name is Dwayne Wade Johnston."

"Small world, huh? Did we receive his court summaries?"

"Yes."

Treehorn drove past the *"Leaving the Navajo Indian Reservation"* sign.

"Open them up and start reading them."

"We'll have something to discuss on the two-hour drive."

Their time passed quickly as the judge's tenure unfolded. Case after case of the scale of justice weighed heavier for the Indian defendants and lighter for the whites.

Raven's telephone pinged from Melanie, *"Doc says we're okay. Is Treehorn pissed?"*

"ER cleared Hopper and Moore." Raven conveyed the update to his partner.

Treehorn glanced at him and didn't comment.

Raven texted, *"Yes."*

Treehorn passed the *"Welcome to Albuquerque"* sign and drove straight to the Whispering Winds Crematorium.

"Are you going to the hospital?"

"Do they need their hands held?" Treehorn snapped.

"No," Raven said, catching the keys that were tossed at him.

Someone needs coffee, he thought.

Entering the crematorium grounds, Treehorn found himself facing a Fed with a gun.

"Stop. Show me your hands."

The agent raised his arms as he said, "Special Agent John Treehorn. My gun and badge are on my right side."

"Hey, Young, he's the reason we've been assigned here."

The agent holstered his weapon.

"Quinn," Treehorn said, acknowledging an agent in his early forties he'd worked with before.

"Owen Young," the other agent introduced himself, holding out his hand to Treehorn.

"What's the deal?" Quinn asked.

"This location keeps resurfacing in our investigation. I have the two dead Indian Posse members up at Four Corners."

"Hernández ordered us to take your lead when you arrived. What do you need?"

"Let me show you."

Treehorn searched and found Betsy Justice's funerary. A single daffodil attached to a wall plate caught the agent's attention.

"This name is somehow connected to my case. I want uniformed State Police walking the perimeter and two agents guarding this crypt until further notice."

"Done."

Two agents remained vigilant outside the curtained area while a third delivered clothing to the patients, who immediately dressed in the dark set with hoodies.

Ronan exited his vehicle, making a beeline for the bushes with his rifle. Then he telephoned the emergency room.

"This is FBI Director Neal Wilson. Would you please inform my two agents that I have a car waiting at the north entrance to transport them as soon as they're discharged?"

FBI Agent Emily Garcia allowed the nurse to enter the secured area.

"Here are your discharge papers. You're free to flee."

Melanie smiled as she and Kendrick signed their paperwork.

"Director Wilson has a car waiting for you at the north entrance."

Kendrick watched as the smile disappeared from Melanie's face.

"Thank you and your staff for everything you did for us."

"It's my job."

Melanie waited until the nurse departed before turning to her partner.

"We're getting out of here."

"Yeah, I know."

She drew her weapon as she explained. "Neal Wilson died last week and he was never a director. We didn't order a driver."

Kendrick opened the curtain a crack and whispered to the two agents, "Step inside here. We have a situation."

The two agents listened to Melanie and Kendrick and the plan.

FBI Agent Simon Layton texted someone and they replied, *"Ride, west entrance."*

Melanie texted, *"What's your ETA?"*

"3"

The Feds readied their weapons.

"Let's go."

The agents pulled the hoodies over their heads and walked toward the entrance.

Melanie texted the driver, *"Sniper."*

The agents waited while a woman exited the hospital in a wheelchair pushed by a male attendant.

A black SUV stopped outside the entrance and the back door opened.

The partners looked at each other.

"Ready?"

"Let's go!"

The hooded agents ran toward the SUV.

The rifle shot rang out as the agent's hoodie fell off her blonde hair.

Ronan searched for the other agents.

The second black SUV skidded to a stop in front of the wheelchair and aide.

Raven shouted, "Need a ride?"

Melanie and Kendrick jumped inside as the bullet struck the rear of Treehorn's SUV.

The two other agents fired their weapons toward the gunshot flash, providing cover for the departing Feds and their vehicle.

"Go, go, go."

Raven floored it as the agents kept their heads down.

Melanie looked at Raven as she said sarcastically, "Add that to Treehorn's pissed-off list."

Raven chuckled.

"You better find a way to get on his good side."

"Can we stop and buy him coffee?"

"You can't delay the inevitable."

"I know, but it may soften the blow."

Trying to postpone the confrontation with her field supervisor, Melanie said, "Kendrick and I will work on locating the inlay guy who duplicated the Colt."

Ronan managed to evade the gun-wielding agents and escape from the hospital before their security spotted him.

Later, the New Mexico State Troopers secured the perimeter of the crematorium which prevented him from taking another shot at the three agents as they returned to the business.

"I'll complete the paperwork on the bullet hole as soon as I return."

Raven stated, "It's worst the longer you wait for him to deal with you."

Melanie winked as she walked to her vehicle. "We'll keep you posted."

Treehorn watched Raven as he limped inside. He made no comment on Hopper and Moore's ongoing evasive tactics.

Ronan telephoned ATF Finch at his home while he tailed the female agent from the crematorium. He wasn't finished with her yet.

"Finch."

"Ronan here."

"I heard the report over the radio. I told you to lay low."

"I went to the crematorium to remove the contents."

"What the hell were you thinking? The place will be crawling with Feds for days. If they connect Betsy Justice's funerary with me, we all go down. *All of us.*"

"I was trying to save *all of us.*"

"Now, all we need is that half-breed prick Treehorn showing up."

"He's already here."

Bethany Justice Finch listened to her husband's one-sided conversation and his swearing as he terminated the call.

Treehorn and Raven sat in front of Betsy Justice's funerary, sipping their coffee as the sun rose.

Treehorn researched her disappearance. The newspaper archives stated she took journalism classes during high school with a focus on Indian rights activism. A prom picture showed her with D. Wade Johnston, a son of a prominent family.

Raven pointed to the locked door as he asked, "What's inside?"

"No warrant, no answers."

"Sorry about the bullet hole. I'll submit the incident report today."

"Wasn't your fault."

"Just like Mel and Kendrick being assaulted here."

"They didn't wait for necessary back-up."

"You've always followed the rules?"

Treehorn didn't respond. Both men already knew the answer.

Melanie drove to the *Texas Inlay Company*, pulled into the parking space with an off-set sign labeled, "*Customers Only*" and shut off the engine.

"This is the last one in the area before we have to expand out."

Kendrick glanced at the little business in the basement with bars on their windows.

"Inlay business must be tough."

The agents entered the small but established shop. There were pictures of famous musicians with guitars, athletic rings with initials, jewelry with gemstones, and finally an area dedicated to guns with their inlays lining the walls, showing the custom work produced over the years.

An older man appeared through a secured door.

"How may I help a pair of Feds today?"

"FBI Agents Melanie Hopper and Kendrick Moore. How'd you know?"

"Your license plate."

The two agents looked toward the vehicle from where they stood and found that the shop had a direct view to anyone's front bumper.

"Your name?"

"Elliot Vernon. Looks like someone didn't know how to treat a pair of federal agents."

"Score one for the bad guy that got away last night," She said as she removed an image from a folder.

"We're looking for the craftsman who did this work."

She presented the man with the glossy photograph of a revolver that Treehorn took eight years earlier at Nez's crime scene.

"My customers don't take kindly to me giving out information."

"So, you know this work?"

The man's lip curled but he didn't provide an answer.

"This gun killed a cop."

The smirk disappeared off Elliot's face.

"An individual walked into an establishment with this gun to be duplicated. He then exchanged the fake gun for the weapon in the ATF depository. Do you know whose gun this is?"

"Maybe."

"Do you know who ordered the work?"

"Maybe."

Melanie informed him, "Deputy Daniel Tsosie was 33 years old when the killer came upon him changing a tire on his patrol car, and for no reason, put a bullet in his head. He left behind a pregnant widow."

"What year?"

"Eight years ago."

The man unlocked a filing cabinet filled with index cards with photographs attached to their fronts. He searched and removed an image of a .45 caliber Colt with mother-of-pearl inlay that spelled "DWJ".

"I recognized the man as soon as he entered my shop. I see him on the television all the time."

Melanie and Kendrick listened.

"You'd be surprised the egos that cross my threshold who want their initials engraved on their possessions. It's not like they can take them with them when they meet their Maker. This request was different. He brought the handgun and a duplicated model."

The craftsman eyed the agents as he said, "I wasn't born yesterday, Missy."

Melanie waited for the man's revelation.

"I did the work and I got paid, but I never forgot it. When you pulled into that parking spot my camera took a picture of your front bumper. The same way it has for every vehicle since day one."

The man flipped the card over.

Melanie's lip curled as she recognized the license plate. She walked past it every morning when she reported to work at the ATF.

"His name's Colin Finch. He's the Assistant Director of the ATF."

The card also held his name and contact information.

"May we take the card?"

"Yes."

The old man's wizened hands dropped the card into an evidence bag that Melanie produced and opened.

Melanie examined it through the plastic.

"Can you tell me what this five-digit code means?"

"I ask for a zip code used as a password from their fondest memory."

"Thanks."

"Go get him." he urged the agents.

"I know someone who will," Melanie assured him.

Kendrick examined the five digits written on the card when the agents returned to their SUV.

"Where's this zip?"

Melanie pursed her lips as she replied, "That's the town where Betsy Justice disappeared."

"How do you know that?"

"Because I downloaded her file and read it at the hospital while you were being x-rayed."

Elliot Vernon telephoned Colin Finch and left a message on his voicemail, "Had a visit today from two FBI agents asking about a 'DWJ' Colt. You told me if anyone ever came asking to let you know and you'd make it worth my while."

Ronan followed the two FBI agents' SUV as it drove from the Texas Inlay Company to the ATF.

Treehorn and his partner sat in the parking lot of the federal court, figuring out their game plan for the appointment Raven had scheduled with Judge Dwayne Wade Johnston.

Raven received a text from Melanie, *"Finch ordered DWJ inlay duplication."*

Treehorn didn't respond.

"You need to give her a break."

"She didn't follow proper procedure," Treehorn reiterated.

Raven bit his tongue on the obvious.

"You take the lead," Treehorn said, handing him a note, "I'll start my questions towards the end."

His partner replied, "I see we're playing *'Red Indian, White Indian'* today."

Treehorn opened his briefcase and inserted his non-prescription green colored contact lens.

"That's one way not to look like an Indian."

Treehorn's lip curled. He knew he needed an advantage before this suspect.

Raven removed his conservative necktie that Dana had given him and replaced it with a beaded Navajo bolo tie.

"That's one way to look more Indian."

The agent chuckled.

Once they entered the building, Raven led the way into the judge's chamber.

"Dwayne Johnston?"

A thin, gray-haired white man glanced at the Indian and the green-eyed agent, "*Judge* Johnston, I earned the title."

"FBI Special Agent Raven Shelly and my partner…"

The Fed held out his hand to shake the judge's, but the man turned away to avoid physical contact. Raven pocketed his FBI identification.

"Do you mind if we sit? It's been a long day." Raven didn't wait for a response. He sat down, then stood back up, and dragged his chair closer to the judge's desk so he could use the corner to write on.

Treehorn watched as the judge's face flushed with anger at his partners insolent behavior. He sat in his assigned chair with his long legs stretched out and crossed casually at the ankles.

Both agents pulled out their detailed notes.

"Did you know Janet Watts?"

"Who?"

"Sorry, that's a different case I'm working on."

As Raven flipped pages in his notebook, he knocked over a pencil holder on the judge's desk.

"Sorry."

"I thought *you* agents were trained."

Raven chuckled, "I am. Did you want to see my ID?"

"There's the door Mr. Shelly."

"It's Special Agent Shelly, I earned the title."

The judge blinked.

"What do you think is the biggest problem in the area?"

The judge glanced at the two agents. "Indians."

"I asked what, not who."

"Indians committing crimes."

"I don't remember seeing those statistics."

The judge sighed.

"Drug dealing of narcotics and opioids. Does your training take longer, Mr. Shelly, because you don't appear too smart on the illegal drug activity, being an FBI agent?"

"I'm qualified. Are you related to the ambulance

chasing lawyer Wade Johnston?"

"Yes, he's my son and no, he doesn't chase ambulances."

Raven burped.

"You're wasting my time." the judge said, raising his voice.

"Do you have any questions?" Raven asked, eyeing his partner.

The judge tapped his pencil on his blotter as he examined the silent green-eyed agent.

"What is your name, *boy*?"

"They call me FBI Special Agent John Treehorn."

The judge squinted, glanced at a smirking Raven, and pursed his lips.

Treehorn started his interrogation, "What happened to your .45 caliber Colt revolver with the 'DWJ' inlay?"

"ATF Colin Finch took possession of it because it killed an *Injun*. I never expected it to be returned."

"It won't be because it killed a cop."

Treehorn caught the slight tell on the judge's lip. As if he had a secret...well, the agent had plenty of those too.

"Tell me about Greyhorse."

"I know how some things may be difficult for your

313

breed when you're working, but if you don't ask a question correctly then you've wasted my time."

"The one that appeared in your courtroom."

"Parker Greyhorse?"

"Yes."

"A criminal lowlife Indian prick from the reservation."

"Tell me about Paul Greyhorse."

"The death of the man listed in the *INDIAN TIMES*?"

"Yes."

"Never knew him."

"Tell me about Peter Greyhorse."

"Don't know him."

"He's married to your daughter."

"I don't have a daughter, Mr. Treehorn."

"Mr. Johnston, can you tell me why you give lighter sentences to white men and harsher sentences to Indians?"

"I don't like what you're implying, Mr. Treehorn. I would need a case to address your insinuation."

"Every case where an Indian has appeared in your courtroom, Mr. Johnston."

"Your time's up."

"What happened to Betsy Justice?"

"Your time's definitely up. There's the door."

As soon as the two agents exited the office, they removed their audio recorders and shut them off.

"I caught more than ten words."

"That should be enough for the lab to make a comparison."

"Let's drop these off."

Treehorn removed his colored contact lens. They served their purpose.

The agents delivered the recorders to the FBI Audio Lab, along with the recorded conversation from Cibola Prison where Guard Louis Henson's conspiracy to commit murder was caught on tape. The technician, Dawn O'Neal, promised to have the results by the next day.

Black Hills Firearms and Ammunition Company

Mark Connelly telephoned Agent Hopper as she arrived at her desk at the ATF.

"Melanie Hopper."

"Mark Connelly, Black Hills FAC. I have that information on the 9mm you requested. The original owner's name is Ronan Ryan. I emailed you a copy of the invoice."

"Let me check to see if it came through."

Melanie clicked on her inbox and hit 'download.'

"I received it. Thanks for your assistance."

Melanie saved the file. She searched the ATF records for the individual's gun permit in his home state of Colorado, which included his fingerprints. She then downloaded the partial print from the Whispering Winds Crematorium and hit 'Match Search.'

As the man's black-and-white image loaded on her screen, she glanced at the permit holder's references. Two were needed and supplied at the time of the application: *Judge Dwayne Wade Johnston and ATF Agent Colin Finch.*

Once the image finished downloading, the man that attacked her and Kendrick stared back at her from the screen.

Her computer dinged 'Match' for the fingerprints at the crematorium.

"Gotcha."

Melanie logged into her FBI account and typed in 'Ronan Ryan' copying his social security number, date of birth, and the home address supplied from the gun permit.

Results: *Special Forces, retired. Specialty: Sniper.*

Melanie texted Raven, *"9mm owner, Ronan Ryan. He's our attacker. His references: Judge DW Johnston and ATF Colin Finch."*

Judge Dwayne Wade Johnston telephoned Colin Finch.

"I was visited by Agent Treehorn."

"Did you keep your mouth shut?"

"They know a lot more than they asked and he questioned me about my Colt."

"What did you answer?"

"I told them that you took possession of it after it killed that Indian."

"The duplicated one is in the depository."

"You need to destroy it. If the Fed figures out it's a copy, we're done."

Finch decided not to inform the judge that Agents Hopper and Kendrick had already tracked down the inlay guy.

"I'll take care of it."

"Do it now."

After terminating the call, Finch walked straight to the depository. However, he found he couldn't access the locker because Michael Hollander, the clerk, had secured the safe with his own security code instead of Finch's.

Chapter Thirteen:
Half-Breed Prick

FBI Agent Melanie Hopper issued an all-points bulletin for Ronan Ryan, for assaulting two agents and the security guard Desmond Vincent of Whispering Winds Crematorium. She requested immediate roadblocks in and around the City of Albuquerque after she added his picture to the legal document, his vehicle description of a black 2018 Chevrolet Tahoe, and considered him ARMED and DANGEROUS.

Treehorn and Raven's phones flashed the APB as they drove away from the federal courthouse.

Ronan listened as the police scanner listed his bulletin across their network.

"Shit!"

He put on a hat and sunglasses before he started his vehicle and exited the ATF parking lot.

Finch's phone activated with details of the FBI's manhunt.

He telephoned his nephew and asked, "Where are you?"

"Heading out of town as we speak."

"Get your ass out of the country. You're compromised."

Ronan hung up as he traveled the back streets to avoid detection.

Treehorn and Raven drove their black Tahoe on Main Street with their emergency lights flashing, searching for the assailant.

Judge Johnston telephoned Finch.

"Just heard of Ronan's misfortune. How in the hell did this happen?"

"He made a mistake. He's leaving the country."

"Have you destroyed the Colt yet?

"No."

"Do it. You can get out of a *'misplacing evidence'* allegation."

"*I'm on it!*" Finch shouted, refusing to listen further.

Treehorn's phone beeped with an incoming text from Agent Hopper.

Raven hit the dashboard 'listen' text icon.

"Finch will destroy the gun and bullets."

"Tell her he's probably already done it," Treehorn ordered Raven.

The agent sent the text, *"Finch probably already destroyed it."*

Melanie responded, *"You have to take him down."*

Raven answered without asking Treehorn, *"Keep the evidence secured."*

Finch telephoned the depository and asked, "Hollander back yet?"

"Still on his break, sir. He left his phone but I can page him for you."

"No, don't do that. Just have him call me as soon as he returns."

Finch thought to himself as he searched the office for Agent Hopper, *Mexico looks good right about now.*

Ronan thought the same as he successfully avoided the police until he merged into a line of traffic that slowed for a roadblock. He looked around at his diminished options.

As the cars in front of him moved forward, Ronan slammed his vehicle in 'Park,' grabbed his briefcase, and exited his vehicle to jog down a side road.

The cars soon backed up behind the black Tahoe so numerous drivers laid on their horns.

The noise alerted a State Trooper who walked up with his pistol drawn to examine the empty vehicle.

A woman shouted to the officer, "A guy just ran away from it. He went that way."

She pointed toward a side street.

The State Trooper activated his handheld radio, "Suspect Ronan Ryan may be on foot near Alameda and Cross Boulevard. State Trooper in foot pursuit."

Treehorn and Raven heard the updated APB information on the police scanner and noted their address on Cross Boulevard, as they overtook the running police officer to search for the fugitive.

Ronan was jogging down the street when the black Tahoe slammed on its brakes and skidded to a stop in front of him. The tinted window lowered and a voice yelled, "*My camarada*."

"Shady!"

Ronan tried the door as he urged, "Let me in."

Shady shook his head.

"What are you doing here?"

"Company business. Saw the APB. You're so screwed. Attacking two FBI agents? You have a death wish and that stain's not going to rub off."

Ronan watched as a black SUV with emergency lights neared with other law enforcement vehicles appearing in the distance.

"Let me in!"

"Why would I do that?"

"I'll owe you a favor."

Shady unlocked the passenger door and Ronan jumped in.

"Can we go?"

"Get down."

Ronan ducked.

Treehorn sped past. Raven glanced to his right as they drove by the parked Tahoe.

"Is Shady Lynch in town?"

"Why?"

"That looked like him."

"Was he alone?"

"I couldn't tell."

"Then why would he have stopped?"

Raven turned on the sirens as Treehorn made a U-turn.

Shady turned down a side street and evaded the other vehicle because he knew he'd been spotted.

"Colin Finch is your uncle? Don't see the resemblance."

"I shot my first body under his tutelage."

"That's family bonding for you."

"Got anything to drink?"

"Cooler's on the floor. Help yourself."

"Just water?"

Shady nodded.

"I'm heading to Mexico. Need a lift?"

"I want a shot at Treehorn. Can you arrange that?"

"Maybe."

"I'll owe you another favor and you know in our line of business that's gold," Ronan said, smirking as he patted his briefcase, "My skills are much appreciated."

Shady thought for a few seconds. "Two favors? Deal."

Ronan finished his water and checked his phone for messages.

"How did Bart Baker and Paul Greyhorse end up in your sights?" Shady asked.

"Judge Johnston hired me to work select cases, if you catch my drift."

"Enlighten me."

"I dealt with Indians that never learned their lessons in a court of law."

Ronan missed observing Shady's hand clench the steering wheel as he spoke.

"Do you know Peter Greyhorse?"

"Long time ago. The judge and I were up at Los Alamos Gun Range. He had me arrange a little meet-and-greet with Bart and his half-brother, Theo, to get rid of Peter Greyhorse who was sniffing around the judge's daughter."

"What happened?"

"Went to hell in a handbasket. Baker's sticky fingers lifted the judge's gun and mine from his automobile. Told us the guns were his security while he went to prison. The judge got his Colt back fairly soon and the damn Feds tracked mine back to me."

325

Shady slowed the SUV to the speed limit where nondescript, commercial-type buildings lined the street.

"Finch told us you got Bart to the Four Corners."

Shady ignored that statement.

"Where's the Colt that put a bullet in Paul Greyhorse and Bart Baker?"

Ronan surrendered the information. "Whispering Winds Crematorium. I can't believe I just told you all of that..."

Shady pulled into the driveway of a red brick building and activated its garage door. Once it cleared the vehicle's height, he drove inside and parked next to several similar black SUVs while the door lowered.

Ronan dropped his phone.

"Shady, I can't feel my hands. Did you drug me?"

"Yeah, bad water."

Shady opened the car's center console and removed a drug-filled syringe. He used his teeth to remove its plastic cap.

Ronan's paralyzed body couldn't move but his eyes followed the hypodermic needle.

"You're going to sleep now and when you awake, your gun will take a shot at Treehorn."

Shady stabbed the needle into Ronan's thigh and

326

pressed the barrel's plunger until its contents emptied.

Ronan whispered a woman's name and funerary into Shady's ear before he passed out.

"You should have secured your weapon better, *my camarada.*"

As a safety precaution, Melanie checked her gun safe to make sure it remained locked. Then she whispered to Kendrick, "You ready?"

Her partner nodded once.

Melanie wrote a note on a yellow sticky pad. Looking around, she typed in the two serial numbers of the two guns from the Four Corners that were secured in her safe, and hit *'Enter'.*

Kendrick read the note she stuck to her monitor.

"Time to go."

Finch's laptop flashed "WARNING ALERT." He examined the details. The missing .38 and .357 from the Four Corners appeared on his screen. He searched for the agent who requested the data: *FBI Agent Melanie Hopper.*

Finch slammed down his laptop screen and rushed out of his office to speak to her.

As he did, his phone rang.

"Finch."

"Hollander. You looking for me?"

"I need to access Theo Nez's locker."

"I'm here."

"Don't move your ass from that chair."

Finch reached Agent Hopper's desk and found her seat vacant. His jaw clenched as he read the note she left stuck to her computer: *The half-breed knows about the guns!*

His staff stepped aside as he hurried to the depository.

Shady's men removed Ronan from the vehicle, handcuffed him to a metal security bar inside a sound-proofed prison cell, and secured its steel door.

"Are we ready for tonight?"

The men nodded.

"Let's go over it one more time."

Michael Hollander watched Colin Finch's arrival at the ATF depository.

"Has anyone asked for access to the locker?"

"Just you, boss, since Hopper."

Hollander typed in his security clearance followed by

328

Finch's who proceeded to the locker as soon as the approval code appeared.

Agents Hopper and Kendrick stood next to the terminal.

Finch removed his telephone and dialed, "Security? Colin Finch. I have two FBI agents here at the depository who are officially terminated from the ATF. I need four officers here *now* to escort them off the premises."

Melanie and Hopper showed their sidearms. Two against one didn't favor Finch.

He stepped away from the two agents while he waited for his staff's arrival.

"You're both fired. That'll leave a permanent red flag on your records."

Melanie's lip curled, "Why do you think Treehorn hates your guts?"

Finch's face flushed an ugly red.

"You two can wait outside."

The FBI agents looked at each other and answered, "No."

Melanie added, "He knows you're dirty."

Four armed security officers approached with their weapons drawn.

"Escort these agents off the premises and revoke their

security clearances immediately."

"Yes, sir."

Finch looked around and saw no one in his area. He typed in his security code and Nez's evidence locker opened. He smirked as he reached for the container then frowned. The box appeared light for its contents.

He opened it. No gun, no bullets, only a simple note: *"You're under arrest!"— FBI Special Agent John Treehorn.*

Finch turned around.

FBI Special Agent John Treehorn held his gun pointed at him.

"You're under arrest."

Melanie removed the box from Finch's hand.

"You're not arresting *me*, you half-breed prick!"

"Yes. I. Am."

Treehorn didn't move a hair.

"Now, raise your hands and place your palms on the wall behind you."

Finch looked left at Agent Hopper and right at Agent Shelly. Both were aiming their revolvers at his chest. Agent Moore stood in the rear with two unknown agents. Treehorn's barrel was aimed directly at his face. This time, he knew without a doubt the Navajo would shoot him if he resisted. Finch saw it in the man's eyes and by the determined look on his face. The agent clearly wanted him *dead.* Finch slowly raised his hands to the top of his head and watched as Treehorn's lip curled. He wondered whether the Indian was more upset with his surrender or his missed opportunity to legally kill him.

Treehorn holstered his gun and unsnapped his handcuffs.

Finch remained silent as the FBI agent placed the cuff around one wrist and wrapped the metal around the other. Then, he suffered the humiliation of a pat-down by the Navajo's hands.

Treehorn continued the arrest, stating the penal charges of tampering with and destroying evidence in Nez's murder investigation, then took pleasure in reciting Finch's rights to him.

"Did you give any thought to your actions? You could have solved Deputy Daniel Tsosie's murder."

Finch answered, "Who cares about a dead Indian?"

"He was a cop."

"He was still an Indian."

Treehorn couldn't prevent the look of disgust that crossed his face.

"What did you do with the Colt and its bullets?"

"It's documented here that Agent Hopper removed them from the depository."

"I'm talking about the original .45, not the one you had duplicated."

"I wish to remain silent since it's my right."

"Let's go."

Finch whispered, "I'll be out in an hour. Then, I'm coming for you."

"Did you just threaten an FBI agent?"

"No, I was giving you my evening's itinerary."

"I suggest you remain silent."

Treehorn purposely slowed Finch's perp walk through the building so his employees could snap photos of their soon-to-be ex-Assistant Director.

"Did you enjoy that?" Finch snarled.

Raven chuckled and answered before his partner, *"I sure did."*

Treehorn whispered into Finch's ear, "Agent Hopper wasn't *just* a liaison between the FBI and ATF. I recommended her placement here to *investigate* you."

Melanie cleared her desk and removed the three handguns from her safe: the duplicated Colt .45, and the two weapons that were found in Bart Baker's SUV after his murder and illegally confiscated from their original owners.

Treehorn hung out at central booking until he possessed a copy of Finch's mugshot, which he sent to Leo Mancuso and the FBI Communications Department.

Treehorn texted Shady, *"I arrested Colin Finch."*
"Got the Colt?"
"Not yet."
"Don't leave town without locating it."

Colin Finch made bail within an hour of his arrest. Reporters, camera operators, and photographers lined his street.

Bethany met him at the door.

"Pack a couple suitcases for a few days. We'll head to camp until this blows over."

"How bad is it?"

"They don't have a gun or bullets in an investigation and they're blaming me."

"That's all it is?"

"Yes."

"I'll pack and then pick up the girls. Why don't you

head out now?"

"I have a couple phone calls to make before I leave."

Finch went to his study and telephoned Judge Johnston.

"Where's the Colt?"

"I gave it to Ronan."

"Did he store it at the crematorium?"

"I would say 'yes' and Treehorn can't access the crypt without a warrant. We stay quiet and all of this will blow over, in time."

"What are the charges?"

"Don't worry about them. The FBI removed the gun from the depository with its bullets. They tampered with it, and in doing so, my charges will now disappear. Have you taken care of things at your end?"

"I have a meeting tonight."

"Good. We're staying at camp for a few days until things quiet down here."

"I'll keep you posted."

Bethany listened to her husband's conversation until he ended the call. A single tear rolled down her face as she accepted the inevitable.

Treehorn tapped on the locked metal door of Betsy Justice's crypt.

"All of our answers may be hidden behind this."

Raven leaned against the wall as his injured foot rested on his cane.

"We'll never obtain a warrant."

"We can't access it when we don't even know who the legal owner is."

"Staff here won't surrender the information to us."

"Where are Hopper and Moore?"

"They cleared their desks at the ATF and were heading to the Ballistics Lab to drop off the guns for additional testing."

Treehorn didn't comment.

"Hopper and Moore have done well."

"They took a chance. It could have ended badly."

"You've trained her well. She searches for the truth, too."

Melanie appeared from around the corner.

"Yes, I do."

Treehorn opened his mouth to respond but Melanie held up her hand and stopped him.

"Do you need to open this funerary?"

"We can't without a warrant, grasshopper."

"How about the person who holds the ownership and legal access rights to the chamber?"

Treehorn and Raven's eyes met.

"Anita Rowland, the administrator, telephoned the owner. I asked her to explain to the person that the FBI would like access to the chamber because we believe it holds evidence of a crime."

Raven gave her a thumbs up.

"Master Treehorn, you taught me well," Melanie whispered for Treehorn's ears and he frowned in displeasure.

"I'd like to introduce you to someone," Melanie said, waving the person forward.

The woman stepped around the corner.

"This is Mrs. Bethany Finch, Colin Finch's wife and Betsy Justice's sister."

Treehorn held out his hand for introductions.

"Special Agents John Treehorn and Raven Shelly," he said.

Raven shook her hand, too.

Melanie winked at Raven, then faced Treehorn.

"I've explained that we can't access this funerary without a warrant and we don't have just cause. Mrs. Finch holds the ownership and access rights to the chamber."

"Do you think a crime has been committed?" she asked, her eyes meeting Treehorn's.

"Yes," he stated in all honesty.

Lost in thought, she touched the single daffodil that hung on the wall.

"My sister dated Dwayne Johnston. She wanted to be a journalist. I purchased this funerary for her as a gift. She told me she knew she would die young and wanted to know where her final resting place would be. She wanted a single chamber so she could lay alone, for she was a solitary woman."

Treehorn and the other agents listened respectfully.

"She's dead, isn't she? My heart's felt that since the day she disappeared."

"We're sorry, Mrs. Finch," Treehorn said gently.

"I believe Dwayne Johnston and my husband know what occurred but they have refused to talk."

"It will be investigated."

"I knew this day would come and I understand you were just doing your job when you arrested my husband."

Treehorn refused to discuss his investigation.

"You've been the bane of my husband's existence for years."

The agent stayed silent.

"Here's a notarized statement allowing the FBI full access to the funerary."

Mrs. Finch handed the legal document to the senior agent.

"My husband isn't a good man, Agent Treehorn. Whatever is behind that door will probably provide you with more proof for criminal charges."

Treehorn examined the document.

"I want to know what happened to her and if the answers lie inside. I gladly grant you access."

Bethany handed Treehorn several additional documents.

"Here is the original contract for the chamber and you'll see that I am the sole legal owner. Here's a notarized letter granting the FBI permission to unlock, remove, and take possession of any and all of its contents."

Bethany squeezed Melanie's arm.

"Here's a picture of my sister, Betsy. I hope you will re-open her case."

Melanie accepted the image.

"All I ask is that you don't forget her. Don't let her justice be denied."

Melanie promised, "You have my word that her file will remain on my desk until she's found. Special Agent Treehorn is my field supervisor."

"I give you my word. She won't be forgotten."

"You've trained her well."

Bethany Finch turned and walked away.

Treehorn and Raven's glances spoke volumes.

Yes, Treehorn *had* trained her well.

Melanie waited for Treehorn's reaction while Raven watched.

"Good work, Agent Hopper, and don't ever call me *'Master Treehorn'* again."

Melanie nodded once, wondering whether he would ever call her *'grasshopper'* again.

Kendrick appeared carrying bolt cutters.

"Melanie said you'd need these."

"Agent Hopper can do the honors."

Melanie's finger traced the one daffodil on the wall plaque, then she turned to look at the three men.

"Did you know that Treehorn gave me a bouquet of

daffodils the day I graduated from the Academy?"

Treehorn's lips raised in a slight grin at the memory while the two other agents shook their heads.

"A bouquet means *'new beginnings'* while a single flower means *'misfortune.'*"

Treehorn eyed the crypt as he said, "Their misfortune was meeting us."

Agent Hopper cut the lock and stepped back.

The three agents went to their vehicles and returned with evidence collection kits, flashlights, and supplies.

Raven opened his kit and handed latex gloves to the agents.

Treehorn collected the cut metal pieces and opened the cast iron door.

The first item he removed was a .45 caliber Colt with a 'DWJ' inlay in mother-of-pearl. He placed it in an evidence gun box and handed it to Melanie who examined it.

"Do you believe this is Theo Nez's murder weapon?"

"Yes."

Kendrick gave his partner a skeptical look as he asked, "How can you be so sure?"

"Because, I shot a dead man with it."

Melanie handed it to Raven who placed it into a serial-numbered evidence box.

"Melanie, I want it tested, fingerprinted, and ballistics conducted on it today as a top priority. I want you and Kendrick assigned to it at all times. Weapons drawn if necessary. You're to arrest anyone who attempts to take possession of it. Mancuso will provide any support needed."

Treehorn shined his flashlight inside the funerary, revealing a criminal treasure trove of photographs, videos, documents, cash, and a .300 Remington rifle.

"Raven, call CSU. Have them bring the whole unit here to secure this."

The agent made the call while Treehorn spotted a manila envelope labeled, *'Parker Greyhorse'* and removed it. Inside, he found the Indian Posse leader's two court cases, a telephone number written on a piece of brown Kraft paper, which he recognized then pocketed, and two 8x10 black-and-white glossy images with red ink on one, and ink with writing on the other.

Raven's eyes rounded when he saw the images and the threat.

Treehorn broke out into a sweat and felt nauseous.

The pictures showed headshots of Treehorn in one

and Shady Lynch in the other. Someone had drawn a rifle target scope on their faces in red. A note, typed and taped to the bottom of Treehorn's image read, *"Parker Greyhorse - PLEAD GUILTY OR THEY DIE."*

Treehorn took out his phone and snapped photos of the two images.

Raven opened a plastic evidence bag. His co-worker inserted the complete folder with the images into it and then sealed it.

Treehorn didn't mention the slip of paper he pocketed or the owner's identity.

"Prioritize the evidence."

Raven nodded.

"We'll document everything in the cabinet until it's emptied."

"Have CSU take it to the conference room and have it all secured."

Raven placed his hand on his friend's arm as he said kindly, "John, we got this. There's someplace you need to be."

Raven called him by his first name only when it became personal.

"Go to your friends."

The two men's eyes met in understanding.

Treehorn removed his gloves and shoved them into his pocket.

"I'll be back tomorrow as soon as the arrest warrant is signed. Call Mancuso if you need anything."

"We'll need the morning. There's a lot here and the staff will need time to catalog, test, and document everything. I'll text you the updates."

"Thanks, Raven."

"Drive safely."

Treehorn nodded and walked away.

"Where's he going?" Melanie asked, watching as Treehorn left an active crime scene.

"Agent Hopper, have you ever wondered why the FBI motto doesn't include loyalty or justice?"

"Because it's a given?"

"Exactly."

"Where's Treehorn going?" Kendrick asked, watching the agent remove his jacket and climb into his SUV to depart.

Melanie respected the man's determination.

"To find answers."

Raven added, "And he won't stop until he has them."

"Who knows the truth?"

Melanie named one, "Parker Greyhorse."

Raven, the other, "Shady Lynch."

Chapter Fourteen:

Unfinished Business

Treehorn topped off his gas tank and purchased extra coffees.

He telephoned Shady before he departed.

The agent's cellphone vibrated as he emerged from hidden brush. His camouflaged black-and-tan painted face glanced at Treehorn's image on his screen. Then he let it go to voicemail.

Sorry, my mojito, can't talk right now.

Shady and his men watched as Bethany Finch and her two daughters arrived at the family cabin. Colin stepped outside and assisted them with their luggage.

Shady's telephone vibrated signaling a text from Treehorn.

"Where are you?"

"Unfinished business."

"I located the Colt."

"Find anything interesting in Betsy Justice's crypt?"

"I'm going to pound you into the ground."

"See you soon, my mojito."

Shady texted his man, who waited at an isolated cell tower ten miles away.

"Ready?"

"Yes."

"Two-minute countdown."

"10-4."

Shady group-texted his men, *"Two minutes."*

Two minute countdown.

"Dad, my phone's not working."

"Mine either."

Colin examined his cellphone: 'No Service.'

"It's probably down for maintenance."

Bethany's eyes rounded as her husband removed his gun from the safe.

"Tell the girls we're all eating in town for dinner."

"Colin, what's happening?" she whispered. "You're scaring me."

"It may be nothing. Get the girls. I'll turn the vehicle around."

As Finch opened the front door, a camouflaged man struck the ATF director's face with the butt of his gun. He went down for the count as his body landed on the cabin floor.

Several men rushed the two entrances and grabbed the three screaming females. Shady turned from where he had nonchalantly leaned against the side of the cabin and bent over Finch, waving activated ammonia to wake him up.

Finch reached for his gun but found it missing. When he raised his eyes, Shady Lynch's eyes met his.

"What do *you* want?"

Shady grinned but the smile didn't reach his eyes. He opened a small metal box and removed a drug-filled syringe. He plunged the needle into Finch's thigh and watched the man's eyes roll back as he surrendered to the drug's effects.

Bethany and her two daughters watched as the same man approached them with his drugs. He replaced one empty syringe and removed another smaller full one. Then he pointed to the youngest girl.

His men understood his silent command.

Bethany begged, "What do you want? Please don't hurt them. Whatever he's done it's not our fault."

Shady's men held the youngest girl down as he injected the drug into her thigh, watching as her body

347

relaxed into sleep.

His staff moved to the next daughter while Bethany struggled in horror.

Shady injected her and watched her succumb to the anesthesia.

Bethany didn't fight the inevitable as he approached her with the last hypodermic needle.

"Why?"

"Someone has to pay the piper."

Shady looked at his men and ordered, "Let's roll."

The men loaded the Finch family into the black van and the convoy headed west to Arizona for the night.

As Treehorn passed the welcome sign for the *Navajo Indian Reservation*, his phone beeped with a text notification from Raven. He hit the *'listen'* button.

"Ballistics lab confirmed the Colt bullets matched Tsosie's, Greyhorse's, and Baker's. Su Hawkins confirmed it matched Nez's too. Duplicated .45 matched Theo's fake bullets on file."

Treehorn didn't respond.

Raven added a comment. *"Thank you for solving*

Daniel Tsosie's murder. I know you paid a price with
Parker."

The agent deleted the last message.

Treehorn drove into the parking lot of the NNP headquarters in Window Rock. He removed a sheet of FBI stationary with its matching envelope and began to write.

Samuel,

The FBI ballistics lab confirmed the Colt revolver we recovered from the crypt today is the murder weapon that killed Deputy Daniel Tsosie. Theo Nez killed him."
—Treehorn

Treehorn removed the brown slip of paper from his pocket that he removed from the 'Parker Greyhorse' file found inside Betsy Justice's funerary. A single telephone number with its area code was written on one side. He wrote two words on the back side then placed it into the folded letter, sealed it, and wrote "Samuel Bear" on the front—not "police chief."

Sitting in his SUV, he watched the hard-working policemen and women exit the station. Some were heading home while others were just starting their patrol. As he entered the building, he approached the counter and not his usual entrance straight through to the chief's office.

Deputy Redfeather raised her eyebrow at the change.

"Can you please deliver this to Samuel Bear?"

"Sure, Treehorn. You want to leave it on his desk?"

The agent shook his head.

"The FBI solved Deputy Daniel Tsosie's murder today."

The officer's face showed surprise but before she could offer her congratulations, the agent turned and walked out of the building.

Treehorn drove to Nettie Tsosie's house. He pulled into her driveway as she stood next to her mailbox and raised its red flag. She waited anxiously as Treehorn approached.

"Did you find Daniel's killer?"

"Yes."

Nettie Tsosie grabbed the mailbox for support. Then, she took a couple deep breaths as she opened the flap and removed the letter inside addressed to Treehorn, the same question she had asked him every week for eight long years.

Treehorn lowered the flag and caught her as she collapsed. He carried her to the front porch where they sat on the bench as the woman cried.

"Mrs. Tsosie, I wish I could tell you Daniel died heroically, but that isn't the case. Theo Nez approached him as he changed a flat tire. He pulled out a stolen gun and shot your son in the head. Then, Theo put the gun in the hands of another victim of his, who was forced to fire the second bullet into his dead body. Your son was moved so he wouldn't be found and suspicion would not lead to the killer. Nez died by the same gun just forty-eight hours later. We recovered that weapon today."

Treehorn held the broken woman in his strong arms until family members arrived to take care of her.

Judges Elgin Watson and Dwayne Wade Johnston sat in front of the quarter-sawn oak desk, admiring its craftsmanship over Cuban cigars and vintage Scotch. Two judges who rose up the ranks together, sharing case conferences, and legal opinions.

Dwayne ran his smooth hands across the desk. "I remember the feel of wood in Daddy's carpentry shop when I was a boy. My favorites were maple and ash."

"Those were the good old days when everything seemed black and white."

"What happened to us?"

Elgin took a hard look at his peer, "What happened to you? Why so much hate? You don't just wake up one morning with it. Something filled you with it, then you fed off it. I have friends at the FBI. There are whispers. Is that why you showed up at my door for the first time in years?"

Dwayne squinted through the cigar haze, "Colin Finch's arrest today put me in an unwanted spotlight."

"How are you two connected?"

Dwayne sighed. "Years ago, a stolen gun of mine killed a cop. ATF took possession of it and now it's missing. Finch's arrest is related to that disappearance."

Elgin knew there was more without having to ask.

Dwayne took a long drag of the expensive Cuban and disappeared into his memories. "I met the woman of my dreams when I was fourteen. I treated her with respect. At age sixteen, I took her to the prom and we made love up at a friend's old cabin. At age eighteen, I asked her daddy for her hand in marriage and he agreed. He asked me to wait until we finished college. I mapped out my life with her at my side."

Elgin watched as the ugliness rose up deep from the man's soul his face pinched with anger and hate.

"She was my everything until I surprised her one afternoon at our hideaway cabin. I found her screwing a Native American activist."

Elgin raised his hand, "I don't need to hear any more."

Dwayne's whiskey-laden spit struck Elgin's face as he said proudly, "I put a bullet in his head and Colin Finch put a bullet in hers."

Elgin visualized the horrific events and his face paled.

"I have your dirty, little secret so now you have mine."

Elgin didn't question Dwayne's and Finch's loyalty to each other.

This story would be forever burned in his own memory.

"When she took her last breath, she took mine, too. I felt nothing when I married Rosemary. I felt nothing when my seed popped out a son. The only time I felt anything is when I passed judgment against an Indian or someone who hurt an Indian."

Dwayne handed his fellow judge a small envelope.

"Here are your photographs."

Elgin grasped them like a lifesaver.

"See, my friend, justice can be bought. You just need the right currency."

Elgin needed to ask, "Are these the only copies?"

"Yes."

He didn't believe it.

"If I'm arrested I'll be appearing in front of you."

Elgin listened because that was the agreement.

Dwayne handed his friend a large manila envelope.

"Here are the instructions for you to follow. Bail, discovery, and future court proceedings which will occur within the shortest window available. I'll waive a jury trial and you'll hear my case. Of course, you'll find me not guilty."

"Is there anything else?"

"When I walk out of the courtroom an innocent man, I'm going to keep my job and I'm going to continue to show Indians their place in the white man's justice system. I'll have one goal until the day I die and that's to destroy that Navajo John Treehorn and take his FBI badge. I call that a win-win."

"Get out and don't ever grace my doorway again."

Elgin spat.

"Can I use your toilet? My prostate is acting up."

"It's out of order. There's one in the hallway you can use on your way out."

"See you at the arraignment, *Your Honor.*"

Dwayne snuffed out his cigar in the ashtray and walked toward the exit. When he looked back at his friend's wooden desk, the man's token gavel sat atop his yellow envelope.

Elgin sat in shock at his desk as Dwayne used his hallway lavatory, then departed his house. At the same time, Judge John Wellington II watched from the man's private upstairs bathroom as Dwayne stepped into his limousine and departed. He flushed the toilet hoping it would be a euphemism for destroying the dirty judge.

"I made a mistake." Elgin placed the two envelopes into the separate evidence bags Judge Wellington held open.

"Yes, you did, and he found it."

"I want to believe it made me a better judge, that I ran a good race, and didn't worry about the finish line."

"You knew this day would come. It was only a matter of time."

"He's going after your son. He won't stop."

"A lot can happen between now and judgment day."

Shady Lynch and his convoy crossed into Arizona as the sun set. Less than an hour later the SUVs and a black van pulled into a commercial building located next to an airplane hangar.

"Unload Ronan first into the soundproof cell. I don't want him or Finch knowing we have the other."

"Okay, boss."

"Put the two young girls together and keep Finch and his wife separated."

"You got it."

"Feed them and let me know when they're settled. I'll be in the office."

Shady chose to do Finch's interview first.

His men politely requested that the ATF agent wash and change. He refused until a couple fists to his ribs made him more agreeable.

When Shady entered the sound-proofed room, he carried a couple of beers, a tablet, and a tape recorder. Finch was handcuffed to the metal table.

When Finch raised his forehead, he sported a swollen bruise from the pistol-whipping earlier.

"I'm not answering any of your questions."

The CIA agent's lip curled.

"You're really not in a position to negotiate." Then he chuckled and added, "I've always wanted to say that."

Finch frowned and stayed silent.

Shady nodded toward the guard who understood the order.

The man opened the door.

Finch's daughters lay asleep on a bench in the next room.

Colin understood.

"Do we let them sleep with their childhood dreams for one more night?"

"I'll answer every question you ask."

And so, the interrogation of Colin Finch began.

"I have four questions. The first three are fairly simple, the fourth not so much."

Finch nodded once.

"Who killed my two Mexican CIA agents in Socorro?"

"Ronan Ryan."

"Why did you step into Melinda Del Toro's art gallery in Tucson?"

"Heard she brokered some ATF-related deals with bearer bonds but it turned out to be Drug Enforcement related."

"Tell me about the Parker Greyhorse roadblock arrest."

"Police Chief Samuel Bear was sick of that little prick and his merry band of renegades. The setup was easy. I personally told Parker that Treehorn was on death's door. He willingly hopped into a drug-filled car and drove it straight into Samuel Bear's roadblock. Judge Dwayne Wade Johnston waited in his courtroom to make sure Greyhorse went directly to jail that night."

The knuckles on Shady's one hand turned white on his beer bottle hidden beneath the table, while his other fingers twitched to remove his knife and slit the man's throat.

But he restrained himself—for now.

"Last question: what ATF operations are of interest to the CIA? You know, the off-the-book ones."

Finch started talking and hours later Shady had gathered enough information to keep him busy for a very long time.

When Shady finally stood and stretched, he rewarded Finch by saying, "You can spend an hour with your wife, in private."

Finch understood. That was all he'd be given.

Shady entered Ronan's cell holding a tiny box.

Ronan rattled the chains that secured his handcuffs.

"This is how I'm treated after everything we've done for each other over the years?" he roared.

"I have a dilemma."

Ronan stopped his movement when Shady opened his syringe box.

"Your uncle told me some unpleasant news about Socorro."

Ronan glanced at the single syringe with its red tape. A lethal injection.

"Did you kill my two agents in Socorro?"

"I don't believe he disclosed their operations."

"He said you killed my men."

"I don't believe you."

Shady's lip curled. He reached into his pocket for his tape recorder and hit 'play'.

"Who killed my two Mexican CIA agents in Socorro?"

"Ronan Ryan."

The CIA agent lifted the syringe while Ronan panicked. First, he tried to kick the syringe out of the man's hand, then attempted to avoid the needle knowing the lethality of the dosage. Shady finally injected the syringe into Ronan's thigh.

"Goodbye, my friend."

Ronan whispered to Shady, "Peyton Greyhorse," right before he lost consciousness.

One of Shady's men opened the door. "Why do you play these games with people?"

"It's my nature."

"He's going to have one hell of a headache when he wakes up."

"Yeah, I know." Shady would interrogate Ronan when the drug wore off to find out why he mentioned Parker's father on a faked deathbed confession.

"When Finch's hour is up, drug him for the night."

His security man nodded once.

"Is the plane ready for Papago tomorrow?"

"Yes."

"I'm going to rest for a few hours."

"Boss, the boys and I were wondering if we could have a little fun." The man looked towards the area where the females slept.

Shady eyed the rooms of the mother and her two daughters.

"Don't touch the young girls."

"Thanks, boss."

Shady hit the numbers on his security door and entered his sound-proofed space that contained a single bed and bathroom. On the nightstand sat a blank photo frame with 0 to 9 digits. He entered a five-digit code and a black-haired, brown-eyed woman in her late twenties appeared smiling on its screen. Shady set the alarm, shut the lights off, and fell asleep as her image illuminated his face.

The neon light of the *BAR NONE* sign reflected on Treehorn's face as he sat in his vehicle in front of the Indian Posse establishment.

Parker Greyhorse knew the answers. Treehorn wondered whether he'd finally surrender them.

Ike, the bouncer, watched the Fed from his comfortable chair.

Treehorn sat pensively in his SUV. Parker went to prison to keep his two friends alive. The agent would bet that Parker wasn't given a time option in the negotiation.

The man needed to face his friend and that's what finally gave him the strength to open his door and step out.

Ike spoke first.

"Evening, Treehorn."

"Ike."

The long-time bouncer didn't budge from his seat as Treehorn walked past and entered the business. Everyone in the room either knew the agent's name or his bearing that identified him as law enforcement. Their voices went silent as they watched him walk over to the bar where Nola was wiping glasses.

"Where's Parker?"

She looked at her boss's lifelong friend.

"Up at his hogan with a cooler full of beer."

The man nodded once.

Treehorn whispered so only she could hear, "If Shady or Peter show up, tell them to meet me at Parker's."

Nola nodded.

As Treehorn turned to leave, he took the time to approach the BAD PENNY display. Members of Indian

Posse lined the board. He touched the empty center slot, turned, and walked out.

Treehorn parked his SUV next to the dusty truck.

Parker sat in front of the campfire trying to find solace in his beer.

Treehorn grabbed one from the cooler and sat down next to him. The agent showed Parker the two images from Betsy Justice's funerary on his phone.

"When did you and Shady make the deal?"

"I called him from the county lockup. My one telephone call."

Treehorn looked at his friend and said two words, "Tell me."

And, he did.

"Ronan Ryan was one of the two men that attacked me after Zane's birth. Indian Posse and I skated around Finch for years with skirmishes here and there with weapons, until the Randy Bonito night. Ronan showed up and we got into a serious fist fight."

"Finch came along and asked whether I had heard the news that you'd been shot. You went by Medivac to the medical center and wasn't expected to live through the

363

night. Randy threw me the keys to his car. He said he'd ride my horse home and catch a ride to his place."

"When I drove into the roadblock, Samuel leaned against his cruiser and laughed. Do you know what he said to me? *'You have two weaknesses: Treehorn and Shady.'* I knew it was entrapment. Lucky for me, Randy made sure it was only marijuana and a little cash in the trunk."

"I looked into Samuel's eyes and told him I knew who killed Daniel Tsosie and that I would take the information to my grave. It took three of his deputies to keep him off me."

"I knew I could fight the charge and I had every intention of doing that, until a white man in a custom suit showed up and had a little talk with me in the interrogation room. It was very simple. He opened his briefcase and presented those two images, the very ones from your phone. You and Shady. The man whispered, 'Plead guilty and they live.' Then he snapped his briefcase closed. He asked whether I needed proof of their ability to follow through. They offered a few names, none of whom I had an ax to grind with. Why take a life who had no business with me or Indian Posse? Then, to sweeten the deal they said they would kill Samuel for free."

"I told the man I would have a decision after I spoke with my attorney."

"You wanted to know what kind of deal Shady could arrange for you?"

The suit stood and said he needed a 'Yes or No' right there. It was non-negotiable."

"What happened?"

"Shady made a deal *they* couldn't refuse. You know his power of persuasion. I pled guilty. The federal sentence served first."

"Shady had your get-out-of-jail card ready to go."

"It wasn't just Sammy. Finch and Judge Johnston set me up. Finch was doing the judge's dirty work all these years. The judge hated the Greyhorses. We may never know why. It seems to go beyond Gina."

"Shady's plan?"

"Pretty ambitious even for him. Bring down Finch, the judge, *and* the right-hand man."

"What plan did you and Shady create?"

"You knew Finch was dirty and I knew the judge was, too. Everything that occurred started with that mother-of-pearl gun. Paul told me the story of Theo and Bart meeting Ronan and the judge at a Los Alamos Shooting Range. The judge wanted Greyhorses gone, but they didn't want it coming back on the judge in any way."

"What they didn't plan on was the fact that Bart and Theo were Indian Posse members, Bart was my brother's lover, and he had sticky fingers. He stole the "DWJ" gun and Ronan Ryan's 9mm, probably as a form of insurance in the transaction. Who knows?"

"Bart and Theo knew Gina was Peter's one weakness and my brother had nothing to do with Indian Posse. So, the two idiots pulled Gina into their car and drugged her. Theo and Bart came upon Deputy Tsosie changing a flat tire. Theo shot the deputy in the head, moved his body so they could have the NNP logo as a trophy in the picture, and had Gina put a second bullet in the corpse. She didn't know he was already dead."

"Why did they move the body?"

"Bart had to report to prison the next day so he didn't want anyone connecting him to the dead deputy. So, Theo and Bart took Gina home, took the naked pictures of her— they didn't touch her whatsoever. That was a strict instruction from the judge. Theo pissed on the pregnancy test she carried. Told her to try again in a month. Peter came home and saw the note and the nude photos, packed his bags, and enlisted in the army."

"Bart caught up with Paul who transported him to the Texas prison. Meanwhile, Theo got his hands on ten kilos of heroin and I found out. I pounded the shit out of him and disowned him from Indian Posse. He hid the heroin and gun with Melanie Hopper. A young thing he sniffed around. Her grandmother shot him soon after with the "DWJ" gun."

"Bart hid the 9mm but no one gave it a thought since he reported to prison. Paul told me the story, then I visited the man in jail. We searched for Peter. Gina found out she was pregnant. She refused my marriage proposal but we went a state over and had her name changed to Greyhorse and told everyone we got married. I gave her my Indian Posse protection. No one would dare touch her. Peter and Gina got back together and married. They didn't tell anyone since her family disowned her and everyone assumed she and I were married."

"Time went by…"

Treehorn removed two more beers from the cooler.

"Finch did something really bad to piss Shady off. I don't know what. I suspect Peter knows but neither one talked."

"Shady had a new plan."

"The judge never forgot Bart's betrayal with that revolver. Shady set up the Socorro deal. You see Finch was selling guns to Mexico. Shady took a cache and delivered them to Bart to take to Four Corners. Shady made the drug deal look good for the New Mexico governor who commuted my sentence, and Shady took some of the CIA's serialized money to screw with Finch."

"Shady set everything up."

"The one thing the man is good at."

"Finch knew Bart would be there so he told the judge and Ronan, his nephew. Those two went there to punish Bart for his sticky fingers."

"Paul knew the judge hated Greyhorses. He knew the judge was dirty for years with his harsh rulings against Indians and easy sentences for whites."

"And, one other plan?"

Parker nodded sadly as he continued, "Shady and Paul did everything. They laid the trap for Finch for setting me up. They knew the judge would be there gunning for Bart for the theft of his revolver from Los Alamos parking lot. Paul's plan was to return home before the men arrived."

"How did you know I would be at the Four Corners?"

"Shady contacted Leo Mancuso. Probably called in a favor. He knew you slept at your grandparents' hogan after difficult cases."

"Shady was there. He left me a penny and he saw how it went down that night."

"Everything was planned as I served my jail time."

"Where are Shady and Peter now?"

"They'll be here tomorrow."

Treehorn grabbed a beer and headed for the hogan.

"I'm going to bed."

"You should leave."

"No. You haven't told me everything," Treehorn stated matter-of-factly.

"I've told you enough."

Parker thought of his brother's death and a tear rolled down his face.

Shady woke Ronan with another injection of drugs that countered the barbiturate he'd injected earlier.

"Good morning, my friend."

"Shady, if I wasn't in these handcuffs you know I'd kill you."

"That's why you're in them."

"Do you have any aspirin?"

Shady handed Ronan two pills and a large coffee.

Ronan wanted to throw it in the man's face but he

knew he'd receive a few broken ribs if he did.

"Tell me what you know about Peyton Greyhorse and I'll make sure you have a pleasant day."

Ronan understood as he downed the pills. His choices were limited but at least he was alive to make them.

"Since my uncle gave me up in the murder of your two dead agents, I might as well give him up on being an accessory to murder in the death of Peyton Greyhorse."

The CIA agent listened and recorded the information.

Shady finished the interrogation and jumped into his jeep to visit his friends. He knew he'd have a favor added to his belt from the FBI by the end of the day.

Chapter Fifteen:

Never Complain and Never Explain

Shady and Peter parked a mile from the men's location as the gray light lit up the horizon.

Treehorn didn't hear the two men's soft-footed progress across the ground outside of the hogan. He slept soundly with his arms wrapped around Parker.

Shady opened the hogan's door.

"Hey, *my mojito*. Playing patty cake with Parker?"

The gun barrel felt cold against Shady's forehead and the sound of the hammer being pulled as the cylinder turned made him stop.

"Wrong, mojito."

"Hello, Parker."

The gun pressed harder against his head.

"I really don't get how you two can sleep together and not have sex."

Shady just didn't know when to keep his thoughts to himself.

"The same way you always seem to be in the doorway watching," Treehorn answered, rolling out of bed in his boxers with his trusted t-shirt and then pulling on his pants.

Parker pressed the gun harder against Shady's head so he was forced backward out of the one-room hut.

"You know how I hate guns, so lower it."

Parker didn't remove the weapon until he heard the sound of a knife opening against Shady's throat.

"Shut up." Peter whispered, "You little pervert."

He then moved the knife up along the skin to Shady's jaw.

Treehorn passed the pair without a comment.

Shady eyed Peter and slowly raised both his hands. His fingers made a derogatory 'O' and finger poke.

Shady gritted his teeth as Peter's knife sliced a half-inch cut into his pale skin. Blood oozed down his neck onto his not-so-crisp white shirt, but the CIA agent didn't move a hair.

Peter whispered, "Do it again."

Shady weighed his cockiness.

Neither Parker nor Treehorn intervened.

"There's thermoses of coffee in my bag."

"Enough." Shady wasn't beneath whining, begging, or pleading.

Peter leaned into the paleface's space and whispered, "Don't screw with my brother's predilections. You damn well know in your depraved mind nothing happened sexually between those two."

Peter sliced another quarter-inch.

"Okay, okay."

Shady's clenched jaw hurt more than the wound.

"How do you think I feel knowing someone cut my brother because they thought he fathered Zane?"

Shady's eyes shifted.

"His life is what he's made it. Do you think for one second I appreciate your comments?"

Peter stabbed the knife in deeper until the point struck bone.

"How do you think I feel when your comments belittle the fact that the only comfort he can find is being held in the arms of a man or a woman?"

Sweat beaded on Shady's face.

Peter softly whispered, "Do you speak of your own dirty, little secret? I left you a scar to remember it daily when you shaved."

The CIA agent remained silent.

"You seem to forget, Shady, that someone's more proficient with a knife than you."

Parker enjoyed his coffee as he watched the

confrontation.

"I won't bring it up again," Shady hung his head in an attempt at an apology.

Peter's response was to slice another quarter inch along Shady's jaw.

"How many times have I heard that?"

"How long is the scar on the other side?" Treehorn asked, stoking the fire.

Parker examined it.

"I'd say an inch. Do you agree, Shady?"

"Yes."

He accepted defeat. He knew he'd have a matching scar and be alive to know it.

"I'll get the needle and suture," Parker said with a chuckle.

"They're in my military bag."

Peter lowered the blade from Shady's jaw and wiped it on the white man's shirt.

"Next time…" The knife disappeared as fast as it had appeared, "…I'll slit your throat."

Treehorn shook his head as Peter walked away.

"Man, you don't know when to shut up."

Shady held his dark handkerchief against the wound

as Parker opened the first aid kit.

"I'm sorry about your brother."

"He made his choice." The men's eyes met in mutual understanding.

Shady gritted his teeth as the needle painfully pierced his skin.

"Have you ever found comfort in the arms of a woman without sex?" Parker asked as he pierced the skin again.

Shady refused to answer but a memory flashed across his face. After a few painful seconds, Shady found his spine, "So what exactly *is* your problem?"

"How many years and you finally asked?" Parker parried.

"I never gave it a thought."

Parker believed him.

"I was born asexual. If you had come into the hospital room the night of my attack, you would have heard everything explained as I cried in Treehorn's arms."

"I couldn't handle your breakdown," Shady said candidly.

"I didn't have a choice. Doctor said that I was lucky to be alive when all I wanted was to die."

"I hunted one of the two men down for you, Parker. I castrated him like he did to you, then I sliced his throat until his blood covered the red earth. He couldn't name his partner."

"Thanks, Shady, I know you did without having to ask. Your badge never stopped you. Treehorn wanted them arrested and jailed."

"What happened to the second man?"

"He disappeared but I found him the night of my roadblock arrest. My stint at Cibola prevented me from finishing the job. I'll kill him one day because now I know his identity."

"I'm sorry I joked about it."

"No, you're not, but I suggest you keep it to yourself because Peter won't forgive you the next time."

Parker tied off the final suture.

"Ouch."

"Are you ever going to tell Treehorn or I how you came to have that scar on the other side?"

"I'll pass on the story today. No sex?" Shady jested.

Parker double-tied the suture and then yanked, *hard.*

"No, Shady, I've never had the ability."

"I'd kill myself."

"I've thought of it."

Their eyes met in understanding.

Shady realized his friend wasn't joking.

"People believe you're bisexual."

"No. I've always let people think that. Bi-romance is a nicer, clinical diagnosis. I seek out companionship and affection from both males and females. It's all I'm capable of. How do you think I feel when you belittle that?"

"Treehorn knows?"

"He's the first person I told and he's given me his loyal friendship during the darkest of my nights. You, my friend, not so much. When you shave, remember that."

"We're our own little broken posse."

Parker snorted, "You thought Treehorn and I had sex?"

"Yes. No. Maybe. Did I ever tell you how my nose got broken on my thirtieth birthday?"

"Treehorn?"

Shady nodded and laughed.

"We were holed up in a cabin with a little stove in a blizzard. We huddled together in a single bed until we could trek out with the morning light. My hand visited a place it shouldn't have as I dreamed of my girl. I woke up with a broken nose. If I thought for one split second that our friend had any gay tendencies, they disappeared in that instant."

Parker laughed as he asked, "What woman would have you?"

"The one I met the day after I graduated from the FBI Academy."

"Is she the reason you left the agency within 72 hours?"

The humor left Shady's face and he didn't answer.

"You changed, Shady. I haven't."

"I promise you we'll get Paul's shooter."

"I know because you planned it. You should tell Treehorn."

Shady and Parker looked at their friend.

"Nah. Jinx."

They both laughed.

Treehorn examined Shady's stitches.

"You'll never learn. Where have you been?"

"Travel itinerary to *Mehico*."

Treehorn knew no good would come of it.

"Finch made bail."

"He's holed up in his cabin in the woods with his family."

"That was your plan, Benito."

"I think I prefer it when you call me Shady in the States and Benito in Mexico."

Treehorn eyed the CIA agent as he asked, "Where's it, Shady?"

"Where's what?"

His not-so-innocent look gathered no support from the three men who stared him down.

"The truth."

Like a conjuring magician, Shady removed his cellphone, activated a video, and handed it to Treehorn.

He turned away and stared off into the distance as the men watched the video of the deaths of Paul Greyhorse and Bart Baker at the hands of Judge Dwayne Wade Johnston and Ronan Ryan. "Everyone knows Judge Johnston. The other man is Ronan Ryan, Finch's nephew."

Treehorn forwarded a copy of the video to his own phone before returning the device to Shady.

"I need the original for court."

Shady removed a micro video cassette from his pants pocket and tossed it to his friend.

Treehorn placed it securely in his travel bag.

"I'll take the judge," Treehorn selected his man.

"I have Finch," Shady stated in skillful deception.

"I'll take the man that knifed me," Parker disclosed.

All three looked at him and understood.

"He was with Finch the night of the roadblock."

Peter volunteered, "I'll help Parker."

Shady held out his hand to Peter in a peace offering, "I'll send him to you."

Treehorn squinted at the CIA agent.

"Shady, why don't you tell us how you came to be at the Four Corners Monument with a video camera?"

"I'll give it some thought."

Treehorn shoved Shady hard as he spat, "It wasn't a *give it some thought* request."

"Tell him, Shady, or we'll hold you down and let Treehorn pound you like he did when you kissed Skyler."

"I loved her, too."

Wrong thing to say.

Treehorn clenched his fist and drew his arm back.

"Enough." Peter yelled, stepping between the two, "Get over it."

"NEVER!" the two men shouted at the same time.

Shady took off on a run.

Peter blocked Treehorn for a second saying, "Got to give my man a head start."

Treehorn shoved the Army Ranger out of his way as he went after Shady.

The two brothers watched as their friends' long strides kicked up dust.

"Run, Shady, as if your life depended on it!"

Peter looked at his older brother and said, "You have to let him go."

The pair watched Treehorn chase Shady.

"Parker, Treehorn will never love you as anything more than a friend. He's shown you that for twenty years."

"I'm afraid I'm not strong enough to live without him."

"It's not healthy."

"It's our choice. We're not hurting anyone."

"It's not *normal*."

"What's normal? It's how I've survived."

Peter took a hard look at his brother, saw the lines on his face, and let the subject drop.

Shady and Treehorn returned to the hogan after a few-mile run with no bloodshed or answers.

Everyone finished the last of the coffee.

"Here's the plan," Treehorn instructed.

Parker and Peter agreed.

Shady didn't disagree nor did he agree. That was the thought that stayed with Treehorn as he drove to Albuquerque to build the case for the arrest warrant against Judge Johnston.

Meanwhile, Parker and Peter stayed at the hogan and waited for Shady's communication.

The CIA agent whistled as he drove his jeep away from his friends. It was never a good sign when Shady appeared happy.

Chapter Sixteen:

I See Mexico

Shady quickly showered and changed into a crisp, white shirt, khakis, and aviator glasses. His crew completed everything for their departure from the hangar complex.

An angry Finch, a crying Bethany, and two scared, young girls sat huddled together between the agency men in the rear of Shady's black Gulfstream G280. A gift from his father when he obtained his pilot's license. Shady absolutely loved flying. It was one of the things he enjoyed most in life other than the obvious. Plus, it came in handy when he had to transport special cargo around the world. Two of his men also carried pilot's licenses since it's wise to always have a contingency plan in an emergency.

Shady leaned over to his second-in-command, Cyrus Ochoto, a retired Special Forces operative and instructed, "As soon as the plane's loaded, you and the boys can deliver the shipment to Denver, then take a couple days off. I've arranged alternate transportation."

"You need help with them?"

"No, they're going to the west compound in the van. How's the house guest?"

Cyrus grunted, "He made us all offers."

"Any takers?"

"None who would live to tell about it."

"Anything good?"

"Not to us, maybe to you. It's recorded. I know you two have a history, but what did he do to piss you off?"

Shady grimaced as he rubbed his suture.

Ochoto and the rest of the crew saw the boss's new stitches but not a single one questioned or commented about them. The same way they never asked about the scar on the other side of his jaw.

"He took a knife to one friend and then he ended up at the wrong place for the other. Both capital offenses."

Ochoto understood. There was a line in their business that no man crossed. When they did, there was a price to pay.

The Gulfstream landed at the CIA hangar southwest of Tucson where Shady's men quickly and efficiently unloaded its passengers into the rear compartment of a black panel van. He headed south to Mexico as soon as the rear doors slammed.

As Shady drove through the raised gate at the US/Mexico border, Treehorn arrived at the raised gate at the Albuquerque FBI parking lot.

Raven sat with his coffee as Treehorn entered the password-protected secured room.

FBI evidence bags lined two long tables.

Treehorn poured a cup and asked, "What do we have?"

"How are you?" Raven didn't beat around the bush.

Treehorn ignored the personal question and asked, "Did the audio lab finish their work on the recording?"

"They said a couple of hours. How are you?"

Treehorn clenched his jaw.

"How are Parker and Shady?"

Treehorn pursed his lips and stayed silent.

"I'll lay money they both showed up and didn't tell you everything."

Treehorn calmed his co-worker, "Their usual modus operandi."

His friend waited.

"Raven, the wheels haven't fallen off yet."

His friend chuckled and understood.

"Where's Hopper and Moore?"

"They are investigating Betsy Justice's disappearance."

"Everyone needs a cold case on their desk to remind them that justice waits. What do we have?"

"The Colt belongs to Dwayne Johnston. I pulled the ownership and permit records. We tested ballistics, fingerprints, gunshot residue, and trace. As the report stated, it's the gun that shot Tsosie, Nez, Greyhorse, and Baker. The weapon had been cleaned prior to its last firing based on gun oil lubricant. The only fingerprints found belonged to its owner."

Treehorn read the report and set it aside.

"Next."

Raven handed him the images of himself and Shady recovered from the funerary.

"We pulled three sets of fingerprints off these: Johnston's, Ronan Ryan's, and one unidentified."

Treehorn moved to the next item, the .300 Winchester rifle.

"Ballistics matched it to Ray Chambers and Jeremy Begay. Unknown owner."

"I suspect this belongs to Ronan Ryan. When he's apprehended, we can ask him if he shot the two men."

"Someone compiled a photo album of Betsy Justice. Stalker-like."

Raven handed Treehorn gloves and opened the

scrapbook from its box.

Treehorn flipped through the pages that were filled with newspaper clippings relating to the disappearance of Betsy Justice. A story regarding the missing Indian activist Peyton Greyhorse was near the front. A shocking photograph labeled "Betsy" with her naked body tied to a bed, her face was bruised and bloodied. Two images labeled "Peyton Greyhorse" followed. The first showed the long-haired Indian sitting stoically tied to a chair. In the second one he was covered with bloody bruises to his face and ribs.

"They are dated the day they went missing."

Treehorn closed the album.

The next box held cash.

"Agent Moore verified this money came from Socorro. Shady's missing money."

Treehorn didn't comment.

"Johnston and Ryan videotaped Greyhorse's and Baker's deaths. Do you want to view it?"

"No. List it for the arrest warrant."

"Why don't you want to watch it?"

"I've seen a variation of it thanks to Shady."

Raven nodded and moved on.

"The next table will keep the justice system busy for

quite some time. These are copies of Johnston's criminal cases. He wrote notes in the sentencing sections on how he intentionally ruled against Indians because of their heritage. Can I arrest him?"

Treehorn nodded once.

"Not only did Johnston hate Indians, but he also made a little criminal enterprise out of it."

Raven opened a small locker that held approximately fifty bags. Each bag held a single sheet of paper and cash.

"What is this?"

"$2.7 million. White defendants or plaintiffs who received reduced sentences, no sentences, or judgments against opposing Indians."

Treehorn's fist clenched in anger.

"Johnston filed the bribe in this folder after he spent the money."

"How much?"

"Another $3.2 million. These transactions started as soon as he took the bench."

"Send them to the courts when we're finished."

Raven reached for one he had put aside.

"Brock Thompson's $25,000 to reduce his attempted assault conviction."

Treehorn examined the details on the kickback.

"He's been transferred to the Albuquerque Medical Center for post-surgery treatment."

"I'll pay him a visit. Do you want to come?"

"No, I'll stay here and work on the cataloging and the arrest warrant."

Mesa Cartel Compound

The Mesa Cartel leader, Diego Del Toro, watched his son's arrival through his compound security gates. He still found it hard to believe he had sired the little paleface, but DNA tests don't lie. He told everyone he adopted the boy since he only had daughters. Shady understood this made him less of a threat to others if they didn't know he carried Diego's blood in his veins.

The black van stopped and Shady stepped out and waved to his sister, Melinda, as she stood on her balcony.

"Welcome home, Benito!" Del Toro greeted his son.

Shady kissed his father on both cheeks.

"I've missed you, Papa."

"You need to visit more often and stay longer."

All the kids in the compound ran to the man to see what treats he brought them. He removed a huge stuffed pinata from his front seat and handed it to one of the

389

children's sitters.

"Have fun."

A chorus of 'thank yous' filled the air along with the children's laughter.

"You spoil them."

"Yes, I do. What time's the meeting?"

"As soon as you change. I'll serve a round of drinks while we wait."

"Gero, have the men remove the packages out of the rear."

Shady grabbed the wrapped artwork from the front seat.

The guards opened the rear of the van and removed the handcuffed and gagged Finch family.

"Scrub them with the hose and take them onto the patio."

"Yes, sir."

Shady pointed to his sister and then to the package he carried. Entering his separate, secured wing of the ornate Mexican hacienda, he quickly showered and dressed.

When Shady entered the sprawling living room, he first paid his respects to his father and then shook the hands of the three men seated next to him.

Manuel Gutierrez, head of the Gutierrez Cartel, and two of his sons, Carlos and Eduardo, sat next to their father.

A single, dark-haired, dark-eyed woman sat quietly behind Del Toro.

"You know my daughter, Melinda."

Shady glanced at his sister whose face matched the image on his alarm clock. He watched the men for any sign of disrespect, but none appeared.

Screams and crying could be heard as Finch, his wife, and their two daughters were soaked from the water hose. They stood on the patio handcuffed to each other and attached to a post.

Shady removed an apple from the bowl next to his chair, opened his pocketknife, and slowly sliced it as he ate one piece at a time.

Melinda sat passively as the men conducted their business.

Del Toro opened the group discussion.

"I owe you much gratitude for your assistance in helping me bring this man to justice."

"No, we owe *you*," Gutierrez gratuitously countered.

Del Toro's men entered the room with three trunks and opened each.

"I would like to offer my thanks for the recent transactions. Even a bad shipment of cocaine has its value."

The men smiled.

"Benito negotiated a worthy deal in New Mexico. As a show of gratitude, I've provided you $10 million in secured bearer bonds for payment, $4 million in cash, and a worthy shipment of arms. My men will deliver everything safely to your compound."

The Gutierrez men looked toward the patio.

Del Toro followed their focus.

"I keep Finch," Benito spoke as he sliced his fruit.

No one objected.

"This Finch made the mistake of approaching my Melinda at her art gallery in Tucson."

No one noticed as Shady's knuckles whitened as he gripped his knife.

"He did wrong."

The men understood that the ATF agent had crossed an invisible line.

"No one disrespects my family."

All the men understood the spoken threat.

Del Toro eyed Gutierrez as he said lasciviously, "You and your sons are welcome to his woman and girls as a grateful thank you for your help."

The three men's lips lifted as they nodded.

"All I need is a photograph and then our business is concluded."

The men shook hands, nodded respectfully at Melinda, and walked out to the heliport for their departure.

Shady winked at Melinda as she walked past him.

Two men came forward, removed the handcuffs from Finch, and stripped off his clothing. They cleaned him and made him presentable in Mexican-designed clothing and then pushed him into a patio chair.

Del Toro sat down next to Finch and handed him a lit cigar and a glass of brandy. A servant laid a copy of a current Mexican newspaper near the decanter.

"Enjoy the cigar and brandy."

Finch looked toward his wife and daughters. It would be the last decent thing he could do for them as the photographer took his picture with Del Toro. A group of unknown men mingled with their backs to the photographer to make it appear to be a party.

Shady snapped a couple images and verified that they showed Finch and Diego Del Toro with the dated newspaper. He texted the best picture to Leo Mancuso.

The FBI Assistant Director's phone beeped. He examined the Mexican image, sent it to his laptop to confirm its details, and then forwarded it to Judge John Wellington II.

The laptop next to Leo dinged with the message, "That should satisfy you."

The judge opened his email to find the picture of Finch and Del Toro smoking cigars and drinking brandy, the Mexican newspaper with its date strategically situated for the shot.

"Are we good?"

The man's lip lifted.

"I'll schedule a news conference. When do we depart?"

"A couple of hours."

"Perfect."

Mancuso texted Shady, *"Thanks for the information. I've forwarded the image to legal services. I'm departing in two hours."*

Shady read the text and finished slicing his apple. Time for the interrogation.

Treehorn entered the Albuquerque Medical Center. In his hand, he carried the bribe document for his sole purpose: to investigate the kickback and referral for criminal prosecution. The smell of the facility churned the agent's stomach and more when he entered Brock Thompson's room.

Two individuals looked at him as he entered and presented his identification.

"FBI Special Agent John Treehorn."

Brock Thompson's father stood up and said, "Geoff Thompson, my wife, Marjorie."

"How is he?" Treehorn asked, looking at the sedated young man.

"How do you think he is after being attacked by a bunch of savages?"

Treehorn squinted at the angry man.

"Have you caught the men who did this? Is that why you're here?"

"I referred your son's case to the Gallup FBI office for assignment. I'm not working his. I'm conducting another investigation."

"On what?"

"What can you tell me about your interaction with Judge Johnston and his decision to sentence your son to 90 days?"

"What are you insinuating?"

"You didn't answer my question."

"Geoff…"

"There's nothing to answer."

"Agent Treehorn…" Mrs. Thompson interrupted.

"Shut up, Marjorie. I know the games they can play."

Treehorn held up an evidence bag labeled, *'Brock Thompson, $25,000'*.

"Geoffrey."

"What, Marjorie?"

"Let the agent speak."

Geoff looked at his wife as he suddenly comprehended.

"What did you do?" he demanded.

"I protected our son."

Brock's mother looked at her only child covered in bandages.

"Did you pay Judge Johnston for a reduced sentence?"

"Agent Treehorn, do you have children?"

Treehorn shook his head.

"You'll understand one day when you do."

"Shut up, Marjorie! Don't say another word."

"Your case will be referred to the District Attorney's office and your son will be referred back to the courts for judicial review."

"Get out of this room."

"Mrs. Thompson, I would hope if I'm fortunate enough one day to have a child I would teach them not to break the law or harm others in the first place."

Treehorn glanced one last time at the sedated young man in the hospital bed, the victim, and walked out.

Mexico

Two guards unlocked Bethany Finch's handcuffs from the post so she could wrap her arms around her daughters.

Del Toro tapped his glass for attention.

"Everyone, dessert and drinks are served inside. Please follow Maria."

As soon as the last guest entered the house, Del Toro turned to Finch.

"Messy business. You made two mistakes, threatening my daughter and then Socorro. Two dead men, stolen money, and missing weapons."

"Is that what this is all about? I'll make amends."

Del Toro glanced at Shady, his El Capitán and mocked sorrowfully, "It's out of my hands."

397

The leader of the Mesa Cartel walked away without a glance, while Shady played with his knife.

"Your wife and daughters will pay the price for your actions."

Two men grabbed Finch as Del Toro returned to his guests.

"I'll do anything you ask to save my family."

Shady shook his head and didn't respond.

Finch laughed.

"What's so funny?"

"I thought you CIA guys had your act together."

"Enlighten me."

"This isn't about me. Dwayne Johnston hated all the Greyhorses. He drove Peter away, put a bullet in Paul, and planned Parker's death in prison. Let my family go and I'll tell you."

"Non-negotiable."

Finch looked at his wife.

"Your whore of a sister started all of this! She screwed around on Dwayne."

"With who?" Bethany Finch asked, trying to understand.

Finch looked at Shady but Ronan had already dropped the penny to the agent.

"Peyton Greyhorse, Peter, Paul, and Parker's father."

As the realization sunk in, Bethany yelled in horror, "What did you do to my sister?"

Finch looked his wife in the eyes and said, "I screwed her and then I put a bullet in her head. She's buried with Peyton Greyhorse three hundred feet behind old Matt Stenson's cabin. Dwayne and I dug a hole and buried them with her car."

Mrs. Colin Finch staggered back from her husband to return to her girls.

"Do you know what you've done to us?" she screamed.

"No one's getting out of here alive," Finch stated the reality.

Shady poked Finch with the end of his knife as he said gleefully, "That's definitely true for you."

Then the knife pointed to Bethany and the girls.

"Gutierrez owns them now and he'll decide their fate."

Bethany and her daughters screamed and struggled as several men pulled them away and loaded them into a waiting black cargo van, which departed as soon as its rear doors closed.

Finch watched in horror as the vehicle departed the

compound. Knowing what would happen, and seeing it, still shocked the ATF agent who'd witnessed plenty during his career.

The two guards hauled a struggling Finch away from the patio and around the building to an isolated area where two strong supports hung with handcuffs and chains. A metal drain, to absorb any blood and bodily fluids, was located beneath one's hung body. The men easily connected the cuffs to Finch's wrists.

"Remove his clothes except for his underwear."

The two Mexicans complied with Shady's order by taking their knives and slicing the clothing off Finch's body. Then they stood back and waited for their next order.

"*Ustedes dos pueden irse.*"

Shady waited for the men to leave as ordered.

Finch waited. His fists clenched and his body taut.

"Your daughters will pay the price with their innocence. Your punishment for when you crossed the line with my Melinda. You should never have approached her in her gallery."

"She's Mexican trash."

Shady kicked Finch in the testicles. He responded by vomiting up the contents of his stomach.

"She's the woman I love," Shady whispered in Finch's ear.

"You're sick."

"I know, right?"

Shady smiled as he removed an expensive watch from his right wrist.

"My father bought me this with Mesa Cartel drug money. I've always been fond of it because it keeps perfect time. I don't want it damaged."

He sat it on the shelf out of harm's way.

Finch's eyes grew round when he saw the tattoo that was beneath it.

Observing his response Shady explained, "The watch keeps company with my loyalty."

On his right wrist, the "IP" Indian Posse brand mark contrasted sharply against his white pale skin.

Finch searched for time.

"Why do they call you Shady *and* Benito?"

Shady's lip lifted.

"Treehorn named me Shady when we were teenagers. My pale skin couldn't take the reservation sun so I was forced to stand in the shade every chance I could."

"Why Lynch?"

Shady laughed.

"What CIA agent *doesn't* have the last name of Lynch?"

"I beg of you. I'll do anything you want…"

Shady ignored the man's plea.

"They call me Benito here because it's my Mexican name in translation. You didn't think Benito's my real name? It's my fake passport."

He focused on the job at hand.

"I want you to know why I'm going to kill you today."

Finch's face beaded with sweat.

"I have two men who I call 'friend'. One is Parker Greyhorse; the other, John Treehorn."

Shady leaned into Finch's personal space.

"I've killed for both of them."

Finch's face paled as Shady honed his knife.

"Do you know Treehorn has a new woman after all these years of being a widow? I even went to Maryland to pay the two people who once attacked her a visit. You may have read about it."

Shock kept Finch silent.

"I would do it again."

"Someone will bring you to justice one day, you piece of shit."

"Tell me about the Randy Bonito roadblock that sent my friend Parker Greyhorse to prison."

Finch stayed silent as Shady opened a metal box that contained five syringes.

"Do you want me to deaden the pain?" Shady asked, removing one hypodermic needle and injecting Finch's thigh.

"Coagulant, that'll slow down the bleeding."

"I'm not telling you shit."

Shady removed another needle and injected Finch's other thigh.

"That one's known to increase pain receptors."

Finch's breathing increased and his pupils dilated.

Shady pointed his blade toward Finch.

"You set Parker up with a car full of drugs. You tampered with evidence to prevent Treehorn from solving a deputy's murder, all because a dirty judge didn't want his daughter involved with an Indian. Does that sound about right?"

Finch didn't deny any of it.

"One last thing for you to put into perspective: I set up

the Socorro deal for Parker. Then I sabotaged the deal so my father would give me permission to go after you. All for Melinda."

Finch's eyes rounded as he comprehended the series of events that delivered him here. Then he watched as Shady's wrist flashed like a cobra's strike. The fine steel cut through the air as it drew first blood across his cheek. The slice felt like a firebrand burning his soul—that one and the countless others, until his pain flowed red and his thoughts faded to black.

Shady's men dumped the corpse into a vat of acid and that ended the reign of Colin Finch's abuse of power.

Treehorn returned to the FBI building with a double lunch to satisfy Raven's appetite while the two men worked on the remaining contents of Betsy Justice's funerary.

Trinity Bessette from the Audio Lab telephoned Treehorn, "Judge Dwayne Johnston's courthouse '*voice*' recording is a match with the man speaking on Cibola guard Louis Henson's telephone call."

"How soon can I have the written report for the arrest warrant?"

"I'll have it to you in an hour."

"I'll be here waiting."

Treehorn telephoned the federal district court in Washington.

The judge's longtime assistant answered the telephone.

"Judge Wellington's office."

"Hello, Harriet, John Treehorn."

"Hello, stranger. How are you?"

"Good. Is my father available?"

"No, he's in Arizona. You can reach him on his cell."

"Thanks, Harriet."

"You take care and visit soon."

"My father's in Arizona," Treehorn updated his co-worker.

"Yes, he is."

Raven pointed to the federal communications monitor where Judge John Wellington II's image appeared in fixed format while an *Indian Times* journalist spoke.

"Jori Lansing reporting, *Federal Judge of the Southwest District John Wellington II filed an arrest and extradition warrant for ATF Assistant Director Colin Finch. Today, images surfaced of him with Mesa Cartel leader, Diego Del Toro, in his Mexican compound. No word if Colin Finch's family accompanied him.*

Raven muted the television.

"Where's Shady?" Treehorn slammed his fist on the table.

Shady stopped his black van at the border crossing barricade and handed Hector Gonzalez a pastry box.

"My father thanks you for your hard work."

The old Indian nodded as he raised the gate. Inside sat two of Rosita's homemade pastries and $5,000 in cash.

Shady whistled as he drove into Arizona past the old Papago Indian Reservation marker which someone painted an 'X' over beneath a larger, newer *'Tohono O'odham Nation'* with an attached *"Welcome to Arizona"* sign.

Melinda sat next to him and smiled.

He stopped the vehicle as he passed the sign.

"I need an updated picture for my alarm clock."

Melinda smiled as he took her picture.

"Let's get you home safely," he whispered as Melinda's finger caressed the old scar on his jaw.

Shady's phone beeped with a text notification.

Treehorn's image appeared.

"Where are you?"

Shady glanced at Mexico in his rearview mirror and

replied, *"Arizona."*

"Arrest tomorrow for Colt owner."

"Old news."

"Tell Parker - Perp Walk."

"I'll ask him if he wants a road trip."

Shady drove his van into the private isolated airport hangar, removed his belongings, and threw the keys to one of his security staff.

The Gulfstream G450 gleamed in the daylight as it waited on the tarmac for his arrival.

He helped Melinda out of the vehicle while his men took possession of her belongings. Shady kissed her on the cheek and whispered something in her ear.

As the agent's security man approached, he ordered, "Daniel, make sure Melinda arrives safely at her gallery."

"Yes, sir."

Melinda begged Shady, "Kiss me."

He grabbed her by her thick black hair and yanked her forward for a passionate kiss.

John Wellington II looked out the plane window and uttered a sound of revulsion. "Is Shady kissing his sister?"

Leo Mancuso leaned around the judge for a view.

Shady's one hand tangled in the woman's hair while the other grabbed her ass.

"Melinda isn't Diego Del Toro's daughter."

Shady finally released the woman. Whatever he said to her put a smile on her face.

"Who's her father?"

Mancuso delayed answering as he picked up the inboard telephone and issued the pilot an update, "We're ready to depart as soon as he's boarded."

Shady sauntered onto the plane, in one hand he carried his knapsack and in the other a string-wrapped pastry box.

He glanced at the men as they sat in their custom made power suits.

Shady spoke to the FBI Assistant Director, "Hey, boss, thanks for the ride." Then his eyes shifted to the other man, Judge John Wellington II, as he said, "Nice to see you, *Pops*."

The judge pursed his lips.

"I see you haven't changed."

"Here for Treehorn's birthday?"

Surprise flickered across the older man's face.

"I see *you* haven't changed," Shady snorted.

"Go sit in the rear of the plane before we test that no

parachute rule."

The agent grabbed his belongings.

"What's in the box?"

"Treehorn's present."

"Benito?"

"Yeah?"

"Thanks for Finch but you knew Treehorn had a plan, right?"

"Really?" he asked with a beguiled look.

"Who do you think placed Agent Hopper with the ATF?"

Shady smirked, "I guess two plans were better than one. As for Finch, he won't screw with..." he glanced from man to man, "...anyone again."

The judge realized Shady voided his signed extradition warrant.

Mancuso understood the implied reference directed toward Greyhorse and Treehorn.

"What happened to Finch's wife and girls?"

"They weren't at the cabin when my team picked him up and we didn't wait for them to appear. Check with my men if you need it verified."

"I already did."

Shady's blank stare met his boss's shrewd one.

"When Treehorn figures everything out, and you know he will, he'll probably put you either in the hospital— or a morgue."

Shady shrugged his shoulders.

"He still thinks I quit the FBI and work for the CIA."

He continued his walk down the aisle whistling George Thorogood's, *"Bad to the Bone"*.

Judge Wellington whispered, "I'm surprised someone hasn't put a bullet in that psychopath's back."

Mancuso chuckled.

"He's a sociopath and, honestly, I thought Treehorn would've killed the little shit by now. You want to lay a wager?"

"I don't bet against my son."

"Neither do I, but you should because if Treehorn ever does find out Shady's history, he'll probably kill him with no remorse."

"I'm not betting on anyone's life or death."

Mancuso glanced at Shady and remembered the history of their deal.

"Since our work is completed, I could give you a few hours for a visit with Anna...and Treehorn while I check in with my Gallup staff."

The judge thought of a couple hours wrapped in Anna Treehorn's arms.

"Thanks, Leo. Arrange it."

Mancuso and the judge watched Shady settle into his seat and stare out the window as if he didn't have a care in the world.

The FBI Assistant Director whispered, "You know when you cross that line and make a deal with the devil?"

"He returns one day without warning."

"Exactly."

"Who's Melinda Del Toro's father?"

"That devil."

Both men knew that day would come because some bones never stopped their rattling.

Agents Hopper and Moore located the diner where Betsy Justice was last seen based on the police report and numerous newspaper articles.

Both agents looked around the one-stoplight village.

"Small town."

"Everyone knows everyone's business."

The two agents entered the little town's eating establishment, *Kellie's Diner*, and settled in for an

411

afternoon drink.

A short, gray-haired waitress with the name-tag 'Kelli' walked up to the pair carrying menus and waters. Three pencils peeked out from her hair.

"Welcome, strangers. What can I start you off with for drinks?"

"Coffees, please."

"Specials listed on the menu. I'll be right back when I find a pencil."

The agents didn't comment on the pencil stash.

Kelli returned with two cups and a thermos of coffee.

Melanie introduced them: "I'm FBI Agent Melanie Hopper and this is my partner Agent Kendrick Moore. We're investigating Betsy Justice's disappearance."

"Sad times. Seems that's all we have nowadays."

Kelli pulled up a chair since there appeared to be only one other customer who sat at the counter eating pie.

"I started waitressing here when she disappeared."

"Is there anything you recall now that you didn't remember then?"

"Funny times back then. White girl disappeared; place swarmed with cops. It's not remembering anything new, missy, it's not forgetting what I saw."

412

"What do you mean?"

"My husband, Mack, towed a car from the parking lot. Same time the white girl Betsy disappeared. Cops couldn't care less about an Indian's abandoned car. People park here all the time, leave for a few hours, and then return to pick up their automobile."

"What was the concern with the Indian?"

"He never returned for his car." Kelli looked at the pie eater, "Hey, Johnny, come here. Feds have a question for you. My son took over the towing business when my husband changed to long-distance hauling."

"Where's the Indian's car that your father towed when the white girl disappeared?"

"It's still in my storage barn waiting for the owner to collect it."

"Can we take a look?"

"Sure. I live five miles away. Just follow my truck."

The agents paid for their drinks and exited the diner.

"It could be just a coincidence," Kendrick poked.

"Treehorn doesn't believe in them," Melanie stated as she followed the tow truck to an unpainted storage barn surrounded by weeds.

The three entered the old but sturdy structure and walked to a vehicle covered with a canvas tarp.

Kendrick typed in the Arizona license plate and the owner's identification appeared as "Peyton Greyhorse."

The agents uncovered a faded red 1985 Jeep CJ7.

"Why wasn't this reported?"

"My father gave the information to a New Mexico State Trooper," Johnny said, opening the glove compartment, removing the vehicle's title and registration, and handing them to Melanie, "Here's his name and badge number."

Melanie copied the information and confirmed the ownership.

"What are the odds that Peyton Greyhorse and Betsy Justice disappeared together?" she asked Kendrick.

"She wanted to be a journalist. He was an Indian activist. I bet they had something to talk about."

Melanie's telephone rang from an unknown caller,

"Agent Hopper."

"Shady Lynch."

"How'd you get my number?"

"Leo Mancuso."

"What do you want?"

414

"A favor."

"I don't have any."

"I know where Peyton Greyhorse's and Betsy Justice's bones are located."

"I heard your style is wild goose chases."

"Town of Emerson."

"I'm listening."

"Deal or no deal?"

"That's the town she disappeared from that's listed on her missing person's report."

"Treehorn's trained you well."

"You're wasting my time."

"Listen, my little grasshopper, because I'm only going to play this once."

"What did you do to my sister, Betsy?"

"I screwed her and then I put a bullet in her head. She's buried with Peyton Greyhorse 300' feet behind…"

The recording stopped.

"Did you find that favor?"

Melanie thought of her promise to Bethany Finch.

"If we uncover them."

"If you cross me, it won't end well for you."

"I figured that."

Shady's lip curled as he spoke, "I'm sending you the

coordinates and satellite imagery."

Melanie waited for the download to her phone.

"A first-day academy graduate could see where the ground has been disturbed with a bulldozer."

"You found a gravesite that's thirty years old?" Melanie scoffed.

"She's buried with her car because they had to hide the evidence."

Shady terminated the call while Melanie examined the location.

Trinity Bessette, the FBI Audio Lab technician, entered the secured conference room where Treehorn and Raven worked.

"Here's your documentation for your warrant."

"Thanks, Trinity."

"We saw the news feed. Finch and Johnston have always been thick as thieves."

"Hopefully justice will prevail."

"Jeez, Treehorn, I always thought you were a realist, not an optimist."

Once again the federal monitor highlighted a news feed: a Federal News Network, FNN, where reporter Cici

Rance's face appeared in the corner of the screen.

"Judge Dwayne Wade Johnston made an announcement today with his wife, Rosemary, and their son, Wade, at his side."

'I'm being investigated by the FBI. They've obtained a doctored video through an illegal search that makes it appear that I've committed a crime. I've never been to the Four Corner's. It's absolutely disgusting what Agent Johnny Treehorn will do to make an arrest. Not only am I innocent of this crime, but I'm going to do everything in my power to make sure this federal employee is terminated for providing fraudulent evidence for prosecution.'

"This statement occurred at 4pm today outside of the US District Court for the District of New Mexico. We'll reach out to Special Agent Treehorn and Hélena Hernández, FBI District Supervisor, for their response."

Trinity Bessette looked at the two agents who watched the monitor without moving a hair.

"Have a good day, Johnny Optimist."

Hélena Hernández's image appeared when the agent's telephone rang. "Treehorn."

"Hello, Johnny."

"We have this under control."

"Did I ask?"

"No."

"Do me a favor?"

"If possible."

"Nail his ass!"

"Yes, ma'am."

"Time frame?"

"9am tomorrow."

"I'll look forward to it."

Treehorn texted Shady, *"Arrest 9am, perp walk follows."*

The agent looked at Raven.

"We need to modify that arrest warrant."

Chapter Seventeen:

Perp Walk

Treehorn entered the empty courtroom at 9am and stared at the Lady Justice plaque that covered the rear wall behind the judge's bench. Justice wasn't blind in this courtroom but color blind.

The court deputy stood guard outside of the Judge's chamber.

"FBI Special Agents John Treehorn and Raven Shelly. We have an arrest warrant."

The white deputy eyed the agents and pointed back to the courtroom doors. "Court clerk's office is just around the corner. Does *your type* know the correct procedure?"

"Step aside or I'll handcuff you for interfering in official business. We're arresting Judge Dwayne Johnston. I won't ask again."

The deputy eyed the agents who removed their pistols from their holsters. He stepped aside and allowed them to perform their duties.

"Where is he?" Treehorn softly whispered.

The deputy pointed towards a single wooden door. "Restroom."

"Is there an exit?"

"No."

Treehorn waited with his gun drawn.

Raven followed suit and whispered, "Overkill?"

Treehorn winked.

The judge dressed in his black gown stepped out from the restroom and came face-to-face with two federal agents with their pistols aimed at his face.

"Dwayne Wade Johnston, you're under arrest. Raise your hands, slowly."

"You're not arresting me."

"Shoot him, Agent Shelly, if his hands disappear."

The judge kept his extremities visible and still.

Treehorn holstered his weapon and unclipped his handcuffs. He snapped one on a wrist and then the other.

The judge remained silent.

"You're under arrest for conspiracy to commit murder against Parker Greyhorse and the murders of Paul Greyhorse and Bart J. Baker. It's listed in your arrest warrant." The Fed then Mirandized him, *"You have the right to remain silent. Anything you say can and will be used against you in a court of law. You have the right to an attorney. If you cannot afford an attorney, one will be provided for you. Do you understand the rights I have just*

420

read to you? With these rights in mind, do you wish to speak to me?"

"No, I don't wish to speak to you, you half-breed."

"Search him, Special Agent Shelly."

"Keep your Indian hands off me."

Treehorn raised the man's handcuffed wrists higher behind as he struggled, this forced the judge's face to be pressed onto his gavel that sat on the desk. The agent's strong arms kept the man pinned down while Raven thoroughly touched the judge from head to toe as he conducted the body search.

"I'll have your badges for this."

"Bigger egos have tried."

Treehorn and Raven walked him out of his courtroom and kept the man dressed in his black judge robe.

The two agents didn't hurry as they passed the spectators, sheriff's deputies, and lawyers who all stopped and watched the scene, many of whom snapped pictures.

Raven, being the pissant, whispered to the judge, "Smile Dwayne."

Treehorn's glance encompassed the people who lined the corridor, "No one is above the law."

Raven chuckled at Treehorn. "I always wanted to say that."

The two men walked the silent offender to their SUV.

Treehorn unlocked and secured their criminal to the vehicle's security bar. Raven opened the rear door, threw in his windbreaker, and secured items in the rear as Treehorn climbed into the driver's side.

Raven shouted, "Can I use the restroom before we leave?"

Treehorn clenched the steering wheel, "You can't wait?"

"He's not going anywhere without us."

"Go and make it quick." Treehorn pursed his lips in displeasure as he started the engine and its air conditioning.

Raven slammed the door and Treehorn pressed the door locks.

"Mr. Treehorn, if you place both of your hands on the steering wheel I'll tell you a story."

"Dwayne Wade Johnston, it's FBI Special Agent John Treehorn. I would like to remind you that I've Mirandized you."

"There's just you and me. There's no one to hear it or repeat it, you prick."

"Remember, I read you your rights and this FBI Agent has told you to remain quiet."

Treehorn placed his hands on the steering wheel and

waited for the white man's diatribe.

The judge regressed into his memories.

"I met the love of my life when I was a teenager. We'll call her Betsy. I took her to a little cabin owned by a family friend and made love to her innocent flesh. She was the love of my life. When you've touched that kind of passion, anything after it leaves an emptiness that can never be filled. Have you ever felt that; you prick?"

Treehorn didn't reply as he glanced at the judge in his rear-view mirror.

"I doubt it. I arranged to meet Betsy at the cabin one afternoon. I had her engagement ring burning a hole in my pocket. Much to my surprise she had arrived early and brought company."

Treehorn observed the bitterness as it crossed the judge's face.

"They didn't hear me arrive because they were too busy screwing each other. Let's call him Peyton Greyhorse. Some Indian activist who made the misfortune of stopping at Kelli's Diner where my gal had stopped for a meal. They talked and realized that they shared a hobby. Cheating on their partners. Betsy calculated I wouldn't arrive for a couple of hours and they could spend the time at the secluded cabin."

The judge met Treehorn's eyes, "Keep your hands on your steering wheel and I'll keep reminiscing. We're getting to the good part and I don't want to see you take any notes."

The judge watched as shadows of individuals passed the SUV's tinted windows. "I grabbed a baseball bat that someone left near the door and swung that maple wood against the Indian's head. Betsy thought I killed the man but he was just laying on her unconscious. Then I slammed the bat once against her head too."

The judge chuckled. "I have to thank my daddy for his little toolbox in the rear trunk of my car. He was one of those auxiliary deputies with the police force when needed. I brought it inside and found it filled with supplies I required. I handcuffed Greyhorse to the chair and tied Betsy to the bed. I called Betsy's brother-in-law. Told him to bring his nephew. We had some business to conclude. I probably could have put a bullet in both of their heads right about then but I got thinking. They needed to pay."

"They owed you nothing," Treehorn spoke.

The judge ignored the agent. "Do you know who I called?"

"Colin Finch and Ronan Ryan."

The judge sneered. "While I waited for the two men to arrive I drove Betsy's vehicle into the garage and spotted a piece of machinery that would work for my purpose. Finch and Ronan arrived and we got to work. Ronan watched the two adults while Finch and I dug a hole in the back field. A nice deep hole that no law enforcement would ever find."

Treehorn wanted to remove his hands from the steering wheel and punish the man.

"The Indian knew his fate that night. He became a human punching bag. All of my anger bruised his body but his spirit held true. He didn't beg for his life, nothing. He didn't even mention that he had a wife and three sons. Meanwhile, Finch confessed to me that he had a little thing for his sister-in-law Betsy but she had threatened to tell his wife if he ever touched her. That would have ended his youthful marriage and his future ATF career he had planned. So, I sat out on the porch and smoked a cigar while the Indian was forced to watch Finch and his nephew have a little fun with Betsy. I can still hear her screams. I had one last time with her, too. For the memories. Betsy got the last laugh on me. The only time I could climax after that was to think about her. I could have killed her again for that alone. I removed the revolver my daddy gave me for my 18th birthday and Ronan carried her kicking and screaming

425

naked body out to the deep hole I dug. I couldn't put a bullet in her but I did shove the diamond engagement ring down her throat. Colin put one in her forehead and he handed the gun to Ronan who put one in her chest. You know, just to have a feel for it."

Disgust lined Treehorn's face.

The judge continued. "Finch and I dragged Greyhorse out to the hole. He heard two gunshots so he knew his fate. I raised the gun and asked him if he had any final words. He whispered, "You couldn't satisfy her but I did.""

"I raised the gun and put one between his eyes. I handed the gun to Ronan and he put a second one in the corpse. I threw in her bouquet of daffodils, pushed her car into the deep grave, and then used the bulldozer to crush and cover everything, dirt to dirt."

"Are you done?"

"Mr. Treehorn, that's the beginning. Every Indian that came in front of me in my courtroom I punished them for Peyton Greyhorse. Some advocate he turned out to be, huh?"

"All of your cases will be re-examined. I'll make the court referrals myself."

"Good luck turning over guilty convictions."

"You must have lost it when Gina fell in love with Peter Greyhorse."

"I don't have a daughter, Indian."

"They call me FBI Special Agent John Treehorn."

"I won't forget your name because I'm coming for you as soon as I'm released from holding. I suggest you take the remaining part of the day and get your affairs in order."

"Did you just threaten an FBI Agent?"

"Yes, I did."

"Do you know why after I book you, fingerprint you, and put you in a jail cell you won't be released on your own recognizance?"

"Why Injun?"

"Because you're a murderer and you deserve to live the rest of your pathetic life behind bars."

"You'll have no proof in a courtroom to back any of this up. I've taken appropriate steps to secure my freedom."

"What did you do? Bribe a judge?"

Judge Johnston smirked.

"Why did you kill Bart J. Baker?"

"Baker, a career criminal and thief to me. No great loss."

"You put two bullets in Paul Greyhorse. Did you know he was Peyton's middle son?"

"No that became bonus points for me."

Treehorn unlocked the passenger door as Raven approached with his slight limp.

The agent slid in and snapped his seat belt.

Treehorn eyed his partner, "How's Dana?"

"Good. She's recording the news to watch me on TV."

"You'll be lucky to have one reporter there." The judge snorted.

Raven spoke, "I disagree. I telephoned all of them and they'll be waiting for you to do your perp walk as you're removed from this vehicle. You'll little walk of shame will be permanently recorded."

"That's all you'll have on me."

The two agents looked at each other.

Raven grinned, "Did he talk?"

"Sang like a bird. I really can't comprehend why the white man lacks the ability to keep their mouths shut after I've arrested them."

"You have nothing on me." The peanut gallery so noted.

"Thanks, Raven, for exiting the vehicle. This pale face

wouldn't have spoken a word with two Indians in the vehicle."

"No problem. I love playing *"Red Indian, White Indian."*

"Too bad you weren't in the vehicle to hear it, Mr. Shelly."

Treehorn looked at Raven, "I told him to remain silent."

"What are you talking about?"

"I witnessed FBI Special Agent Treehorn properly Mirandize you, right?"

"Yes, *he did.*" Spat the criminal.

"Did he tell you to remain silent?"

"Yes, *he did.*"

"And you chose not to?" Raven chuckled.

"It's not like an Indian's a credible source around here."

Treehorn shook his head as he merged into traffic, "End of recording," and his finger pressed a button on the dash.

"What, *'End of recording'*?"

Raven chuckled.

"What's so funny?"

Raven faced the judge. "I recorded your

conversation."

"You're lying."

Raven's eyebrow rose, "Would you like to hear the playback?"

"You weren't smart enough to hit a record button."

Raven looked at Treehorn, "Can I do the honor for His Honor?"

Treehorn's lip curled and nodded to his wing man.

Raven pressed the button with an orchestras conductor's flourish.

"Dwayne Wade Johnston, it's Special Agent John Treehorn and I've Mirandized you and I recommend that you keep your mouth shut against any self-incrimination."

"There's just you and me. There's no one to hear it or repeat it, you prick."

"Remember I read you your rights and this FBI Agent has told you to remain quiet."

The judge decided he wanted the last word as the vehicle entered the FBI parking lot.

"I'll be back, and I'll be coming for your badges."

Treehorn simply stated, "Many have tried, all have failed."

"If I spend a night in jail, I want you to know I have a

430

very long reach."

Raven took his turn, "Many have tried, all have failed."

"I'm different. I'm a dirty white judge and my sole purpose in life will be to bury you."

"I'm an FBI Special Agent and I'll use every remaining days of my life to keep you off the bench." Treehorn countered.

"You don't have the ability."

"Yes, I do. I'm a lawyer, I know justice, and she'll never be denied."

"That sounds like a threat."

"That's a promise."

Treehorn looked at his co-worker and offered him his thanks, "Would you like to do the honors for the spirits of Peyton Greyhorse and Betsy Justice?"

Raven eyes rounded, "Thanks, Treehorn."

"You've earned it my friend."

The agent parked far enough away from the gathered crowd of reporters and photographers so they would have ample time to record Dwayne Wade Johnston as he wore his black gown for the perp walk.

Treehorn hoped it would be the last time the man

431

would be allowed to wear a robe in judgment. A promise the agent silently made to every Indian the man harmed as he ruled from the courtroom. As he conducted his law enforcement perimeter sweep he spotted Parker and Shady, two lone figures sitting on the bench watching the events unfold.

Agent Amelia Morales, another dedicated agent who excelled at investigative research and avoiding the spotlight, exited the building.

Treehorn caught her eye and waved her over as his co-worker removed the judge from the SUV.

"Can you help Raven do a perp walk?"

Agent Morales's eyes grew round when she saw the suspect. "Can I?"

"Sure. Raven, don't forget to look good for Dana."

The agent caught sight of Treehorn's friends watching the activity, "We'll see you inside."

Parker and Shady watched as Treehorn approached them.

"Long way to drive to see the song and dance."

"We had nothing better to do."

The three men viewed the perp walk. It provided little satisfaction to any of the them.

"It won't change anything."

No one argued the point.

Treehorn addressed Parker, "I have news of your father's disappearance."

Shady interrupted, "Dwayne shot him."

Treehorn grabbed his friend. "How did you know that?"

"A confession came my way. Dwayne stumbled upon Peyton and Betsy." Shady did the derogatory finger in the circle poke again.

"What else do you know?"

"Betsy's buried with Peyton."

"Where's their grave?"

"I've assigned Agent Hopper to it."

"At what cost?"

"A favor."

Treehorn frowned as he released Shady and shoved him back.

"Let's go, Parker. We saw what we came for."

"Thanks, John." Parker shook his friend's hand.

Treehorn turned on Shady, "When's this going to end?"

"When you hit the ground."

As the two mischief makers ambled away, Treehorn's

433

mood turned pensive then angry.

Melanie Hopper's caller ID identified Treehorn.

"Hopper."

"What kind of deal did you make with Shady?"

Melanie broke out in a sweat. *Shit.* "Bones for a favor."

"You've learned *nothing* from me."

Shit. Shit. Shit.

"Remember that when Shady calls in the marker." Treehorn terminated the call.

Melanie felt the bile rise in her throat.

"What did you do?" Kendrick handed her a water.

"A mistake."

Melanie and Kendrick arrived at the cabin located from Shady's image and GPS.

The agent removed a copy of a photograph that showed a bloody and beaten Peyton Greyhorse cuffed to a chair. Behind him stood a stone fireplace. Any other time the beauty of it would be foremost in a rustic architecture magazine. Today, a murder scene.

Melanie knocked on the entrance with her credentials.

An older couple opened their door.

"FBI Agents Melanie Hopper and Kendrick Moore."

The man looked at his wife, "What did you do now, Margaret?"

"Clifford."

"We've been married forty years and I can still get her to shout my name."

The agent's tried not to crack a smile.

Margaret laughed, "Yes, at mealtimes."

Clifford hugged his wife as he opened the door wider, "What's this about?"

"We're investigating a crime that may have occurred here."

"Why don't you come inside and tell us about it."

Agents Hopper and Moore entered the structure and saw the focal point, a stone fireplace that matched the photograph Melanie held in her hand.

Clifford and Margaret listened as the agents told the basic details of the murders of Peyton Greyhorse and Betsy Justice.

The older couple walked the agents to a field 300 feet behind their cabin.

"Nothing grows here but flowers."

The FBI forensic team arrived along with a heavy-duty excavator and started their dig.

The Crime Scene Unit and the two agents watched and waited for the appearance of the rattling bones.

Treehorn observed Raven and the FBI staff as they processed Dwayne W. Johnston. He downloaded the man's mugshot and texted it to Leo Mancuso with the little handcuff emoji. The federal monitor on the wall flashed the updated news.

"Jori Lansing with the Indian Times reporting, soon to be ex-judge Dwayne Wade Johnston was arrested today by Navajo FBI Special Agent Raven Shelly on a three-count criminal charge. Conspiracy to commit murder against Parker Greyhorse and the murders of Paul Greyhorse and Bart Baker. The two dead men were found last weekend at the Four Corners Monument. The lead investigator for the FBI was Special Agent John Treehorn. The FBI has no further comment at this time."

Dwayne Johnston retained the legal services of Jack Mahoney, a custom-suited arrogant lawyer who crossed paths many a time with Treehorn.

The agent handed the attorney a copy of the arrest warrant.

"Did you frame my client?"

"No actually, a video of him killing the men made it easy for us."

The lawyer snatched the document. "The evidence will be suppressed, the charges dropped, and I'll have your badge."

"Bigger *'JACK'* asses have tried." Treehorn turned to walk away.

"All it takes is one person to bring you down."

"As an attorney, I know it's not you. What's the count? The 25th time you've attempted to practice law in my investigations?"

Mahoney's face flushed red to his receding hairline. "You've never taken a bullet, why don't you eat one?"

Treehorn charged the attorney.

It took all of Raven and Agent Quinn's strength to hold Treehorn back. "He's not worth it." His friend whispered.

The lawyer wouldn't stop, "A dead Indian is still a dead Indian."

Treehorn stepped back and shook his friends' hands off him.

Raven chirped in, "Hey, Baloney, don't matter how expensive the suit you wear, it still covers a jackass."

Quinn tagged teamed, "It'll be 27 if Treehorn joins the Rathburn investigation."

Raven smelled blood as Mahoney's eyes widened at the news.

"Where's my client?" he demanded.

"Probably wishing he had a different attorney." Treehorn taunted as he walked away.

Raven whistled as he entered their office area.

Treehorn packed his belongings and papers, "We're done here. Gather your things and let's go."

"I want to stay for the arraignment."

Treehorn observed his friends serious face.

"He's a dirty judge and I grew up with Paul."

"We'll leave as soon as it's over."

"Deal."

Federal District Attorney Susie Shipley's eyebrows rose when the two agents appeared in the courtroom, but she didn't comment on their attendance for the proceedings.

Treehorn always felt that justice appeared one case at a time. Inimitable.

Raven texted Dana while Treehorn sat silent.

The bailiff watched as the courtroom filled with lawyers, their clients, and bystanders who settled in for the arraignments.

A court stenographer soon entered and checked her equipment.

Two court deputies guided a handcuffed Dwayne Johnston to his seat.

Attorney Jack Mahoney glanced at the agents, once, as his client's restraints were removed.

Behind the defendants, Rosemary Johnston and their son Wade sat somberly.

Bailiff announced, "All rise. The United States District Court for the District of New Mexico is now in session, the Honorable Judge John Wellington II presiding."

Everyone stood as the judge entered.

Raven leaned over, "Did you know your father would be here?"

Treehorn shook his head.

Dwayne appeared visibly upset with the entrance of the black robed man.

Everyone remained standing until the judge sat.

John Wellington II eyed the room's occupants and spotted Treehorn. "Please be seated."

The defense attorney asked the obvious to calm his client, "Your Honor, where's Judge Watson?"

"He was transported to the hospital an hour ago. I'm hearing arraignments today. Let's proceed."

"District Attorney Susie Shipley for the prosecution."

"Jack Mahoney for the defense."

"In the US vs. Dwayne Johnston, how do you plead on the first count of....."

Dwayne interrupted, "I plead not guilty on all three charges, your Honor."

"Are you waiving the charges being read?"

"Yes." Jack Mahoney and Dwayne answered at the same time.

"Is there a request for bail?"

"Your honor, we're challenging the arrest warrant. Evidence was taken from a funerary that the FBI had no authority and no warrant to access."

"Ms. Shipley?"

"The FBI had written permission from the crypt's legal owner to access the contents, your Honor."

"This crypt is a poison tree."

"Ms. Shipley, was any of this evidence from the crypt used to obtain the arrest warrant?"

"Not a single item, your honor. If you examine the

attached documentation, you'll see, in the first charge of conspiracy to commit murder Mr. Johnston communicated with a Cibola guard, Louis Henson to arrange a murder for hire. The FBI obtained a copy of that conversation."

"I object," Dwayne shouted.

"Mr. Mahoney, please control your client."

"Ms. Shipley?"

"Second, a video tape obtained showed Dwayne Johnston as he shot Paul Greyhorse and Bart Baker to death."

"Your honor, that videotape was inside the crypt."

"Ms. Shipley?"

"No, your honor, a Federal agent witnessed and recorded the shootings. He then delivered the tape to the FBI."

"Mr. Johnston, how did you know the crypt contained a videotape?"

Mahoney whispered to Dwayne, "Shut up, you fool."

"Your honor, we provided a third and last piece of evidence for the warrant. Mr. Johnston stated on the news last night that he'd never been to the Four Corners Monument. Then, can he please tell the court how his urine was found there? Navajo Nation Police Chief Samuel Bear recovered a sample and delivered it to the FBI Crime Scene

Unit."

Mahoney grabbed Dwayne's arm. "Don't say a word."

"Your honor, we're requesting bail so Mr. Johnston can fight these charges."

"The US is requesting that bail be denied. The defendant has substantial means to disappear."

Judge Wellington II eyed all of the lawyers in the room including his son and issued his ruling, "Bail's denied at this time, but I'll recommend a hearing at a future date. Defendant is reprimanded to federal holding until further notice. Case is adjourned."

Raven looked at Treehorn. "Let's go home."

Chapter Eighteen:
A Right-Hand Man

Treehorn and Raven eagerly climbed into the SUV for their return trip to the reservation. The two-hour drive passed quickly as the two men discussed their caseloads.

Treehorn's muscles tensed as he drove past the *"Welcome to the Navajo Indian Reservation"* sign and saw the roadblock being conducted by the Navajo Nation Police.

Raven turned on their emergency lights and a deputy, with a wave, permitted them to bypass the line of cars.

Treehorn drove past Samuel as he and one of his deputies examined a computer tablet.

Raven looked at Treehorn and asked, "Are you going to discuss it with Sammy?"

Treehorn didn't respond as the police chief spotted the Feds' vehicle detour around the barricade.

"It needs to be resolved," Raven said, offering his unwanted opinion.

"Drop it."

Raven didn't discuss it again as he spotted his wife waiting for him in the FBI parking lot.

Four Military Police Humvees lined the perimeter. It appeared the Army Rangers figured out Connor's impersonation and the search for Peter Greyhorse, their AWOL soldier, had resumed.

Raven nodded toward the camouflaged vehicles.

"You going inside for an update?"

Treehorn shook his head.

"No. I have Shady to track down."

"Good luck with that."

Dana Shelly grabbed her man as soon as he opened his door.

"Thanks, Treehorn for bringing him home safely."

Raven landed a kiss on his wife's lips like a seasoned driver.

"Daniel Tsosie's memorial is tomorrow. We'll save you a seat," Dana said, updating them as Raven grabbed his bags.

"I'll see you later."

Raven eyed his partner as he said, "Good work, John."

Treehorn's lip raised and he nodded once.

The agents knew nothing else needed to be said.

Treehorn's phone beeped with a text message from Agent Hopper: *We found two sets of human remains each* buried with their driver's license. Peyton Greyhorse and Betsy Justice. Diamond ring too."

The agent responded, *"Notify Mancuso. I'm no longer your field supervisor."*

Treehorn texted Shady, *"In Gallup. Military Police are here."*

A quick response, *"My mojito."*

"Where's PG?"

"Pony dancing."

"Where's PG?"

"Pony dancing."

Code for Peter and Parker evading the authorities on horseback.

Shady waited for Treehorn's penny to drop.

"Where's the sniper?"

"Heard he's at a low point on the Rez."

Treehorn clenched his jaw.

"2 hours. Bring water. I have the tequila."

Treehorn glanced at his FBI watch. He had time to shower and change.

Shady texted Parker, *"Highpoint. 2 hours."*

Parker's response was an image of two badge-wearing

Indians riding horses.

Shady chuckled.

Highpoint Stone Peak

Shady packed his jeep with all of the necessary items including his Panama hat, sunscreen for his face, and a bottle of tequila.

One hour after texting Treehorn and Parker, Shady whistled as he arrived at the Highpoint Stone Peak in his vehicle with its canopy lowered. He loved seeing the expanse of the desert with its red sandstone, a land he grew up on while his mother worked with the Navajos.

He sat the bottle of tequila on the ground approximately 1,500 feet from the sandstone outcropping. As teenagers Treehorn, Parker, and he would race from the column to the bottle of liquor. Whoever had the quickest time, won the prize, but the boys created a game of chicken first to start the contest.

Grinning at his youthful memories, Shady drove up the hill to the overlook. He opened the rear hidden compartment in his Jeep and whistled as he lifted Ronan's unconscious body from it. Then he dragged him across the red dirt, onto a swinging plank, and precariously placed him on the prepared monolithic peak.

He returned to the rear of his 4x4 and placed the two metal cases on the tailgate. He snacked on a red apple as he opened the larger one that contained Ronan's rifle components and assembled the gun like a seasoned pro.

Shady's fingers flew across his phone as he typed in a message but didn't press 'send'. Instead, he placed the scope on the rifle and looked into it as the black FBI-issued SUV arrived from the main road.

The vehicle stopped at the tequila.

Treehorn stepped out from the SUV, picked up the full liquor bottle, and sat it on the black hood.

The sun prevented him from seeing in detail the Highpoint Stone Peak, one of his teenage hangouts. He saw the dust stir on the horizon and assumed it was Shady but his binoculars soon identified Parker and Peter on their horses.

Shady watched Treehorn use his binoculars through the rifle scope. He sent the text and watched as Treehorn glanced at his phone.

Shady pulled the trigger.

The tequila bottle exploded as Treehorn hit the ground.

"Oops." Shady chuckled, "He's going to be so

pissed."

Treehorn stood and yanked off his red, muddy, tequila-soaked shirt.

"I'm going to put you in the hospital," he shouted.

Shady texted Treehorn again, *"Oops, my mojito!"*

The gunshot woke Ronan.

"I wouldn't move around there, partner," Shady warned, opening the smaller metal case, removing a tranquilizer gun, and shooting a syringe into Ronan's leg, "A little stimulant to wake you up. Get the heart racing."

Ronan removed the needle and tossed it, but he took Shady's advice and didn't move as he took in his surroundings. He found himself perched on sandbags above a deadly drop-off.

"It's thirty-five feet in the front and over seventy-five in the back."

"Shady, what the hell?"

"See those two horse riders in the distance? That's Parker and Peter Greyhorse, Paul's brothers. You and your knife know Parker. I don't think you've met Peter. He's a trained killer... like you."

Ronan felt his heart race as the drug flowed through his bloodstream.

"See the black SUV? That's FBI Special Agent John

448

Treehorn. I'm going to give you a choice as to which direction you want to run."

"I don't like those options."

Ronan eyed his gun on the Jeep and said, "Hand me my rifle and three bullets. I'll end them right now."

Shady shook his head.

"I thought you said I'd have a shot at him."

"No, I believe I said your *'gun will take a shot at Treehorn'* and it did."

Ronan clenched his jaw and fists.

Shady finished his apple and tossed it.

"I've called two men 'friends' since my youth. Parker Greyhorse and John Treehorn. We played this foolish game."

Ronan's face beaded with sweat from his racing heart.

Shady removed his watch, placed it safely inside the Jeep's glove box, and removed his 9mm.

Ronan saw the pistol and then the Indian Posse brand mark on the man's wrist.

"You always said you hated guns."

"I do, but I never once said I couldn't fire one."

Bang, bang.

The bullets struck the sandbags Ronan was lying on and sand started to pour out.

Ronan gradually stood to his full height, making sure his feet were safely grounded.

"You can jump to your death in the rear if you so choose. Although it'll be a slow death of broken bones and coyotes."

"What's Plan B?"

"You jump forward and make a run for Special Agent."

Shady shot two more bullets into the sandbags as Ronan shifted his weight.

Treehorn heard the small pistol gunfire coming from Highpoint Stone Peak and searched the area with his binoculars.

What is Shady doing?

The agent found Ronan Ryan standing on the rock formation. Treehorn's lips pursed as he figured out Shady's plan and knew its subsequent outcome.

"It's best to jump *before* the sand empties because there are spears beneath your feet."

Bang, bang. The sand poured out faster.

Ronan looked at the approaching horses and the FBI vehicle.

Shady shot three more bullets into the sandbags.

"The Greyhorse brothers will kill you."

Ronan jumped, landed, and then rolled safely across the pile of sand. He gave Shady the finger as he stood.

"Run, Ronan, as if your life depended on it—because it does."

Ronan stumbled through the sand and when his feet hit the hard red soil, he sprinted toward the waiting FBI agent.

Shady whistled as he disassembled Ronan's gun, replaced it in its case, and returned it to his hidden compartment. Then he placed his own drug case and 9mm on the Jeep seat and drove toward his friends.

Treehorn returned his binoculars to the SUV and waited for everyone's arrival.

Ronan reached the agent covered in sweat and gasping for air.

Treehorn pointed his gun at Ronan and tossed his handcuffs to the suspect.

"Get on your knees, hands on your head and snap one on your wrist. You're under arrest."

Ronan complied with every demand.

451

Treehorn cuffed Ronan's wrist behind his back and assisted him to his feet.

Parker and Peter arrived on their horses and observed the shattered glass, wet ground, and one filthy agent.

They watched Shady as he arrived in his 4x4. Then the man showed an audacity to tap his nose as he exited the driver's side.

The brothers knew it foreshadowed a bloodied fist punch in the man's not-so-distant future because of Treehorn's red-faced, angry glare.

The FBI agent eyed Peter, Parker, and Shady. Any of them would kill Ronan if he weren't in his custody. He gave the prisoner a little push toward the men.

Ronan's eyes rounded in fear for a split second before he hid his emotions.

As Shady climbed onto the hood of his Jeep and honed his knife, he asked the obvious question, "Why?"

"Peyton Greyhorse and Betsy Justice."

Treehorn gave Ronan another shove as he snapped, "Explain!"

Ronan smirked at Parker and Peter because he knew they couldn't touch him.

"Dwayne Johnston killed your father with a single

bullet to his head. Then, he handed me the gun and instructed me to fire another bullet into the man. Even though he was already dead, I almost passed out with the rush it gave me. Sixteen, and I knew at that moment my future held a gun."

Parker and Ronan's eyes met in hatred.

"Why did you attack me?"

"Judge paid me. Someone told him you fathered his grandson."

Shady rolled the knife blade as if to say, *continue.*

Peter's angry face met Treehorn's.

"He's *ours.*"

The agent shook his head.

"Tell us about Four Corners."

"Simple. Judge wanted Bart Baker dead. You know the details, Shady, since you set it up."

"True, but I targeted Finch."

"Finch called the judge, and the judge called me with the details."

"And Paul Greyhorse?"

"Wrong place, wrong time."

Shady lifted his lip and Treehorn caught the tell.

Shady's lying.

Treehorn opened the rear door of the SUV.

"He's going to prison."

Peter aimed his gun at Treehorn.

"He's not worth losing your wife and son over."

Parker added, "I'll wait for him the day he's released."

Ronan snorted, "I'll never see the inside of a prison cell and you know it. Good luck, Injuns. I'll be gone like the wind with your spirits by the end of the day."

Shady spoke, "Could you clarify that for the record?"

Ronan sneered at the men, "I'll be out within a couple of hours, then I'll disappear. I'll come for each of you and there's not a single thing you can do to stop me."

Treehorn's and Parker's eyes met.

Peter and Shady watched as Treehorn gave Parker a signaled message behind Ronan's back.

The agent's hand flew in a simple silent message as he raised one eyebrow, *'You, me, even?'*

Parker sat stoically on his horse. He could take the deal offered or ride away.

Peter and Shady watched Parker make his decision. All the men knew it would be the hardest verdict he'd ever judge.

Treehorn tapped his watch. The one his father gave him the day he graduated from the FBI Academy. *Fidelity,*

Bravery, and Integrity. Loyalty, sometimes it's a given.

The agent looked at the men.

"Time's up."

Parker looked across the Land of his People and couldn't meet Treehorn's eyes.

"Yes."

Treehorn opened his driver's door and tossed something inside.

The click of the handcuffs being released sounded like a gunshot and then he shoved Ronan forward.

The man stumbled to the ground and stared up at Treehorn in disbelief.

"I'm a man of two worlds and I've never once forgotten where I've come from."

Treehorn eyed Shady, Peter, and lastly Parker as he flatly spoke the words, "He's all yours."

"You can't do this. You're a federal agent." Ronan shouted, glancing at Treehorn's waist.

The agent's FBI badge no longer hung on his belt.

Shady jumped off the Jeep and stabbed Ronan in the thigh muscle, intentionally missing his artery.

"That's for Paul."

Ronan grunted in pain.

Treehorn turned away so no one saw his reaction.

Parker understood his friend and wondered, "Will you be at the BBQ tonight?"

Treehorn slammed his rear door. "Maybe." He climbed into the driver's seat, started his SUV, and locked its doors.

Ronan jumped up and pounded on the window.

As Treehorn's SUV peeled away, the sand and gravel splattered against the criminal. The agent eyed his gold badge on the seat and then looked in the rearview mirror.

Peter and Parker approached Ronan who lowered himself to his knees and appeared to be begging for his life.

Shady focused his attention on the Highpoint Stone Peak instead of on the three men at his back.

Treehorn stopped his vehicle a couple of miles down the road and used the water to cleanse himself of the liquor and his vomit.

When he arrived at his mother's yard, he found his father's magistrate's vehicle parked next to her Jeep. He quickly showered and dressed, then packed his saddlebags with select items. Neither of his parents appeared before he departed.

Treehorn arrived at the Indian Posse BBQ on horseback. The nighttime ride placed everything into perspective for the Navajo and lawman.

As he walked through the desert toward the campfire, he thought of his forefathers whose feet were dragged over the desert floor, hung for no reason other than being an Indian.

Treehorn removed his watch, the timepiece his father gave him the day he graduated from the FBI Academy. He rubbed its face and then placed it in his pants pocket. Concealed beneath it was his Indian Posse 'IP' branded mark.

In his hand, he carried two items: a branding iron and a cloth. The end of each member's branding iron all carried the same symbol except Treehorn's. The 'IP' became a 'TP' when the bottom of the 'I' broke off one day when Paul Greyhorse used it to brand his horses. So, he understood Paul's message when he left 'TP' in stones at the Four Corners Monument.

A few men and women glanced his way when he entered the campfire circle but no one approached him.

He placed his iron into the fire with the others and found an empty log to sit on. Then he tied and adjusted the rectangular piece of cloth around his face so he could see through the openings, while the remaining sections covered his nose and high cheeks. Each Indian's mask was decorated with a combination of red and black paint and then covered with select petroglyph images. His was a bristlecone pine tree with a black wolf standing next to it.

Treehorn watched as Nettie Tsosie delivered food to each member of Indian Posse. He wasn't hungry but accepted it out of respect. This was a period of quiet reflection for the members.

Soon after, the three elders started drumming and chanting songs as old as time, asking for the spirits of the past to join them—including those of Daniel Tsosie and Paul Greyhorse.

Ronan Ryan lay staked to the ground. The gag muffled his screams that bled with the cries of generations before him who begged for mercy and found none. No one spoke but everyone heard him. Every foot stomped represented the weeks, months, and years taken from the lives of Indians before their time.

Treehorn knew Ronan had suffered at the hands of the three men from the amount of blood stained on the man's clothing and zippered trousers. Retribution for the crime he inflicted years earlier on Parker, now similarly occurred to him.

Nettie Tsosie, the sixty-three-year-old mother to Daniel, stood to Parker's left, followed by Peter, out of respect for Paul. Then, each man and woman connected to the next by joining their right hand to the other's left hand, until a circle formed with one last slot remaining at Parker's right for his friend.

Treehorn didn't raise his hands to connect the final link in the chain of Indians; instead, he whispered to the Indian Posse leader, "You have to let me go."

Parker didn't respond as his eyes met Treehorn's. Once again, faith and loyalty stood the test of time for the two.

"Please!"

Treehorn, who once begged for his wife's life, now begged for his own.

Parker relented and nodded his head, which allowed Treehorn to step back.

No one spoke. Everyone in the circle watched and understood. The last person now joined with Parker's hand while Treehorn stood alone outside of the circle.

The drums started again as the circle shuffled their feet in unity. It stopped when the last note of the spirit song reverberated and they dropped their hands. Each Indian went to the fire and removed their branding iron whose ends glowed red. Every person walked to Ronan, except Treehorn.

He stood tall and alone as the dying embers of the campfire cast a shadow on his face and the 'IP' brand on his wrist. He found no solace as he looked into the darkness of the Land of his People.

Chapter Nineteen:

Whispers and Secrets

While everyone participated in the activity, Treehorn went to his saddlebags and removed Nettie's and Parker's letters. He solemnly placed all of Nettie's into the fire and watched as their sparks joined Daniel's spirit in the sky.

Then he stacked Parker's letters next to him and used his jack knife to slit open the first letter he received while his friend was incarcerated at Cibola.

John,

I know you. You will read this letter and none of the future ones so I'll make it good. Don't worry about me. Shady's made a plan. It's what he's good at. All you need to do is your job. Everything else will fall into place in time. Will you come when the darkness gathers?

They assigned a psychiatrist to me. He and the warden visit me almost daily to play their little Hannibal Lecter games. It's a little trick pony show.

The psychiatrist started to bore me so I told him about his wife's extracurricular activities. He stopped his visits. Truth hurts most.

Thoughts of you have kept me alive. I miss the Rez. A jail cell is no place to live, just survive.

Shady visited today. He holds a deep secret and I think Peter knows it. He had a nice cut on his jaw stitched up. He didn't tell me how he came to have it, but there's only one man quicker than him with a knife and that's Peter.

A visit would be appreciated. Bring a photo.

I haven't told anyone that I've wanted to commit suicide. The only thing that's prevented me was you.

I love you.

Parker

When Treehorn finished reading it, he threw it into the campfire. He read each, burned each, and then wiped the tears that streamed down his face. He readied the two horses, his Pinto and Parker's painted pony. As the group emerged from the darkness and dispersed, he silently handed his friend the horse's lead.

Both Navajos looked at the campfire for one last time as they sat atop their rides. Treehorn's branding iron was now forever buried beneath the dying embers.

They say a man can withstand pain for days until he succumbs. The thing about being branded, the pain is indescribable. As Treehorn rubbed his IP brand, he remembered Parker Greyhorse's words he spoke at Cibola that the agent would never find Paul's killer.

Parker was right.

Treehorn was right.

It's one thing identifying a killer and it's another finding his body.

FBI Special Agent John Treehorn identified Paul's shooter and no one ever found Ronan Ryan's body.

The two men galloped across the reservation to Parker's hogan.

Shady had come and gone by the sight of the beer and ice-filled cooler. He'd never attended the BBQ but stayed in the shadows of its perimeter, always silent as he searched the stars for answers.

Treehorn stoked the campfire and placed a poker in it to heat up as he drank a beer. He wrapped his hand around a stick and placed his white handkerchief between his teeth to bite down on.

Parker's foot pressed the stick into the ground which prevented the agent's hand from moving.

Treehorn whispered, "Do it."

Parker pressed the solid hot circle brand mark into Treehorn's "IP" mark. The smell of burnt flesh wasn't pleasant for either man.

Treehorn turned away so any sign of weakness would be kept private.

Parker applied an ointment and bandage from his first aid kit and then covered it with Treehorn's Indian Posse bandana. The last time it would be used before it would be discarded.

"You can leave now."

"I'm not going anywhere, tonight."

"You need to leave and never return."

Parker walked away from Treehorn. He undressed and climbed into his bed. His bones felt tired for all of the tragedy that he carried in his thirty-five years. Choices made, some pleasant, and some not so. His sobs filled the hogan.

Treehorn entered and undressed to his boxers and

trusted t-shirt. He covered his friend with a light blanket and wrapped his arms around him as he cried.

"Let me go," Parker whispered.

"If I do, I know you'll kill yourself."

Parker didn't deny it.

Treehorn handed his friend a rag as he stretched out on the bed.

"Why didn't you try to stop Paul from killing himself?"

Parker sighed as a weight was finally lifted off his chest.

"When did you figure it out?"

"I suspected it immediately at the Four Corners Monument, but only confirmed it the next day when Shady left the penny on the hill. Things didn't add up. There was never a gun deal. Bart was transporting the guns stolen from the ATF in Socorro. Shady let Finch know that Bart and his guns were there for pickup. Paul left me a sign and stones in his pants pocket. The cash was tagged and I followed the guns."

"I asked Shady to recover Paul's penny, but he'd left it there for you to find."

Treehorn knew it was a sign of suicide.

"The penny. I thought it was Shady's at first playing his games since the name was ground off and his print on it, but then I realized that it was Paul's."

Treehorn looked at the Indian Posse leader, removed the copper coin from his pants pocket, and placed it on the window ledge.

"Paul gave it to Shady when they planned the night. No Indian Posse member lets another one die alone."

"Why did he want to end his life?"

"He was tired of living with his illness. I screamed at him from jail. I told him I didn't want to see him again if he wanted to end his life, something he didn't know that I struggled with on a daily basis."

"And Bart?"

"Paul wanted to die with that piece-of-shit he loved. Of course, he failed to tell Bart the plan that night."

"When was all of this planned?"

"When I was in county lockup after the Bonito arrest."

"Paul visited me. He told me he wanted to end his life and he wanted my help. I refused."

"He wrote the letters to you and Peter."

Treehorn remembered the two letters he recovered from Paul's cabin that had gathered a year's worth of dust.

"Paul's letter to Peter told him he was sorry about Gina. In mine, he said he was sorry for his suicide. He signed his death certificate at the Four Corners because he knew Ronan and Johnston would arrive with death and murder on their agenda."

"Shady put the wheels in motion," Treehorn surmised.

"True and it doesn't take much effort when Shady and I put our heads together and figure out the end-game."

"Finch and Johnston."

"Finch crossed Shady. I don't know the details but the ATF leader did something to piss our friend off."

"And Johnston?"

"Paul knew over the years how he treated Indians. It wasn't a secret."

"And you?"

"The last line was crossed when the custom-suited, briefcase-holding man showed me the photographs of you and Shady with the scope target drawn on each face."

"What happened next?"

"I accepted the prison deal to give Shady time to do his wheeling and dealing. He targeted Finch and left the judge for you."

"Finch and family?"

"I didn't ask but we all know someone had to pay the piper."

Parker knew Treehorn would address it with Shady.

"Paul sent a letter to my office in Washington."

Treehorn removed the envelope from his jeans and handed it to Parker.

Treehorn,

I know you'll figure it out. Please thank Shady for me. I'm sorry I didn't come forth sooner with the truth. Thank you for being a good friend to my brothers.

Paul Greyhorse

"It's time for you to let me go," Parker whispered.

"Promise me you won't kill yourself."

"I can't make that promise."

"Then I won't let you go until you can," Treehorn said, turning away from Parker.

"You need to tell your woman the truth or you need to stop coming here."

Treehorn didn't respond but he knew he needed to sit down and speak to Samantha when he returned to Washington.

"Go to sleep, my friend. We'll keep the ghost-riders away."

Parker covered Treehorn with the blanket and wrapped him in his arms. In no time, both men found the sleep that eluded them for such a long time. It wasn't sexual, just a brotherhood others wouldn't understand and they, themselves, couldn't comprehend. All they knew was that it kept them both alive.

The hearse transported Paul Greyhorse's and Bart Baker's bodies together to the *Farmington Last Rites Spiritual Center* during the silence of the night. The staff gently placed their bodies together with their arms wrapped around each other inside the cremation chamber. They loved together, died together, and their spirits rose together.

After Treehorn arrived on horseback at his mother's home, he showered and changed into a set of dress clothes.

When he entered the living room his father and mother sat at the breakfast table.

"Good morning, son," his father greeted him.

"Good morning."

"Hungry?"

Anna spotted the bandage on her son's wrist but said nothing.

Treehorn shook his head.

"In town long?"

"Leaving today," his father replied without glancing up from his newspaper.

"Going to the memorial service for Daniel?" Anna asked, handing her son a slice of toast on a napkin.

"I'll be at Paul's funeral with Parker and Shady."

"Give him my condolences," Anna offered.

Treehorn kissed his mother's cheek as he said, "I will."

Anna whispered, "Your shoulders are strong. Are Parker's?"

The younger man's lip lifted in understanding.

He looked at his father. "Have a safe trip back to DC."

As the two men's eyes met, the judge nodded.

"You too."

Treehorn grabbed his gun and badge as he walked out.

The judge threw down his newspaper. Anna watched out the window as her only child drove away.

"I can't for the life of me understand how our son continues to be associated with those criminals Greyhorse and Lynch."

As Anna thought of the choices her son had made, and the ones she did too, a tear rolled down her cheek. The truth hurts the most and it was time he heard it.

"The night John buried his wife, he planned on killing himself. That man you call a criminal, wrapped his arms around our son and held him tight, listened to his pain, and cried with him until the darkness passed. Shady stood guard because he loved Skyler, too. So, the next time you have a bad word to say about his friends, choose your words well."

"I'm..."

Anna held up her hand.

"The darkness still competes with the light after all of these years."

"I didn't know."

"Why would you when you've never been a full-time

father? You see your life through a white man's eyes while I see it through an Indian's. Our son somehow lives on the fence between our two lands. Sometimes, it's justice. Sometimes, it's the law. And, sometimes it's his survival. Pack your bags and leave, now."

Fort Defiance Cemetery

Police Chief Samuel Bear and his wife, Alisha, the majority of the NNP and numerous law enforcement officers listened to Chaplain Dennis Begay conduct Deputy Daniel Tsosie's memorial service.

An empty chair sat between Samuel and Raven.

Dana glanced at the vacant spot and raised her eyebrows at her husband.

"Where's Treehorn?" Raven whispered to Samuel as he looked for his co-worker in the crowd.

Samuel knew the answer. Entrapment, an ugly word for an innocent man's conviction.

He rubbed his watch. Beneath it lay the original "IP" brand Preston Greyhorse had burned on his skin, now covered by the solid burn mark Parker placed there when he took over the Indian Posse leadership several years later. Treehorn knew the mark existed and its history.

Samuel unfolded his clenched fist and flattened out the piece of Kraft paper he held.

Alisha Bear noticed the number and asked, "Why are you holding your old phone number?"

"Treehorn found it in a folder."

Samuel didn't tell his wife that the agent also left two newly written words on the back: *"I know."*

CIA Assistant Director James Dieter stood next to a framed picture of US Army Ranger Peter Greyhorse, his wife Gina, and their son Zane.

Addressing his opening statements, he addressed the point of the news conference to the audience, *"The CIA would like to thank the US Army Rangers for their participation in a recent joint operation with the FBI in Mexico: their attempt to locate ATF Assistant Director Colin Finch after his arrest and arraignment this week at the United States District Court for the District of New Mexico. His sighting in Mexico led to an issuance of an extradition warrant for his capture and return to the United States.*

Earlier reports stated US Army Ranger Peter Greyhorse was declared AWOL, but in actual fact, it was a cover disguise for the joint operation. This was the second time Ranger Greyhorse assisted in a joint US/Mexican operation. We're pleased to announce that Mr. Greyhorse has extended his enlistment contract with the Rangers. At this time, we have no further comment on the matter."

"Nice spin, Shady," Mancuso whispered to himself as he shut down his computer.

Chapter Twenty:

You'll Never Die Alone When Someone's Killing You

Cimarron Federal Prison

The guard unlocked Dwayne Wade Johnston's protective custody cell door and called, "Mail."

Inmate *'87521'* accepted a single postcard.

It had been sent locally. A Mesa Cartel logo printed on the front. On the back was a headshot of his son, Wade Johnston, dressed in his custom suit as he carried his briefcase. Someone had taken a red marker and drew a rifle target scope on the man's face and labeled it *"Justice, she'll never be denied."* —Indian Posse

As Johnston focused on the threatening mail he didn't realize that the guard, who had a large wristwatch on his right hand, had left his cell door open to the general population.

Two large, muscular Indians entered the single-prisoner cell and closed its sound-proofed door immediately.

"Remember me?"

"And me, too?" the other asked.

Johnston lost count of the number of men who entered and exited his cell that day, seeking retribution for his done deeds. Death would have been welcomed but none of them sought that resolution. Broken ribs, beatings from head to toe, and a broken nose. Through the pain, he was grateful that he wasn't sexually assaulted.

The Native American guard who unlocked the door for the mail delivery returned for one last visit. He wanted his pound of flesh, too, and when he finished he whispered into the judge's ear, "I'll call that ambulance now but remember this: we can, we will... reach you anywhere, any time. By the way, your son-in-law says 'Hello'."

Johnston, who couldn't see out of his blackened, swollen eyes didn't see the Indian Posse's tattoo peek out from beneath the guard's wristwatch or see as the man pocketed the Mesa Cartel postcard.

Window Rock Park

Peter and Shady smiled at each other in their dress suits.

Shady whispered, "When your tour's up, the CIA will have a spot for you."

"I don't know, Shady. I'm thinking the other side of the fence is where I apprehend criminals."

"There's no fun in that, plus you'd be spending all of your time chasing Parker."

"And you, too. By the way, I believe Treehorn owes you a bloody nose. What were you thinking when you fired that rifle at the tequila?"

Shady glanced at Treehorn.

"I was hoping he'd forget."

Peter glanced at the FBI agent and laughed, "Not likely."

The agent glanced at the two men who stood on the other side of the chaplain with Parker next to him.

"Why do I have a bad feeling when I see your brother and Shady with their heads together?"

Parker chuckled.

"Could be worse. I could be standing with them."

Chaplain Roger Thompson opened his bible as the cellist started to play *"Cuts Like a Knife"* by Bryan Adams.

"Nice choice," Shady whispered to his compadre.

Peter Greyhorse watched proudly as his son accompanied Gina as she walked towards him in her blue wedding gown to renew their vows.

As they spoke of their love, the gold bands sat on the cremation box labeled 'Paul Greyhorse and Bart J. Baker.'

Treehorn, Parker, and Shady—three solitary men—listened solemnly to their family and friends' marriage commitment.

BAR NONE: An Indian Posse Establishment

The wedding reception was in full swing as the men sat and drank their beers.

A plane flew low over the establishment.

"Was that Shady?"

"The lengths he'll go to," Peter joked.

Parker glanced out the window to verify the plane's owner.

"Where's he going?"

Peter answered, "Tucson."

"What's there?"

"The woman he's been shagging since the Academy."

Treehorn squinted at Peter.

"I thought he was gay."

"Why would you think that?"

Treehorn frowned.

"He's never mentioned a woman since his infatuation

478

with my wife."

The Greyhorse brothers smiled because they knew.

Treehorn explained, "We were holed up in a cabin on his thirtieth birthday. He grabbed my privates while we slept in a twin bed for survival. I broke his nose, again."

Peter and Parker looked at each other and laughed.

"You both heard this story?"

The brothers nodded but Peter added, "Shady told me he dreamed of her that night."

Treehorn grinned and said, "He should have told me before I swung."

Peter laughed again as he left to find his wife for a dance.

Parker and Treehorn glanced at the *BAD PENNY* board and then at each other. They knew what had to be done.

Treehorn removed his watch from his left wrist where he'd worn it while his right wrist healed. He rubbed its crystal face. Fidelity, bravery, and integrity. No loyalty. He knew that wasn't true. He turned the watch over and popped open the custom backing he had added to hold Parker Greyhorse's penny. He removed the coin and handed it to his friend who had asked him to keep it safe so many years earlier.

Parker reached down to his belt buckle of three horses and removed the hidden compartment. Inside sat John Treehorn's coin. Parker handed it to his friend and then placed his own engraved coin back into the fitted circle.

Treehorn walked to the board and inserted his penny into the empty center slot.

Everyone in the bar watched him and no one said a word.

Meanwhile, Leo Mancuso watched the news as *Indian Times* reporter Jori Lansing spoke, *"Today the FBI issued a statement that Agents Melanie Hopper and Kendrick Moore have recovered the skeletal remains of two missing bodies identified as Indian activist Peyton Greyhorse and Betsy Justice. Their bodies were found buried together in a grave behind a cabin that once belonged to Matt Stenson, a family friend of Judge Dwayne Wade Johnston. Betsy Justice was the ex-girlfriend of Judge Johnston and the sister-in-law of ex-ATF Assistant Director Colin Finch. The coroner on the scene, Dr. Samantha Reynolds, has ruled the deaths as homicides."*

"The latest from Cimarron Federal Prison is that Judge Johnston was transported via ambulance to

Albuquerque Medical Center after being attacked by multiple inmates who he had sentenced to the facility over the years. A prison spokesperson stated they couldn't comment on the investigation as to why Johnston was in the general population at the time of the attack. In other related news, the FBI and the New Mexico District Attorney's office has launched an investigation into Judge Johnston's acceptance of bribes to reduce the prison sentences of white defendants whose criminal cases were brought against Native Americans.

It's noted that Navajo FBI Agents John Treehorn and Raven Shelly were in charge of the investigation. They arrested Johnston on conspiracy to commit murder against Peyton Greyhorse's oldest son, Parker, and the murders of Greyhorse's other son, Paul, along with Paul's partner Bart J. Baker. This is Jori Lansing reporting."

Treehorn stood in the doorway and sipped his coffee while he wore his sunglasses.

Beer cans littered the ground around the campfire, a testament that two old friends drank together to dull the pain of their existence, at least for a short while.

"You look like hell."

Treehorn felt like it, too.

Parker's eyes squinted in the morning light.

"Thanks."

"You needed sleep and that's always been my gift to you. When was the last time you slept a whole night?"

"I don't recall."

Treehorn did. Parker remembered, too.

"What are you going to do about Samuel?"

Treehorn met Parker's eyes as he asked, "Why did he set you up?"

"You'll have to ask him."

"Will he give me a straight answer?"

"Samuel laughed at me as I sat in the police cruiser. When did you realize the roadblock wasn't a coincidence?"

"When you said it occurred on Daniel Tsosie's birthday. I knew the deputy's date of birth because I examined his file every time I received a letter from Nettie asking if I had solved her son's murder. I had the details memorized."

"Don't blame Samuel. I'm sure he had a reason. We should thank Shady for this crap shoot."

"Really?"

"My father's disappearance was solved and his bones have stopped rattling."

Both men heard Shady's Jeep's low-gear grind as it slowly traveled across the desert to their location. Their friend arrived with his Panama hat and white sunscreen on his nose. The men were so used to the sight it no longer seemed out of place.

After they finished a second pot of coffee, Parker departed in Shady's vehicle.

"Nice flight to Tucson?" Treehorn asked, watching as the Jeep departed.

Shady rubbed the old scar on his jaw.

"Yes, it was. You know I'm not into parties. I prefer one-on-one contact."

Treehorn eyed the man and knew the game was still on.

"Who is she?"

Shady ignored his question, instead saying, "I'm glad you two kissed and made up."

"You could have told me the truth earlier and saved me a lot of trouble."

"Where would the fun be in that?" Shady asked, looking at Treehorn, "Sometimes, it's the planning that becomes the fun part."

Treehorn's telephone rang and when he saw the caller was Leo Mancuso, he walked far enough away from Shady for privacy.

"Treehorn."

"I just wanted to let you know that I'm giving Agents Hopper and Moore merit awards for locating Betsy Justice and Peyton Greyhorse's remains."

"They earned them. I'm recommending Agent Hopper for Special Agent status."

"Why?"

Treehorn squinted at Shady. "She made a mistake. Just like I did."

"What did she do?"

"She granted Shady Lynch a favor."

Mancuso inhaled a quick breath.

"When did you make a mistake?"

"The day Shady and I graduated from the academy."

"What happened?"

"He went home to Tucson for the weekend. When he returned Monday, he resigned from the FBI."

"I remember. I still hold his resignation letter."

"I asked him why he resigned."

"He joked and said, "Give me a favor and I'll tell you.""

"And, you gave him a favor."

"Yes, I did and then he told me why he quit."

"What happened next?"

"I pulled out my service weapon to shoot him but before my gun cleared its holster he called in the favor."

"Which was?"

"I would never kill him."

Mancuso actually chuckled, "Then, what happened?"

"I swung and broke his nose."

"How many times was that?"

"That was the second of three."

"I honestly thought you would have killed him by now but that explains everything. Shady knew you would and that was his prevention policy."

"Anything else, sir?"

"Why are you friends with Parker Greyhorse?"

Mancuso felt the chill come over the communication.

"You could ask my father the next time you're having drinks but I know he won't tell you. I choose not to discuss the matter."

"So, what you're saying is that I don't need to know and to keep my nose out of your private life."

"I'm alive to do my job at the end of the day. That's what's important."

"I'll support your recommendation and by the way. I'm submitting a merit award for you, too, in solving Deputy Daniel Tsosie's case. Keep up the good work."

"Yes, sir."

Navajo Nation Police Department

"Hey, chief, someone hand-delivered a note for you earlier this morning."

Deputy Redfeather handed him the blank envelope labeled 'Samuel Bear'.

The man opened it and removed the single postcard of a blackbird image labeled, *'The Raven'*. When he flipped it, he felt his body break out in a sweat. A Mesa Cartel logo covered the back with a written threat, *"I know and you're going to pay."*

Samuel's hand shook as he pinned the postcard and the brown slip of paper to his bulletin board. He accessed the security feed from his office and watched the video. A man dressed in a dark hoodie with sunglasses, who kept his head lowered, walked from the perimeter of the parking lot into the entrance. There, he handed his deputy the envelope and departed the same way he came. The police chief hit the zoom button as Lucy Redfeather took possession of the note from the stranger. On the man's right wrist, an Indian Posse tattoo was branded.

Treehorn and Shady sat drinking coffee in front of the campfire.

Shady rubbed his Indian Posse tattoo and stared at Treehorn's burn.

"Have you ever asked Parker how he survives with his injury?"

"Would you let it go?"

"I'm curious."

"I suggest you don't bring it up again, like ever."

"Would you be there for me if it happened? I couldn't live with such cruelty."

"Shady, I would hold you while you cried your last tear."

"I appreciate that, my friend. I don't want to die alone."

"You'll never die alone when someone's killing you."

"Good point. I brought you a copy of the *Indian Times*. We'll call it the *'Perp Walk Edition'*. Finch is in handcuffs pictured with you, while a dethroned Johnston in gown and cuffs is pictured with Raven Shelly."

"When did you target Finch?"

Shady's eyes flickered. He wasn't stupid.

"You and Parker believe it was when he called me from jail after the Bonito roadblock arrest, but it was before that."

Treehorn saw Shady's facial tell for a second and then it disappeared. He would share only what he wanted to share.

"Parker's arrest provided me with the plan and an end-goal."

Treehorn wondered whether the true backstory would appear.

"Someone told Finch that Parker had two weaknesses. You and me, *my mojito*."

"His friends."

"Finch made a fatal mistake. He assumed you'd play by the FBI rule book, me not so much. What you didn't know is that he and I had a couple of axes to grind for quite some time."

"This was never a simple murder."

"No, but when are they ever?"

"He didn't plan it alone."

"No, my friend. He had help."

"The man who hates Parker Greyhorse as much as Finch hated you."

Treehorn knew who.

Shady continued, "Parker knew Samuel coordinated with Finch for the NNP roadblock. I visited him at the jail while his case was being processed. We knew Judge Johnston—Peter's father-in-law who hated the Greyhorses—would throw the book at Parker. I called in a couple favors and the District Attorney made the deal with his sentencing. Judge Johnston agreed to it. He didn't have a choice and he knew he would have been exposed. Everything fell into place after that. I had plenty of time to set Finch up to make him pay—and he *has*."

"Where *is* Finch?"

Shady's blank stare met Treehorn's as he handed his friend a pastry container.

"I know it's not your birthday. You needn't worry yourself about those pesky details."

Treehorn opened the box. A tongue and two thumbs lay inside.

"Like I said, Finch won't bother my friends, *ever again*."

Treehorn threw the box into the campfire.

"I'm glad you and Parker had the night to work out your friendship issues."

Shady kicked the beer cans scattered on the ground.

Treehorn added a couple logs to the fire.

"You're a good man, John Treehorn. I stood outside of the hospital room when you held Parker in your arms as he wept. The strength you gave him that night allowed him to survive. Your words washed over me, too, as I listened. I wasn't strong enough to face Parker."

"He knew that, and so did I."

"I hunted one man down."

"We knew you would."

"You never asked."

"I didn't need to."

"I skinned him alive. I castrated him, too. He needed to know the pain he had caused Parker. I knew you wouldn't cross that line."

"I don't know, Shady. Sometimes, I wish I had. What kind of posse are we if the three of us don't stick together in our time of need?"

Treehorn and Shady sat in front of the campfire, introspective of their existence, long after their friend's departure. Parker fought his inner demons while Shady fought his outer ones, and Treehorn always felt on the fence with the two. Each of them still a solitary man.

490

Treehorn entered the hogan. It takes a lot for a man to sleep with another man. Not sexual. Parker lost something a long time ago and he never re-attained it. Treehorn held him the night of the attack while he cried, his body forever broken.

He held Parker the night his mother crawled into a bottle and never came out. The teenager had cried for hours not for the loss of his mother, but for never having one that was worthy enough for him and his brothers.

He held Parker the night two men attacked Paul for being a homosexual. The agent held him that night so he wouldn't hunt the men down. He never asked but he assumed Paul, Parker, and Shady dealt with the perpetrators in time.

Treehorn never forgot that it was Parker that held him the day he buried Skyler. That night he wanted to crawl into the ground next to his wife and never re-emerge. Parker was there for him during the subsequent nights over the years when his sporadic depression covered the light of his reality, and a night's sleep wasn't to be found. The criminal investigations of dead children, missing women, and senseless murders where the questions never stopped being asked and the answers were never to be found, took its toll.

Shady, as always, stood guard. Staring out toward the stars—searching for, but never finding, what he sought.

This time was different. Deputy Daniel Tsosie's murder put Treehorn on this path. Being in the middle between Parker's manipulation for wanting to be held in one man's arms for his survival, and Samuel's years of friendship and loyalty. Treehorn knew in the end neither man was to be blamed for their agenda. No, there was only one man to blame and Treehorn stared at him now.

Treehorn's private ringtone sounded. It played Ennio Morricone's, *'The Good, The Bad, and The Ugly'*.

Shady chuckled.

Treehorn glanced at the image of Parker on his screen and at his message, "Thanks for the favor, last night." He pocketed his device.

"Shady, tell me about Socorro."

"I set up Finch after he'd set up Parker. I knew about the weapons being sent to Mexico. A bad batch of drugs made the New Mexico governor look good. I switched out the money with serialized currency from my department. He stole cash that he couldn't spend. I sent the guns to Four

Corners to get Finch there, but Finch didn't show that night. Johnston and Ronan showed instead. Finch crossed a line with the Mesa Cartel. Parker and I knew you would work the investigation and everything would be resolved."

"What do you know about the man who killed Agent Dennis Donovan in Williston, North Dakota? The same man killed your two agents in Socorro with the same gun."

"Really."

"Shady?"

The man lowered the *Indian Times* newspaper.

"Yes, my mojito?"

"Where are Finch's wife and daughters?"

"Someone had to pay the price, John. That's the business we're in."

Treehorn let his fist fly, knocking Shady backwards, and landing him on his ass on the red dirt.

His bloodied and broken nose a testament that Treehorn's first fist hit the mark.

"Why'd you do that?" he wailed, trying to stem the flow of blood.

"You got Parker Greyhorse released from Cibola."

"So?"

Even though Treehorn had two extra inches on Shady Lynch, the paleface was a mean, little scrapper. An all-out

493

brawl followed between the two men who supposedly called each other 'friend.'

Matamoras, Mexico

The Central Intelligence Agency lost a man for two weeks while he recuperated from surgery for his broken nose.

Melinda slowly peeled her white dress down her naked body as Benito watched from his reclined position on their king-sized bed. His face swollen, eyes blackened, and his two broken ribs securely wrapped while his raven tattoo peeked out from his bandages. His lips curved into a smile.

Washington DC

The Federal Bureau of Investigation lost a man for a week while he recovered from his injuries. The FBI won the bet against the CIA.

Samantha accompanied Treehorn back to Washington DC. When they arrived at their apartment, he told her about his friendship with Parker. He thought she'd understand.

She didn't. He recuperated, alone. He remembered Parker's words, when you hold something dear, you become vulnerable. Treehorn knew the enemy awaits.

Shady Lynch never learned the cost Treehorn paid Parker Greyhorse for solving Deputy Daniel Tsosie's murder. All he knew was that it made FBI Special Agent John Treehorn a very angry man.

THE END

Made in United States
Orlando, FL
14 May 2023

33130206R00300